Society and Culture in Medieval India

Society and Culture in Medieval India

Dr. A.K. Saxena

ABD PUBLISHERS

Jaipur ■ New Delhi

ABD PUBLISHERS

Regd. Off. "Bony Residency", Gate No. 2
Opp. Tilak Public School, Vishweswariya Nagar,
Gopalpura Road, Jaipur - 302018, India
Ph: 0141 - 2761280, Telefax: 2761381
Email: abdpublishersjpr@gmail.com

Delhi Office: 102, 1st Floor, Satyam House,
4327/3, Ansari Road, Darya Ganj,
New Delhi - 110002, India
Ph: 011-45652440

visit us: www.oxfordbookcompany.com

Distributed By
KEYA INTERNATIONAL PRESS LLP
E-mail: keyainternationalpressllp@gmail.com

Published in India, 2025

ISBN: 9788183766661

Typeset by Shivangi Computer, Jaipur

Printed and bound in India by Thomson Press Ltd.,
New Delhi

Contents

Preface

Muslim rule in India coincides with what is known as the Middle Ages in Europe. The term Middle Ages or the Medieval Age is applied loosely to that period in history which lies between the ancient and modern civilizations. In Europe the period is supposed to have begun in the fifth century when the Western Roman Empire fell and ended in the fifteenth century with the emanation of Renaissance in Italy, Reformation in Germany, the discovery of America by Columbus, the invention of Printing Press by Guttenberg, and the taking of Constantinople by the Turks from the Byzantine (or the Eastern Roman) Empire. In brief the period of Middle Ages extends from C.E. 600 to 1500. Curiously enough the Middle Age in Europe synchronises exactly with what we call the medieval period in Indian history. The seventh century saw the end of the last great Hindu kingdom of Harshvardhana, the rise of Islam in Arabia and its introduction into India. In C. 1500 the Mughal conqueror Babur started mounting his campaigns. And since these foreign Muslim invaders and rulers had come not only to acquire dominions and extend territories, but also to spread the religion of Islam, war and religion became the two main currents of medieval Indian Muslim history.

The Hindus hated the Muslims and called them Mlechchhas. They were not prepared to interdine with them or to have marriage relations. There was a feeling among the Hindus that by doing so they would fall in life. Most of the Hindus cared for their self-respect. Their superiority was undoubted. They were known for their love for justice and were not prepared to give it up in actual life. In their professions, they were known for honesty and worthy of confidence. In all spheres of life, Hindus were respected for their qualities of head and heart. It is true that the religious and intellectual leaders of the Hindus were not influenced by Muslim conquest of India and they maintained their standard of nobility and superiority, but the ordinary Hindu was affected by Muslim conquest. On account of lack of independence, there was a fall in Hindu society. The Sultans of Delhi and other Muslim rulers regarded the Hindus as their enemies. With a few exceptions, no Hindu was given any position of responsibility in the state by the Muslim rulers. Even the right to life was given to them if they agreed to pay Jizya. For political reasons, Ala-ud-Din Khalji treated the Hindus of the Doab with great severity. He humiliated the Khuts, Chaudharies and Muqaddams. No Hindu could raise his head. There was no sign of any gold or silver coin or even Jital in their houses. They could not ride on horse. They had no arms or good clothes, Birani tells us that their lot bad become so bad that their wives were forced to work as maid servants in the houses of the Muslims. The Muslims state offered many concessions to convert the Hindus to Islam. Ibn-Batuta tells us that when a Hindu desired to become a Muslim, he was taken in the presence of the Sultan who gave him valuable clothes and articles of gold. The orthodox Muslims hated the Hindus. When the condition of Hindus improved a little during the reign of Khusrau, Birani wrote in sadness that the Hindus had again begun to live in comfort and had become happy. Brahamanas were not taxed to Jizya but Firuz Tughlaq imposed Jizya even on the Brahamanas. Sikandar Lodi also started persecuting the Hindus and their condition became miserable. This book should be useful to the students and teachers of medieval Indian history.

—Dr. A.K. Saxena

Chapter 1

Introduction

Muslim rule in India coincides with what is known as the Middle Ages in Europe. The term Middle Ages or the Medieval Age is applied loosely to that period in history which lies between the ancient and modern civilizations. In Europe the period is supposed to have begun in the fifth century when the Western Roman Empire fell and ended in the fifteenth century with the emanation of Renaissance in Italy, Reformation in Germany, the discovery of America by Columbus, the invention of Printing Press by Guttenberg, and the taking of Constantinople by the Turks from the Byzantine (or the Eastern Roman) Empire.

In brief the period of Middle Ages extends from C.E. 600 to 1500. Curiously enough the Middle Age in Europe synchronises exactly with what we call the medieval period in Indian history. The seventh century saw the end of the last great Hindu kingdom of Harshvardhana, the rise of Islam in Arabia and its introduction into India. In C. 1500 the Mughal conqueror Babur started mounting his campaigns. And since these foreign Muslim invaders and rulers had come not only to acquire dominions and extend territories, but also to spread the religion of Islam, war and religion became the two main currents of medieval Indian Muslim history.

Kingship

War is the work of kings turned conquerors or conquerors turned kings. Therefore it was necessary for the medieval monarch to be autocratic, religious minded and one who could conquer, rule and subserve the interest of religion. Such was the idea about the king in medieval times, both in the West and the East.

The beginnings of the institution of kingship are obscure. Anatole France attempts to trace it in his *Penguin Island*, a readable satire on

(British) history and society. That is more or less what he writes: Early in the beginning of civilization, the people's primary concern was provision of security against depredations of robbers and ravages of wild animals. So they assembled at a place to find a remedy to this problem. They put their heads together and arrived at a consensus. They will raise a team of security guards who will work under the command of a superior. These will be paid from contributions made by the people. As the assembled were still deliberating on the issue, a strong, well-built young man stood up. He declared he would collect the said contributions (later called taxes), and in return provide security. Noticing his physical prowess and threatening demeanour they all nodded their assent. Nobody dared protest. And so the king was born.

In whatever manner and at whatever time the king was born, he was, in the Middle Ages, personally a strong warrior, adept at horsemanship, often without a peer in strength. He gathered a strong army, collected taxes and contributions and was surrounded by fawning counsellors. They bestowed upon him attributes of divinity, upon his subjects those of devilry, thus making his presence in the world a sort of a benediction necessary for the good of mankind. Once man was declared to be bad and the king full of virtues, there was hardly any difficulty for political philosophy and religion to recommend strict control of the people by the king.

There were thus monarchs both in the West and the East and in both autocracy reigned supreme. Still in the West they could wrest a Magna Carta from the king as early as in 1215 C.E. and produce thinkers like Hobbes, Locke, Rousseau, Montesqueue and Bentham who helped change the concept of kingship in course of time. But in the East, especially in Islam, a rigid, narrow and limited scriptural education could, parrotlike, repeat only one political theory-Man was nasty, brutish and short and must be kept suppressed.

In the *Siyasat Nama*, Nizm-ul-Mulk Tusi stressed that since the kings were divinely appointed, they must always keep the subjects in such a position that they know their stations and never remove the ring of servitude from their ears. Alberuni, Fakhr-i-Mudabbir, Amir Khusrau, Ziyauddin Barani and Shams Siraj Afif repeat the same idea. As Fakhr-i-Mudabbir puts it, if there were no kings, men would devour one another. Even the liberal Allama Abul Fazl could not think beyond this: If royalty did not exist, the storm of strife would never subside, nor selfish ambition disappear. Mankind (is) under the burden of lawlessness and lust. The glitter of gems and gold in the Taj Mahal or the Peacock Throne, writes Jadunath Sarkar, ought not to blind us to the fact that in Mughal India, man was considered vile;-the mass of the people had no economic liberty, no indefeasible right to justice or personal freedom, when their oppressor was a noble or high official or landowner; political rights were not dreamt of. The Government was in effect despotism tempered by revolution or fear of revolution. Consequently, medieval Muslim political opinion could recommend only repression of man and glorification of king.

The king was divinely ordained. Abul Fazl says that No dignity is higher in the eyes of God than royalty Royalty is a light emanating from God, and a ray from the sun, the illuminator of the universe.

Kingship thus became the most general and permanent of institutions of medieval Muslim world. In theory Islam claims to stand for equality of men, in practice it encourages slavery among Muslims and imposes an inferior status on non-Muslim. In theory Islam does not recognize Kingship; in practice Muslims have been the greatest empire builders. Muhammadans themselves were impressed with the concept of power and glamour associated with monarchy. The idea of despotism, of concentration of power, penetrated medieval mind with facility. Obedience to the ruler was advocated as a religious duty. The ruler was to live and also enable people to live according to the Quranic laws. In public life, the Muslim monarch was enjoined to discharge a host of civil, military and religious duties. The Sultan was enjoined to do justice, to levy taxes according to the Islamic law, and to appoint honest and efficient officers so that the laws of the *Shariat* might be enforced through them.

At times, he was to enact *Zawabits* (regulations) to suit particular situations, but while doing so, he could not transgress the *Shariat* nor alter the Quranic law! His military duties were to defend Muslim territories, and to keep his army well equipped for conquest and extension of the territories of Islam. The religious duty of a Muslim monarch consisted in helping the indigent and those learned in the Islamic law. He was to prohibit what was not permitted by the Shara. The duty of propagating Islam and carrying on *Jihad* mainly devolved on him. *Jihad* was at once an individual and a general religious duty. According to a contemporary *Alim*, if the Sultan was unable to extirpate infidelity, he must at least keep the enemies of God and His Prophet dishonoured and humiliated. It must be said to his credit that the Muslim Sultan, by and large, worked according to these injunctions, and sometimes achieved commendable success in his exertions in all these spheres.

As said earlier, there were autocratic monarchs both in the West and the East. Still in the West there appeared a number of liberal political philosophers who helped to change the concept of kingship in course of time. But Muslims could not think on such lines, so that when in England they executed their king after a long Civil War (1641-49), in India Shahjahan, a contemporary of Charles I ruled as an autocrat in a golden age. Even so autocracy took time to go even in Europe and there was no check on the powers of the king in the Middle Ages, except for the institution of feudalism.

Feudalism

Feudalism was a very prominent institution of the Middle Ages. It was prevalent both in Europe as well as in India, although there were many differences between the two systems. In Europe feudalism gathered strength on the decline of the Western Roman Empire. After Charlemagne (800-814) in particular, there was rapid decline in the monarchical power throughout Europe, and governments failed to perform their primary duty of protecting their peoples. The class of people who needed protection the most was the petty landowner. In the earliest times the lands were free whether these were held by ordinary freeman or a noble. In the absence of strong monarchy, the possessor of the free land, threatened or oppressed by powerful neighbours, sought refuge in submitting to some lord, and in the case of a lord to some more powerful lord.

In the bargain he surrendered his land. For, when he begged for protection, the lord said: I can protect (only) my own land. The poor man was thus forced to surrender the ownership of his land to his powerful and rich neighbour, receiving it back in fief as a vassal. (The word feudalism itself is derived from the French *feodalite* meaning faithfulness). His children were left without any claim on that land. He was also obliged to render service to his superior lord. In return he was promised protection in his lifetime by his lord. The origins of feudalism are thus to be traced to the necessity of the people seeking protection, and exploitation by those who provided it.

Conditions were not the same everywhere, but the system was based on contract or compact between lord and tenant, determining all rights and obligations between the two. The vassal was obliged to render military service, take his cases only to his own lord and submit to the decisions of the lords court, and pay certain aids to the lord in times of need, like free gifts or benevolences, aids at the marriage of the chiefs daughter, some tax when the chief was in trouble or as ransom to redeem his person from prison. These aids varied according to local customs and were often extorted unreasonably.

On the other hand, for providing security to the vassal, it became common for a chief or lord to have a retinue of bodyguards composed of valiant youths who were furnished by the chief with arms and provisions and who in turn devoted themselves to his service. These companions received no pay except their arms, horses and provisions. With these companions or troops the lords also conquered lands, and gave certain portions of it to their attendants to enjoy for life. These estates were called *beneficia* or fiefs, because they were only lent to their possessors, to revert after death to their grantor, who immediately gave them to another of his servants on the same terms. As the son commonly esteemed it his duty, or was forced by necessity, to devote his arms to the lord in whose service his father had lived, he usually received his father's fief, or rather he was invested with it anew. By the usage of centuries this custom became hereditary. A fief rendered vacant by the death of the holder was taken possession of by his son, on the sole condition of paying homage to the feudal superior.

In the feudal system, therefore, the vassal and the lord benefited from one another, although the latter much more, at the cost of the king. Junior vassals could become powerful and rise in hierarchy to become sub-lords or even great lords. They could have their own subordinate vassals in sub-infeudation. Kingly power, as always, continued to exist, but under feudalism it was widely diffused. The privileges the lords enjoyed often comprised the right of coining money, raising armies and waging private wars, exemption from public tributes and freedom from legislative control. Sometimes the kings had to make virtue of necessity even to the extent of granting titles and administrative fiefs to Counts etc. to be administered by them. But the struggle between royalty and nobility (as in England under William the Norman), continued. Of course, and ultimately, it ended in the power of the lords sinking before that of the king.

In India feudalism did not usher in that spirit of civil liberty which characterised the constitutional history of medieval England. Here the king remained supreme whether among the Turks or the Mughals, and the assignments of conquered lands were granted by him to lords, soldiers or commoners or his own relatives as salary or reward in consideration of distinguished military service in the form of *iqtas* or *jagirs*, sometimes even on a hereditary basis, but they were not wrested from him. This system was bureaucratic. There was also a parallel feudalistic organisation but the possessor of land remained subservient to the king. It was based on personal relationship. The vassals were given *jagirs* and assignments primarily because of blood and kinship. On the other hand, the practice of permitting vanquished princes to retain their kingdoms as vassals, or making allotment of territories to brothers and relatives of the king, or giving assignments to particular families of nobles, learned men and theologians as reward or pension were feudalistic in nature. Some feudatories would raise their own army, collect taxes and customary dues, pay tributes, and rally round the standard of their overlord or king with their military contingents when called upon to do so. But the assignee had no right of coining money. (In fact, coining of money was considered as a signal of rebellion.) He maintained his own troops but he had no right of waging private war. He could only increase his influence by entering into matrimonial alliances with powerful neighbours or the royal family. In the

Sultanate and the Mughal empire the feudal system was more bureaucratic than feudalistic, in fact it was bureaucratic throughout. Here the feudal nobility was a military aristocracy which incidentally owned land, rather than a landed aristocracy which occasionally had to defend Royal lands and property by military means but at other times lived quietly.

But there were also many points of similarity between Indian and European feudalism. In India *Nazrana* was offered to the lord or king when an estate or *jagir* was bestowed upon the heir of the deceased lord (*Tika*), like the feudal relief in Europe. As in Europe, here too the practice of escheat was widely prevalent. Aids, gifts or benevolences were common to both. These consisted of offerings at the ascension of the king to the throne, his weighment ceremony, on important festivals, cash and gifts at the marriage of the chief's daughter or son, gifts or a tax when the chief was in trouble. In India the king always stood at the top of the regime. Feudal institutions are apt to flourish in a state which lacks centralised administration. The vastness of India makes it a veritable subcontinent, and the ruler's position was naturally different in each kingdom or region according to local condition found there. But there was a central authority too. The idea of a strong monarch was inseparable from Muslim psyche and Turco-Mongol political theory. In India, under Muslim rule, great importance was attached to the sacrosanct nature of the king's person. The Indian system arose from certain social and moral forces rather than from sheer political necessity as in Europe, and that is why it survived throughout the medieval period.

Whatever its merits and demerits, Indian feudalism recognised division of society into people great and small, strong and weak, haves and have-nots. Nobles were not equal to nobles; there were great Khans and petty Amirs. Men were not equal to men; some were masters, others their slaves. Women were not equal to men; they were subservient to men and considered to be their property. Perhaps the most prominent characteristic of the Medieval Age was the belief and acceptance of the 'fact' that men are not born equal, or at least they could not be recognised as such.

Feudalism in Europe gradually disappeared with the coming of Renaissance and Reformation, and formation of nation-states. In India phenomena such as these did not occur. There was nothing like a Renaissance in medieval India. There could be no reformation either, because innovation in religious matters is taboo in Islam. Some Muslim monarchs were disillusioned with the state of religion and the power of the Ulama (religious scholars). Thai is why, probably, Alauddin Khalji (C.E. 1296-1316) contemplated founding a new religion, Muhammad Tughlaq (1325-51) was credited with similar intentions; and Akbar (1556-1605) actually established the *Din-i-Ilahi*.

Muslims feared that Alauddin's new religion must be quite different from the Muhammadan faith, and that its enforcement would entail slaughter of a large number of Musalmans. He was dissuaded by his loyal counsellors from pursuing his project. All the same it is significant that Alauddin Khalji and Jalaluddin Muhammad Akbar did think of some sort of Reformation in Islam, but the former was scared into abandoning the idea and the latter contented himself by just organising a sort of brotherhood of like-minded thinkers. Such endeavours, strictly prohibited in Islam, could hardly affect India's Muslim feudalistic society.

Europe in the middle ages too lived under a Roman Catholic imperium. Its unity was theological, while its divisions were feudal. After Renaissance the unity of the theological imperium was shattered and so were the old divisions. European societies, after centuries of theological and territorial wars, learnt to aggregate around a new category of the nation-state. In India Muslim theological imperium never came to an end, nor persistent resistance to it. Hence, the idea of a secular nation-state never found a ground here.

Among other chief agencies that overthrew the feudal system were the rise of cities, scouring of the oceans for Commercial Revolution and the spread of knowledge, scientific knowledge in particular. In India there was urbanisation under Muslim rule, but it has been grossly exaggerated. India had large urban centres before the arrival of Muslims. Arab geographers become rapturous when describing the greatness of India's cities-both in extent and in demography-on the eve of Muslim conquest and immigration. During his sojourn in India Ibn Battuta visited seventy-five cities, towns and ports. Under Muslim rule many old cities were given Muslim names.

Thus Akbarabad (Agra), Islamabad (Mathura), Shahjahanabad (Delhi) and Hyderabad (Golkunda) were not entirely new built cities, but old populated places that were given new Islamic names, mostly after the ruling kings. Giving new names to old cities was not an extension of urbanisation as such, although it must be conceded that Muslims loved city life and encouraged qasba like settlements. Urbanisation in Europe gave impetus to industry and personal property and founded a new set of power cluster-the middle class. The rise of this new class, with its wealth and industrial importance, contributed more than anything else to social and political development in Europe before which the feudal relations of society almost gradually crumbled.

The rise and spread of this class in India and its impact on society remained minimal and rather imperceptible. Edward Terry noted that it was not safe for merchants and tradesmen in towns and cities, so to appear, lest they should be used as filled sponges. Moreland on the testimony of

Bernier and others, arrives at the conclusion that in India the number of middle class people was small and they found it safe to wear the garb of indigence. Europe broke the shackles of feudalism by embarking upon Commercial Revolution and took to the seas for the same.

The Mughals in India fared miserably on water. Even the great emperor Akbar had to purchase permission of the Portuguese for his relatives to visit places of Islamic pilgrimage. Throughout medieval India there was little change in the field of scientific learning and thought.

Religious Wars

Such unparalleled feats of success were one day bound to be challenged by the vanquished. As a result Christians and Muslims entered into a long-drawn struggle. The immediate cause of the conflict was the capture of Jerusalem by the Seljuq Turks in 1070 and the defeat of the Byzantine forces at Manzikart in Asia Minor in 1071. For the next two centuries (1093-1291) the Christian nations fought wars of religion or Crusades against Muslims for whom too these wars meant the holy *Jihad.*

Christianity thus found a powerful rival in Islam because the aim of both has been to convert the world to their systems. In competition, Islam had certain advantages. If because of its late arrival, there was any problem about obtaining followers, it was solved by the simple method of just forcing the people to accept it. Starting from Arabia, Islam pushed its religious and political frontiers through armed might. The chain of its early military successes helped establish its credentials and authority.

It was also made more attractive than Christianity by polygamy, license of concubinage and frenzied bigotry. It sought outward expansion but developed no true theory of peaceful coexistence. For example, it framed unlimited rules about the treatment to be accorded to non-Muslims in an Islamic state, but nowhere are there norms laid down about the behaviour of Muslims if they happen to live as a minority in a non-Muslim majority state. Its tactic of violence also proved to be its greatest weakness. In the course of Islamic history, Muslims have been found to be as eager to fight among themselves as against others.

The Crusades (so called because Christian warriors wore the sign of cross), were carried on by European nations from the end of the eleventh century till the latter half of the thirteenth century for the conquest of Palestine. The antagonism of the Christian and Muhammadan nations had been intensified by the possession of Holy Land by the Turks and their treatment of the Christian pilgrims to Jerusalem. In these wars, the pious, the adventurous, and the greedy flocked under the standards of both sides.

The first crusade was inspired by Peter the Hermit in 1093, and no less than eight bloody wars were fought with great feats of adventure, heroism and killings. In the last crusade the Sultan of Egypt captured Acre in 1291 and put an end to the kingdom founded by the Crusaders. Despite their want of success, the European nations by their joint enterprises became more connected with each other and ultimately stamped out any Muslim influence in Western Europe. But the most fruitful element in the crusades was the entry of the West into the East. There was a constant conflict and permanent contact between Christianity and Islam.

In this contact both sides lost and gained by turns, both culturally and demographically, for both strove for expansion through arms and proselytization. The successors of Saladin, who defeated the Christians in the last crusade, were divided by dissensions. By the grace of those disenssions the Latins survived. A new militant Muhammadanism arose with the Mameluke Sultans of Egypt who seized the throne of Cairo in 1250.

However, shortly afterwards there was a setback to Muslim power when the Caliph of Baghdad was killed by the Mongols in 1258. On the other hand, the prospect of a great mass conversion of the Mongols, which would have linked a Christian Asia to a Christian Europe and reduced Islam to a small faith, also dwindled and disappeared. The (Mongol) Khanates of Persia turned to Muhammadanism in 1316; by the middle of the fourteenth century Central Asia had gone the same way; in 1368-70 the native dynasty of Mings was on the throne and closing China to foreigners; and the end was a recession of Christianity and an extension of Islam which assumed all the greater dimensions with the growth of the power of the Ottoman Turks.

But a new hope dawned for the undefeated West; and this new hope was to bring one of the greatest revolutions of history. If the land was shut, why should Christianity not take to the sea Why should it not navigate to the East, take Muhammadanism in the rear, and as it were, win Jerusalem a *tergo*. This was the thought of the great navigators, who wore the cross on their breasts and believed in all sincerity that they were labouring in the cause of the recovery of the Holy Land, and if Columbus found the Caribbean Islands instead of Cathay, at any rate we may say that the Spaniards who entered into his labours won a continent for Christianity, and that the West, in ways in which it had never dreamed, at last established the balance in its favour..

Crusades saved Western civilization in the Middle Ages. They saved it from any self-centred localism; they gave it breadth-and a vision. On the other hand, Muslim victories made Muslim vision narrow and myopic. So that today Christians are larger in numbers and technologically and militarily more advanced than Muhammadans. As these lines are being written (August 1990), their armies and ships are spreading all over the West Asian region beginning with Saudi Arabia.

To return to the medieval period. Religious wars between Christians and Muhammadans alone did not account for killings on a large scale. The

Christians also fought bloody and long-drawn wars among themselves. The Thirty Years War (1618-1648), for instance, decimated one-fifth population of the region affected by it. Then there was the Inquisition. Inquisition was a court or tribunal established by the Roman Catholic Church in the twelfth century for the examination and punishment of heretics. England never introduced it, Italy and France had only a taste of it. But in Spain it became firmly established towards the end of the fifteenth century.

It is computed that there were in Spain above 20,000 officers of the Inquisition, called *familiars*, who served as spies and informers. Imprisonment, often for life, scourging, and the loss of property, were the punishments to which the penitent was subjected. When sentence of death was pronounced against the accused, burning the heretic in public was ordered as the church never polluted herself with blood. The number of victims of the Spanish Inquisition from 1481 to 1808 amounted to 341,021. Of these nearly 32,000 were burned at the stake.

Islam outstripped Christianity in contributing to large-scale killings in wars waged for religion or persecution of heretics. Each human being has an idea or image of God in his mind. Consequently, there can be as many Gods as there are human beings. Even according to one outstanding Sufi, the paths by which its followers seek God are in number as the souls of men. In view of this it is presumptuous to claim that there is only one God or there are many Gods or there is no God at all. And yet in the name of One God, and at that Merciful and Compassionate, what cruelties have not been committed in the history of Islam Arabia was converted during the life-time of Muhammad.

Immediately after the death of Muhammad, to borrow the rhetoric of Edward Gibbon, in the ten years of the administration of (Caliph) Omar (634-644) the Saracens reduced to his obedience thirty-six thousand cities or castles, destroyed four thousand churches or temples of the unbelievers, and edified fourteen hundred moschs (mosques) for the exercise of the religion of Muhammad. In these unparalleled feats the number of the killed cannot be computed. Since many pages in this book will be devoted to Muslim exertions in their endeavour to spread Islam in India we may feel contented here to state that in this scenario religion and religious wars became the very soul of thought, action and oppression in the Middle Ages.

Censorship

Middle Ages is also known as Dark Ages. It is so called because there were restrictions placed on the freedom of thought and any aberrations were punished as heresy. Any idea away from the traditional was looked upon with suspicion. New conceptions or knowledge gathered on the basis of new experiments was taboo if it came into conflict with the Church or contravened the Christian scriptures. This restriction on any new notions made the period a dark age.

But it required constant monitoring of people's thoughts and actions. The invention of printing and the rapid diffusion of opinion by means of books, induced the governments in all western countries to assume certain powers of supervision and regulation with regard to printed matter. The popes were the first to institute a regular censorship (1515) and inquisitors were required to examine all works before they were printed. Only one example would suffice to illustrate the position. Nicholas Copernicus was born in Poland in 1473: he taught mathematics at Rome in 1500 and died in Germany in 1543. He researched on the shape of the Earth, and concluded that the Sun was the centre round which Earth and other planets revolved.

In his *De Orbium Celestium Revolutionibus* (On the Revolutions of the Celestial Orbs) he even measured the diameter and circumference of the Earth fairly accurately. But the Church believed the Earth to be flat, and the fear of Inquisition discouraged Copernicus from publishing his outrageous researches till about the close of his life, for the Church could do little harm to a man about to die. Even so, his book was forbidden to the Roman Catholics for long. The Inquisition freely used torture to extort confession; heretics were broken on the wheel, or burnt at stake on crossroads on Sundays for punishment as well as an example for others.

In the medieval India under Muslim rule there was no printing press and no research of the type done by Copernicus. The need for censorship arose because Islam forbade any innovation in the thought and personal behaviour of Muslims. Beware of novel affairs, said Muhammad, for surely all innovation is error. What was not contained in the Quran or Hadis was considered as innovation and discouraged. That is why Muslim learning in India remained orthodox, repetitive and stereotyped. Free thought and research in science and technology were ruled out. Fundamentalist writers like Khwaja Baqi Billah (1563-1603), Sheikh Ahmad Sarhindi (1564-1624) and Shah Waliullah (1702-1763) were considered as champion thinkers.

As Muslims must live in accordance with a set of rules and a code of conduct, there was an official Censor of Public Morals and Religion called *Muhtasib*. It was his duty to see that Muslims did not absent themselves from public prayers, that no one was found drunk in public places, that liquors or drugs were not sold openly. He possessed arbitrary power of intervention and could enter the houses of wrongdoers to bring them to book. Sir Alexander Burnes relates that he saw persons publicly scourged because they had slept during prayer-time and smoked on Friday. I. H. Qureshi writes, It was soon discovered that people situated as the Muslims were in India could not be allowed to grow lax in their ethical and spiritual conduct without endangering the very existence of the Sultanate. Hurriedly converted, half-trained, Indian Muslims were prone to reverting to their original faith which was full of freedom.

Therefore, all the sultans were very strict about enforcing Islamic behaviour on Muslims through the agency of Muhtasibs. Balban, Alauddin Khalji and Muhammad bin Tughlaq were known for their severity in this regard. Muhammad bin Tughlaq regarded wilful neglect of prayers a heinous crime and inflicted severe chastisement on transgressors. Women too were not spared; Firoz Shah and Sikandar Lodi in particular forbade women from going on pilgrimage to the tombs of saints. The Department of Censor of Public Morals was known as *hisbah*. Non-Muslims suffered even more because of censorial regulations.

Tradition divided them into seven kinds of offenders like unbelievers, infidels, hypocrites, polytheists etc. who are destined to go to seven kinds of hell from the mild *Jahannum* to the hottest region of hell called *Hawiyah*, a bottomless pit of scorching fire. A strict watch was kept on their thought and expression. They were to dress differently from the Muslims, they could not worship their gods in public and they could not claim that their religion was as good as Islam. A case which culminated in the execution of a Brahmin may be quoted in some detail as an example.

A report was brought to the Sultan (Firoz Tughlaq 1351-88) that there was in Delhi an old Brahman (*Zunar dar*) who persisted in publicly performing the worship of idols in his house; and that the people of the city, both Musalmans and Hindus, used to resort to his house to worship the idol. This Brahman had constructed a wooden tablet (*muhrak*), which was covered within and without with paintings of demons and other objects.

On days appointed, the infidels went to his house and worshipped the idol, without the fact becoming known to the public officers. The Sultan was informed that this Brahman had perverted Muhammadan women, and had led them to become infidels. (These women were surely newly converted and had not been able to completely cut themselves off from their original faith). An order was accordingly given that the Brahman, with his tablet, should be brought in the presence of the Sultan at Firozabad.

The judges, doctors, and elders and lawyers were summoned, and the case of the Brahman was submitted for their opinion. Their reply was that the provisions of the Law were clear: the Brahman must either become a Musalman or be burned. The true faith was declared to the Brahman, and the right course pointed out, but he refused to accept it. Orders were given for raising a pile of faggots before the door of the darbar. The Brahman was tied hand and foot and cast into it; the tablet was thrown on the top and the pile was lighted. The writer of this book (Shams Siraj Afif) was present at the *darbar* and witnessed the execution the wood was dry, and the fire first reached his feet, and drew from him a cry, but the flames quickly enveloped his head and consumed him. Behold the Sultan's strict adherence to law and rectitude, how he would not deviate in the least from its decrees.

The above detailed description gives the idea of burning at stake under Muslim rule. Else similar cases of executions are many. During the reign of Firoz himself the Hindu governor of Uchch was killed. He was falsely accused of expressing affirmation in Islam and then recanting. In the time of Sikandar Lodi (1489-1517) a Brahman of Kaner in Sambhal was similarly punished with death for committing the crime of declaring as much as that Islam was true, but his own religion was also true.

Astrology and Astronomy

Most medieval people of all creeds and countries believed in astrology. Astrology literally means the science of the stars. The name was formerly used as equivalent to astronomy, but later on became restricted in meaning to the science or psuedo-science which claims to enable people to judge of the effects and influences of the heavenly bodies on human and other mundane affairs. Astrology was not to the medievals an unscientific aberration. It was based on the understanding that the relationship of man to the Universe is as the microcosm (the little world) is to the macrocosm (the great world). Thus a knowledge of the heavens is essential for a true understanding of man himself. A knowledge of the movements of the planets and their position in the heavens, would therefore be of the utmost importance for man since, in the medieval phrase, superiors (in the heavens) ruled inferiors (on earth): and not only man but all were subject to the decrees of heavens, which themselves expressed the will of God. Roger Bacon (1214-1292) considered astrology as the most practical of sciences.

Astrology was practised by Muslims as by all other medieval people. Muhammad bin Qasim, the first invader of India, was despatched on his mission only after astrologers had pronounced that the conquest of Sind could be effected only by his hand. Mahmud of Ghazni too believed in the predictions of astrologers.

Timur the invader writes in his *Malfuzat*: About this time there arose in my heart a desire to lead an expedition against the infidels and become a ghazi, and felt encouraged when he opened a *fal* (omen) in the Quran which said: O Prophet, make war upon infidels and unbelievers and treat them with severity -and he launched his attack on Hindustan. The practice of consulting the Quran for *fal* was common among medieval Muslims. The savant Alberuni gives details of Hindu literature on astrology and astronomy seen by him. By and large Muslim kings and commoners in India decided their actions on the advice of the astrologers, soothsayers and omen mongers.

People's faith in astrology was reinforced for seeking solution to their immediate problems and their curiosity to know their future. The first was done by astrologers and palm-readers by examining the hand and face of the applicant, turning over the leaves of the large book, and pretending to make certain calculations and then decide upon the *Sahet* (saiet) or propitious moment of commencing the business he may have in hand. Amulets and charms were also prescribed for warding off distress, removing fear, obtaining success in an undertaking or victory in battle and a hundred other similar problems.

The second was done by preparing a horoscope. As usually practised, the whole heavens, visible and invisible, was divided by great circles into twelve equal parts, called *houses*. The houses had different names and different powers, the first being called the house of life, the second the house of riches, the third of brethren, the sixth of marriage, the eighth of death, and so on. To draw a person's horoscope, or cast his *nativity*, was to find the position of the heavens at the instant of his birth. The temperament of the individual was ascribed to the planet under which he was born, as *saturnine* from Saturn, *jovial* from Jupiter, *mercurial* from Mercury and so on. The virtues of herbs, gems, and medicines were also supposed to be due to their ruling planets.

Kings and nobles gave large salaries to astrologers. The astrologers prepared horoscopes of princes and the elite. Muslim kings got horoscopes of all princes like Salim, Murad and Daniyal cast by Hindu Pandits. Jotik Ray, the court astrologer of emperor Jahangir used to make correct predictions after reading the king's horoscope. He was once weighed against gold and silver for reward. There were men and women *Rammals* (soothsayers) and clairvoyants at the court. In short, the practice of consulting astrologers was common with high and low. The people never engaged even in the most trifling transaction without consulting them. They read whatever is written in heaven; fix upon the *Sahet*, and solve every doubt by opening the Koran. No commanding officer is nominated, no marriage takes place, and no journey is undertaken without consulting Monsieur the Astrologer. Naturally, the astrologers who frequented the court of the grandees are considered by them eminent doctors, and become wealthy.

But there were charlatans also. They duped and exploited the poor and the credulous. Besides some people then as now had no faith in astrology. The French doctor Bernier was such an one. Describing the bazar held in Delhi near the Red Fort, Francois Bernier (seventeenth century) says that Hither, likewise, the astrologers resort, both Mahometan and Gentile. These wise doctors remain seated in the sun, on a dusty piece of carpet, handling some old mathematical instruments, and having open before them a large book which represents the sign of the Zodiac. In this way they attract the attention of the passenger by whom they are considered as so many infallible oracles. They tell a poor person his fortune for a *payssa* Silly women, wrapping themselves in a white cloth from head to foot, flock to the astrologers, whisper to them all the transaction of their lives, and disclose every secret with no more reserve than is practised by a penitent in the presence of her confessor. The ignorant and infatuated people really believe that the stars have an influence (on their lives) which the astrologers can control.

Astrology and astronomy are closely interlinked. In medieval times astronomy was also considered a branch of psychology and medicine. Astronomy has an undoubtedly high antiquity in India. The Arabs began to make scientific astronomical observations about the middle of the eighth century, and for 400 years they prosecuted the science of *najum* with assiduity. The Muslims looked upon astronomy as the noblest and most exalted of sciences, for the study of stars was an indispensable aid to religious observances, determining for instance the month of Ramzan and the hours of prayers. Halaku Khan (Buddhist) founded the great Margha observatory at Azerbaijain. One at Jundishapur existed in Iran.

In the fifteenth century Ulugh Beg, grandson of Amir Timur (Tamerlane), built an observatory at Samarqand. In Europe Copernicus in the fifteenth and Galileo and Newton in the seventeenth century did valuable work in the field of astronomy. In medieval India many Muslim chroniclers wrote about the movements of planets and stars, but the name of Sawai Jai Singh II of Jaipur has become famous for his contribution to the science of astronomy. He built observatories or *Jantar-Mantars* at many places in the country for the study of the movements of stars and planets. A reputed geometer and scholar, Sawai Jai Singh II built the Delhi Jantar-Mantar in C.E. 1710 at the request of Mughal emperor Muhammad Shah.

The observatory was used for naked-eye sighting, continuously monitoring the position of the sun, moon and planets in relation to background stars in the belt of the Zodiac. His aim was basically to make accurate predictions of eclipses and position of planets. He devised instruments of his own invention - the Samrat Yantra, the Jai Prakash, and the Ram Yantra. The Misr Yantra was added later by Jai Singh's son Madho Singh. The Samrat Yantra is an equinoctial dial. The Yantra measures the time of the day, correct to half a second; and the declination of the sun and other heavenly bodies. Other Jantar-Mantars of Jai Singh were built at Ujjain, Mathura, Banaras and Jaipur.

Alchemy, Magic, Miracles and Superstitions

Alchemy flourished chiefly in the medieval period, although how old it might be is difficult to say. It paved the way for the modern science of chemistry, as astrology did for astronomy. In the medieval age alchemy was believed to be an exact science. But its aims were not scientific. It concerned itself solely with indefinitely prolonging human life, and of transmuting baser metals into gold and silver. It was cultivated among the Arabians, and by them the pursuit was introduced into Europe.

Raymond Lully, or Lullius, a famous alchemist of the thirteenth and fourteenth centuries, is said to have changed for king Edward I mass of 50,000 lbs. of quicksilver into gold. No such specific case is found in medieval India, although there was firm belief in the magic or science of alchemy. A Sufi politician of the thirteenth century, Sidi Maula by name, developed lot of political clout in the time of Sultan Jalaluddin Khalji (1290-1296). He built a large *khanqah* (hospice) where hundreds of people were fed by him every day. He used to pay for what he bought by the queer way of telling the man to take such and such amount from under such and such brick or coverlet, and the *tankahs* (gold/silver coins) found there looked so bright as if they had been brought from the mint that very moment. He did not accept anything from the people but spent so lavishly that they suspected him of possessing the knowledge of *Kimya va Simya* (alchemy and natural magic).

The general solvent which at the same time was supposed to possess the power of removing all the seeds of disease out of the human body and renewing life, was called the *philosopher's stone*. Naturally, there was a keen desire to get hold of one. India was known for possessing knowledge of herbs which prolonged life.

Alberuni writes about the science of alchemy (*Rasayan*) about which he so learnt in India: Its (*Rasayan's*) principles (certain operations, drugs and compound medicines, most of which are taken from plants) restore the health and give back youth to fading old age white hair becomes black again, the keenness of the senses is restored as well as the capacity for juvenile agility, and even for cohabitation, and the life of the people in this world is even extended to a long period. In *Jami ul Hikayat* Muhammad Ufi narrates that certain chiefs of Turkistan sent ambassadors with letters to the kings of India on the following mission. The chiefs said that they had been informed that in India drugs were procurable which possessed the property of prolonging human life, by the use of which the kings of India attained to a very great age. The Rais were careful in the preservation of their health, and the chiefs of Turkistan begged that some of this medicine might be sent to them, and also information as to the method by which the Rais preserved their health so long.

The ambassadors having reached Hindustan, delivered the letters entrusted to them. The Rai of Hind having read them, ordered the ambassadors to be taken to the top of an excessively lofty mountain (Himalayas) to obtain it. In the same book a story refers to a chief of Jalandhar, who had attained to the age of 250 years. In a note Elliot comments that this was a favourite persuasion of the Orientals. But Alberuni's conclusion is crisp and correct. He writes: The Hindus do not pay particular attention to alchemy, but no nation is entirely free from it, and one nation has more bias for it than another, which must not be construed as proving intelligence or ignorance; for we find that many intelligent people are entirely given to alchemy, whilst ignorant people ridicule the art and its adepts.

Belief in magic too was a universal weakness of the middle ages. The invocation of spirits is an important part of Musalman magic, and this (*dawat*) is used for the following purposes: to command the presence of the *Jinn* and demons who, when it is required of them, cause anything to take place; to establish friendship or enmity between two persons; to cause the death of an enemy; to increase wealth or salary; to gain income gratuitously or mysteriously; to secure the accomplishment of wishes, temporal or spiritual.

So, magic was practised both for good purposes and evil intentions, for finding lucky days for travelling, catching thieves and removing diseases as well as inflicting diseases on others. The first was called spiritual (*Ilm-i-Ruhani*) and the latter *Shaitani Jadu*. Although Islam directs Musalmans to believe not in magic yet the belief was universal. It involved visit to tombs, use of collyrium or *pan* (betel), and all kinds of antics and ceremonials for desiring death for others and success for self. There were trained magicians (Sayana). They fleeced the fools, both rich and poor, to their hearts content. A highly popular book on magic among the Muslims in the medieval period was *Jawahir-i-Khamsa* by Muhammad Ghaus Gauleri.

Belief in magic and sorcery and worship of saints living and dead was linked with belief in miracles and superstition. The argument was that the elders and saints helped when they were alive, they could still help when dead and so their graves were worshipped. There was belief in miracles for the same reason. An evil eye could inflict disease and there was fear of witchcraft. A blessing could cure it and so there was faith in the miraculous powers of saints. In medieval times physicians were few, charlatans many, and even witch doctors flourished. Amir Khusrau mentions some of the powers of sorcery and enchantment possessed by the inhabitants of India. First of all they can bring a dead man to life. If a man has been bitten by a snake and is rendered speechless, they can resuscitate him even after six months.

There is nothing surprising about the belief in miracles by medieval Muslims, in particular about their Sufi Masheikh. In theory Islam disapproved of miracles. In practice it became a criterion by which Sufi Sheikhs were Judged and the common reason why people reposed faith in them. Many Sufi Sheikhs and *Faqirs* were considered to be *Wali* who could perform *karamat* or miracles and even *istidraj* or magic and hypnotism. Sheikh Nizamuddin Auliya held that it was improper for a Sufi to show his *karamat* even if he possessed supernatural powers. But belief in alchemy and miracles was common even among Sufi Masheikh and there are dozens of hagiological works and biographies of Sufi saints containing stories of such miracles including *Favaid-al-Fuad, Siyar-ul-Auliya* and *Khair-ul-Majalis* which are considered by many Muslims to be pretty authentic.

There are unbelievable stories, hardly worth reproducing. It is difficult to say when the stories of the *karamat* of the Sufi saints began to be told. But they helped the Sufis take Islam to the masses. It is believed that impressed by these stories or actual performance of miracles, many Hindus became their disciples and ultimately converted to Islam.

Belief in ghosts of both sexes was widespread. Nights were frightfully dark. Right upto the time of Babur there were no candles, no torches, not a candle-stick. Even in the Mughal palace utmost economy was practised in the use of oil for lighting purposes. The common man lived in utter darkness after nightfall. And ghosts, goblins and imaginary figures used to haunt him. Sorcerers and witch doctors tried to help men and particularly women who were supposed to have been possessed by ghosts.

Tenor of Life

The chief amusement of the nobles of the ruling class was warfare. In this they took delight that was never altogether assuaged. If they could not indulge in this, then, in later ages, they made mock fights called jousts or tournaments. If they could not always fight men, they hunted animals. Every noble learned to hunt, not for food-though this was important too-but for pleasure.

They developed the art of hunting birds as well as taming and flying birds. Some nobles were learned, humble, polite and courteous but such were exceptions rather than the rule. Since there was little academic activity, most of the elite passed their time in field sports, swordsmanship and military exercises. Their coat of mail was heavy and cumbersome; a fall from horse was very painful and sometimes even fatal. Such a situation was common both in Europe and India. But in Europe the medieval age was an age of chivalry. It tended to raise the ideal of womanhood if not the status of women. Chivalrous duels and combats were generally not to be seen among Muslims in India. Such artificial sentimentality has nothing in common with (their) warrior creed.

The medieval age, by and large, conjures up vision of times in which everything was backward. Life was nasty, brutish and short. The ruler and the ruling classes were unduly cruel. Take the case of hunting animals and birds. In the process fields with standing crops were crushed and destroyed, often wantonly. The common man suffered. Man wallowed in ignorance. Man was dirty, there was no soap, no safety razor. Potable water was provided by rivers, else it was well-water or rainwater collected in tanks, ponds and ditches.

Political and religious tyranny, the institution of slavery, polygamy and inquisition or *hisbah* rendered life unpalatable. Men had few rights, women fewer. Wife was a possession; *parda* was a denial of the dignity of woman as woman. Medicine was limited, treatment a private affair, medicare was no concern of the state. Police was nowhere to be seen for seeming redressal of grievances while sorcery and magic, and ghosts and goblins were ever present to frighten and harm. Means of transport and communication were primitive. Most people hardly ever moved out of their villages or towns. Society was closed as was the mind.

But there was no scarcity of daily necessities of life. True, in medieval India there was no tea, no bed-tea. Coffee came late. It is mentioned by Jahangir in his memoirs. Tomato or potato did not arrive before the sixteenth century. Still, there was no dearth of palatable dishes for the medieval people to eat. Wheat and rice were common staples. Rice is said to be of as many kinds as twenty-one. *Paratha, halwa* and *harisa*, were commonly eaten by the rich, *Khichri* and *Sattu* by the poor. Muslims were generally meat-eaters and mostly ate the flesh of cow and goat though they have many sheep, because they have become accustomed to it. Fowls, pigeons and other birds were sold very cheap. Vegetables mentioned in medieval works are pumpkin, brinjal, cucumber, jackfruit (*kathal*), bitter gourd (*karela*), turnip, carrot, asparagus, various kinds of leafy vegetables, ginger, garden beet, onion, garlic, fennal and thyme. Dal and vegetables were cooked in ghee, tamarind was commonly used, and pickles prepared from green mangoes as well as ginger and chillies were favourites. There were fresh fruits, dry fruits and sweets.

Apples, grapes, pears and pomegranates were for important people. Melons, green and yellow (*kharbuza* and *tarbuz*), were grown in abundance. Orange, citron (*utrurj*), lemon (*limun*), lime (*lim*), *jamun*, *khirni*, dates and figs were in common use as also the plantains. Sugar-cane was grown in abundance and Ziyauddin Barani, writing in Persian, gives its Hindustani name *ponder*. Mango, then as now, was the most favourite fruit of India. Sweet-meats were of many kinds, as many as sixty five.

Some names like *reori*, sugar-candy, *halwa* and samosa are familiar to this day. Ibn Battuta's description of the preparation of *samosa* would make one's mouth water even today: Minced meat cooked with almond, walnut, pistachios, onion and spices placed inside a thin bread and fried in ghee. Wine and other intoxicants like hemp and opium, though prohibited in Islam, were freely taken by those who had a liking for it. Betel (then known by its Sanskrit name *tambul*) was an after dinner delicacy.

Muslim elite were very fond of eating rich and fatty food, both in quality and quantity. Their gluttony was whipped up as much by the love of sumptous dishes as by their habit of hospitality. It also received stimulus from the use of drinks and drugs and was best exhibited during excursions, picnics and arranged dinners.

According to Sir Thomas Roe, twenty dishes at a time were served at the tables of the nobles, but sometimes the number went even beyond fifty. But for the extremely poor, people in general enjoyed magnificent meals with sweetmeats and dry and fresh fruit added. All this was possible because food grains were extremely cheap throughout the medieval period as vouched by Barani for the thirteenth, Afif for the fourteenth, Abdullah for the fifteenth and Abul Fazl for the sixteenth centuries. The poor benefited by the situation but the benefit was probably offset by the force and coercion used in keeping prices low as asserted by Barani and Abdullah, the author of *Tarikh-i-Daudi*.

In matters of clothing also, India was better placed than many other countries in the middle ages. The textile industry of India was world-famous. The Sultan, the nobles and all the rich dressed exceedingly well. The costly royal robes, the gilded and studded swords and daggers, the parasols (*chhatra*) of various colours were all typically Indian paraphernalia of royal pomp and splendour. The use of rings, necklaces, earrings and other ornaments by men was also due to Indian wealth and opulence.

The dress of the Sultan and the elite consisted of kulah or headdress, a tunic worked in brocade and long drawers. The habit of dyeing the beard was common. It added in the old a zest for life as did the slanting of cap in the young. The Hindu aristocracy dressed like the Muslim aristocracy, except that in place of *kulah* they used a turban, and in place of long drawers they wore *dhoti* trimmed with gold lace.

The Muslims dressed heavily but the Hindus were scantily dressed. They cannot wear more clothing on account of the great heat, says Nicolo Conti. The orthodox Muslims wore clothes made of simple material like linen. The dress worn by scholars at the Firoz Shahi Madrasa consisted of the Syrian *jubbah* and the Egyptian *dastar*. But there was no special uniform for any one, not even for soldiers. In the villages the poor put on only a loin-cloth (*langota*) which Babur takes pains to describe in detail.

Muslim women dressed elaborately and elegantly. The inmates of the harems of the kings and nobles, indeed even their maids and servants dressed in good quality clothes. *Lehanga, angia* and *dupatta* were the common set for women as seen in medieval miniatures. They wore shoes made of leather and silk, often ornamented with gold thread and studded with precious stones. Besides women all over the country wore all kinds of ornaments, the rich of gold and silver, pearls and precious stones, the poor of silver and beads. Care of the teeth, painting the eyes, use of antimony, lampblack, *henna*, perfumed powders, sandal-wood, aloes-wood, otto of roses and wearing of flowers added elegance to personality and beauty to life.

Cities in medieval India were few, but they were large and impressive. Foreign visitors like Athnasius Nikitin and Barbosa give a favourable comparison of Indian cities with those of Europe. Cities and towns generally were built on the pattern of the metropolis of Delhi. Shihabuddin Ahmad, the author of *Masalik-ul-Absar* (fourteenth century), writes: The houses of Delhi are built of stone and brick The houses are not built more than two storeys high, and often are made of only one. Besides, there must have been hut-like houses of the poor huddled together in congested localities.

In the Delhi of the medieval period there was the fort and palace of the Sultan, cantonment area of the troops, quarters for the ministers, the secretaries, the Qazis, Sheikhs and *faqirs*. In every quarter there were to be found public baths, flour mills, ovens and workmen of all professions. In the villages, the peasants lived in penury.

But if there was little to spare, there was enough to live by. There were indoor and outdoor games for all to play-chess, backgammon, *pachisi, chausar*, dice, cards, kite-flying, pigeon-flying, polo, athletics; cock, quail and partridge fighting; and children's games. Public entertainments, as on the occasion of marriage in the royal family, comprised triumphal arches, dancing, singing, music, illuminations, rope-dancing and jugglery. The juggler swallowed a sword like water, drinking it as a thirsty man would *sherbet*. He also thrust a knife up his nostril. He mounted little wooden horses and rode upon the air Those who changed their own appearance practised all kinds of deceit. Sometimes they transformed themselves into angels, sometimes into demons.

Education

Belief in astrology and alchemy, magic and witchcraft, miracles and superstition was there both in the West and the East in the middle ages. Europe released itself from mental darkness sooner because of spread of education and early establishment of a number of universities. Oxford was set up in the twelfth century, Cambridge in 1209. Paris University came into being in the twelfth, Angers in the thirteenth and Orleans in 1231. In Italy, Salerno was founded in the tenth century, Arezzo in 1215, Padua 1222, Naples 1224, Siena 1246, Piacenza 1248, Rome 1303, and Pisa 1343. Such was the situation throughout Europe. The emergence of universities in such large numbers, with still larger number of schools whose selected pupils went to the universities, led to a spurt in learning which may explain the birth and flowering of Renaissance in Italy and Reformation in Germany. Martin Luther, who created a revolution in religion, was a student at the University of Erfurt founded in 1343.

In the early years of Islam the Muslims concentrated mainly on translating and adopting Creek scholarship. Aristotle was their favourite philosopher. Scientific and mathematical knowledge they adopted from the Greeks and Hindus. This was the period when the Arabs imbibed as much knowledge from the West and the East as possible.

In the West they learnt from Plato and Aristotle and in India Arab scholars sat at the feet of Buddhist monks and Brahman Pandits to learn philosophy, astronomy, mathematics, medicine, chemistry and other subjects. Caliph Mansur's (754-76) zeal for learning attracted many Hindu scholars to the Abbasid court. A deputation of Sindhi representatives in 771 C.E. presented many treatises to the Caliph and the *Brahma Siddhanta* of Brahmagupta and his *Khanda-Khadyaka*, works on the science of astronomy, were translated by Ibrahim al-Fazari into Arabic with the help of Indian scholars in Baghdad.

The Barmak (originally Buddhist Pramukh) family of ministers who had been converted to Islam and served under the Khilafat of Harun-ur-Rashid (786-808 C.E.) sent Muslim scholars to India and welcomed Hindu scholars to Baghdad. Once when Caliph Harun-ur-Rashid suffered from a serious disease which baffled his physicians, he called for an Indian physician, Manka (Manikya), who cured him. Manka settled at Baghdad, was attached to the hospital of the Barmaks, and translated several books from Sanskrit into Persian and Arabic. Many Indian physicians like Ibn Dhan and Salih, reputed to be descendants of Dhanapti and Bhola respectively, were superintendents of hospitals at Baghdad.

Indian medical works of Charak, Sushruta, the *Ashtangahrdaya*, the *Nidana*, the *Siddhayoga*, and other works on diseases of women, poisons and their antidotes, drugs, intoxicants, nervous diseases etc. were translated into Pahlavi and Arabic during the Abbasid Caliphate. Such works helped the Muslims in extending their knowledge about numerals and medicine. Havell goes even as far as to say that it was India, not Greece, that taught Islam in the impressionable years of its youth, formed its philosophy and esoteric religious ideals, and inspired its most characteristic expression in literature, art and architecture.

Avicenna (Ibn Sina) was a Persian Muslim who lived in the early eleventh century and is known for his great canon of medicine. Averroes (Ibn Rushd), the jurist, physician and philosopher was a Spanish Muslim who lived in the twelfth Century.

Al Khwarizmi (ninth century) developed the Hindu nine numbers and the zero (*hindisa*). Al Kindi (ninth century) wrote on physics, meteorology and optics. Al Hazen (Al Hatim C. 965-1039) wrote extensively on optics and the manner in which the human eye is able to perceive objects. Their best known geographers were Al Masudi, a globe-trotter who finished his works in 956 and the renowned Al Idrisi (1101-1154). Although there is little that is peculiarly Islamic in the contributions which Occidental and Oriental Muslims have made to European culture, even this endeavour had ceased by the time Muslim rule was established in India.

In the words of Easton, when the barbarous Turks entered into the Muslim heritage, after it had been in decay for centuries, did Islam destroy more than it created or preserved. For instance, Ibn Sina had died in Hamadan in 1037 and in 1150 the Caliph at Baghdad was committing to the flames a philosophical library, and among its contents the writings of Ibn Sina himself. In days such as these the Latins of the East were hardly likely to become scholars of the Muhammadans nor were they stimulated by the novelty of their surroundings to any original production.

Similar was the record of the Turks in India. No universities were established by Muslims in medieval India. They only destroyed the existing ones at Sarnath, Vaishali, Odantapuri, Nalanda, Vikramshila etc. to which thousands of scholars from all over India and Asia used to seek admission. Thus, with the coming of Muslims, India ceased to be a centre of higher Hindu and Buddhist learning for Asians.

The Muslims did not set up even Muslim institutions of higher learning. Their *maktabs* and *madrasas* catered just for repetitive, conservative and orthodox schooling. There was little original thinking, little growth of knowledge as such. Education in Muslim India remained a private affair. Writers and scholars, teachers and artists generally remained under the direct employment of kings and nobles.

There is little that can be called popular literature, folk-literature, epic etc. in contemporary Muslim writings. The life of the vast majority of common people was stereotyped and unrefined and represented a very low state of mental culture.

REFERENCES

Armand Maass: *Social Problems as Social Movements.* Philadelphia: Lippincott, 1975.

Currie, P.M. *The Shrine and Cult of Muin-ul-din Chishti of Ajmer*, Oxford, Delhi, 1989.

Joe R. Feagin: *Social Problems: A Critical Power-Conflict Perspective,* Englewood Cliffs, N.J.: Prentice-Hall, 1986.

MacIver R.M. : *Society, An Introductory Analysis*, Rinehart and Company, New York 1949.

Chapter **2**

Religious and Social Culture under Muslim Sultanate

SOCIAL CONDITION IN DELHI SULTANS

As the rigid Islamic law could not be applied in India, the Sultans of Delhi allowed the Hindus to live in India as Zimmis which means people living under a contract as second rate citizens, Jizya was imposed on them. It was fairly high and amounted to 48, 24 and 12 silver coins for the rich, the average and poor Hindus respectively. Monks, beggars, blind men and children were exempted. Originally, Brahmans were also exempted but Firuz Tughlaq imposed Jizya even on them. The imposition of Jizya was considered as a badge of inferiority. The peculiar thing about the payment of Jizya was that the payers of that tax had to pay it personally to the Collector and behave humbly and obsequiously at the time of payment. The idea behind the payment of Jizya was that on account of sheer economic pressure and discriminatory treatment at the time of payment, the bulk of the Hindu's would one day be obliged to become Muslims, but that did not happen.

In addition to the payment of Jizya, the Hindus were not allowed to worship in open and carry on religious propaganda. Many legal disabilities were imposed on the Hindus. Their evidence in a court of law against Muslims was not considered worth anything. In social matters, Hindus were not given the respect due to their rank or position in life. During the reigns of Ala-ud-Din Khalji, Firuz Tughlaq and Sikandar Lodi, the Hindus were not allowed to put on fine clothes, ride on horse-back or even to possess good arms. Sometimes, they were not allowed to chew betel or to put on the same kind of dress as the Muslims did. Hindus were forbidden from building new temples or repairing the old ones. Not only during war but even during peace-time, Hindu temples were razed to the ground and their images were broken to pieces. Firuz Tughlaq writes that at a time of peace. He rode to the village of Maluh where Hindus had, gathered to worship by the side of a tank and a fair was being held. The Sultan not only stopped the worship and destroyed the idols but also ordered the worshippers to be put to death. Firuz Tughlaq also razed the Keshav Deva temple at Mathura to the ground at a time when there was no rebellion or disturbance of peace. When the Hindus rebuilt it, it was destroyed by Sikandar Lodi. Many sacred shrines of the Hindus in Northern India were destroyed by the Muslim rulers and their broken images and statues can be seen in various Indian museums. Mosques, mausoleums and tombs were built on the sites of the ancient Hindu shrines out of the material of those very shrines. Some of the Sultans like Firuz Tughlaq and Sikandar Lodi made it the chief object of their policy to convert the Hindus to Islam by offering them many inducements and exerting all kinds of pressure on them. Firuz Tughlaq announced that whoever embraced Islam and repeated the Kalima would be exempt from Jizya. He himself writes that his policy was successful and many Hindus became Muslims. The Muslims considered it as their duty to propagate Islam and to convert Hindus to their religion. Some of them offered temptations to the Hindus to become Muslims and some of them used force in their Jihad (Holy war) against Hinduism. There were many Mullahs who called for such a Jihad against the Hindus. The result was that the Hindus during the Sultanate period did not enjoy religious freedom, liberty of conscience worship.

No individual in the Sultanate was allowed to speak a word against the Prophet of Islam or point out any defect in Islam. Those who were guilty of such offences were put to death. In the reign of Sikandar Lodi, a Brahman maintained that both Hinduism and Islam were true religions and he was put to death. Islam did not allow the conversion of Muslim to Hinduism or the re-conversion of Hindu converts to Islam. Those who were guilty of seducing Muslims from their religion were put to death. A similar punishment was given to those who reconverted Hindu converts to Islam. The only Muslim ruler who showed exceptional toleration in this respect was Zain-ul-Abadin of Kashmir. Sometimes, Muslim rulers converted Hindus to Islam in large numbers. Sikandar, the ruler of Kashmir, converted thousands of Hindus to Islam and expelled those who refused to become Muslims. Jalaluddin of Bengal (1414-1430) forcibly converted hundreds of Hindus and persecuted the rest. The same was done by Firuz Tughlaq and Sikandar Lodi.

Most of the Muslims in India were very orthodox in their religion and most of them were Sunnis. They considered the Shias also as their enemies like the Hindus. They suppressed the Shias, Karmanis, Mahadavis and other religious sects who were not Sunnis. Their leaders were persecuted in every way. Many of them were put to death. The Shia rulers of Bijapur and Golconda were persecuted. Firuz Tughlaq particularly persecuted the Shias. Their religious books were burnt by him in public. No Shia was taken in the service of the state. When the Karmanians revolted during the reigns of Iltutmish and Razia, they were put down ruthlessly. Many Sufi saints were also persecuted.

According to the law of Islam, the Hindus were not entitled to any kind of religious toleration. However, practical considerations compelled Mohammed-bin-Qasim, the conqueror of Sind and Multan, to accord to the Hindus of those provinces the same treatment as was given to the Christians and Jews in Arabia and other parts of the Caliphate. This practice was also followed by the Sultans to Delhi. However, as the Quran and the Hadis did not permit the Muslim rulers to allow Hindus to live under a Muslim Government but to give them the choice between Islam or death, the Ulama pressed the Sultans from time to time that the Quranic law should be enforced in India and the Hindus should be compelled either to embrace Islam or be butchered in cold blood.

There are many instances of such orthodox Ulama making this demand on the Sultans from time to time. During the reign of Iltutmish the Ulama made a united demand that the Hindus should be confronted with the choice of either embracing Islam or facing death. The Sultan referred the matter to his Wazir, Nizam-ul-Mulk Junnaidi. The Wazir agreed with the interpretation of law made by the Ulama but made the following recommendation : "At the moment India has newly been conquered and the Muslims are so few that they are like salt in a large dish. If the above orders are applied to the Hindus, it is possible that they might combine and a general confusion might ensue and the Muslims would be too few in number to suppress this general confusion, However, after a few years when in the capital and in the regions and the small towns, the Muslims are well established and the troops are larger, it will be possible to give the Hindus the choice of death or Islam."

In the reign of Ala-ud-Din Khalji, Qazi Mughis-ud-Din of Bayana made a similar demand in these words, "God has himself commanded their (Hindus) complete degradation in as much as the Hindus are the deadliest foes of the Prophet, The Prophet has said that they should either embrace Islam or they should be slain or enslaved and their property should be confiscated to the state. No one except the great Dr. Abu Hanifa allows the imposition of the Jizya upon the Hindus, while other scholars are of the opinion that there is no other alternative but death or Islam." It is clear from above that the Quranic law could not be enforced completely on above that the Quranic law could not be enforced completely on account of the vast numerical superiority of the Hindus and their military and economic strength. However, writers like Barani continued to lament that the fundamental Islamic law were ignored by the Sultans of Delhi.

Many causes were responsible for the conversion of Hindus to Islam. Some Hindus who came into contact with all powerful and prosperous Muslims, joined their faith. Some Hindus became Muslims to secure good jobs in the state. Some were tempted to become Muslims on account of the favours offered to them. Many Hindus were made Muslims through sheer force. Many Hindus of low castes became Muslims in order to raise their status, but their number was not large. There were very few Hindus who became Muslims as a result of the influence of the principles of Islam. One important reason was that there was at that time bitter hatred among Hindus against the Muslims who bad persecuted them and also humiliated them. There were many orthodox Hindus and they were so much devoted to their religion that the question of their embracing Islam could not arise. Although for about five centuries the Hindus and Muslims lived near one another they remained separate. The Hindus had to suffer terribly due to religious and political causes but they continued to oppose the Muslims. There is hardly any example of this period when a Hindu family established a matrimonial alliance with a royal family. In the 14th century, Tughril Shah forcibly married the daughter of Ranamal Bhatti and the consequences were disastrous. Feelings of enmity were aroused in the minds of the Hindus against the Muslims.

Not only the Sultans but other Muslims also considered it as their religious duty to convert Darul Harb (Land of the Kafirs) into Darul Islam (Land of the Muslims). Those Muslim rulers who tried to convert Hindus to Islam were praised by Muslim historians who belonged to the Ulama class. Instructions were issued to convert the Hindus to Islam. One of the reasons why that could not be done was that most of the time of the Sultans was spent in fighting against the Mongols and also in suppressing rebellions in various parts of the country.

There was a decline in the character of the Muslims. The Muslim invaders were brave people but as a result of their stay in India with a lot of money, power and luxury, they deteriorated. The early Muslim soldiers were prepared to sacrifice their lives for the sake of Islam and were ready to fight battles for the conquest of India. However, the luxurious life in India took away their courage and bravery. Too much of drinking and beautiful women finished their bravery. They lost their spirit of self-reliance. They lost self-respect and courage. Instead of being an asset, they became a burden to the state. They began to shun hard work and fighting. They became big landlords. They bad to pay only one-tenth of the produce to the state. As they got too much of wealth without exertion, their decline started.During the Sultanate period, the Mahayan form of Buddhism was prominent. Many scholars were born during this period. They put emphasis on Bhakti and not Nirvana. They acknowledged Buddha as the highest power. They worshipped Bodhisattavas. Buddhism had great influence in North-West and Central India. They had to struggle every day against the Brahman Pandits and philosophers. As a result of that, their influence declined.

There were four important Sampradaya, of Vaishnavism. Their names were Shri Sampradaya, Brahm Sampradaya, Rudra Sampradaya and Sanakadi Sampradaya, Ramanuja propagated Shri Sampradaya. His followers believed in Advaitvad. The original Guru of Brahm Sampradaya was Brahma but it was propagated by Madhavacharya. Its followers were Dvaitvadis. The followers of Rudra Sampradaya were Advaitvadi. It was propagated by Vishnuswami and Vallabhacharya. The followers of Sanakadi Sampradaya were Dvaita Advaitvadi. It was propagated by Nimbarkacharya.

There were many Sampradayas of Saivism. The important among them were Pasupat, Kapalik, Virsaiv, Shiv Sidhanta, Lingayat etc. Saivism was a very old religion and it spread in all parts of India. Many Sampradayas came into existence. The Saivas collected a lot of knowledge. They started the cult of Vam-Marg. When the Muslims attacked India, at that time Vijrayani Buddhists and Kapalik Saivas were spread from Bihar to Assam and Kalinga. As a result of the preachings of Sankaracharya, Buddhism lost its hold. Sankar gave Gyan Marg for the Pandits and worship for the ordinary people. In this way, he won over people belonging to all walks of life. There were some pandits who regarded the views of Sankar as not attractive and they put emphasis on Bhakti.

The religious order to which the Yogis belonged was known by different names : Gorakh-Panthi (followers of the path prescribed by Gorakhnath), Nath and Kanphata (split-eared). The literal meaning of the word Nath is master. The Yogis regarded Siva as Adi Nath (Original Master). There was nine human Naths who were really superior Yogis. To that category belonged Matsyendranath and Gorakhnath who were supposed to have attained immortality and as a consequence became objects of worship. The term Kanphata had reference to the practice of splitting the cars which tradition ascribed to Gorakhnath. A Siddha was a Yogi who had attained the stage of perfection, a semi-divine stage, through the practice of Yoga. The Siddhas were supposed to have acquired "extended life and miraculous powers." Usually, the Yogis used the sacred thread. A secular Yogi was known as Rawal. He earned his living by begging, fortune-telling, singing and similar practices. There was another sect of Yogis known as Aipanthis, i.e worshippers of the Mother Goddess. A female disciple of Gorakhnath named Bimla Devi was called Mai.

The Yogis were primarily devotees of Siva in the Bhairava form which represented his most terrible aspect, although some attention was paid to Vishnu. Sometimes Siva and Gorakhnath were identified. Gorakhnath was worshipped as a manifestation of Shiva in some Shaivite temples. In general, the Yogis worshipped many gods and goddesses of the Hindu pantheon. They also worshipped nine Naths and 94 Siddhas living in the Himalayas.

The Kanphata order admitted not only Sudras and low caste recruits but also Muslims. Caste restrictions were not observed in respect of inter-dining among the Hindu Yogis) but the Muslim Yogis took their food separately. Two principal vows had to be taken and those were to live by begging and to maintain celibacy.

The Gorakh-panthis succeeded in evolving an integrated system of thought and practice. They drew a clear line of distinction between a Yogi and a philosopher. Intellectual speculation had no relevance for a Yogi. He aimed at direct spiritual experience of the Truth on a supra-intellectual plane of consciousness. He devoted himself to the practice of various courses of self-discipline until he reached the stage of Samadhi which conferred upon a Yogi all that was worth knowing and attaining. It destroyed all fetters of Karma and all imperfections such as ignorance, ego, attachment, aversion and lust of life. That stage was called Nirvana.

The Yogi view of the world was not pessimistic. The world is not the creation of any Satanic force. It is not to be discarded as an evil. The constitution of the individual body is very important in the Yoga system.

The rigorous disciple of the Yoga system was very hard for the ordinary seeker. Hence, it degenerated to the level of self-delusion or even conscious fraud. Hatha Yoga became popular because it was supposed to bring miraculous powers which could be used for worldly purposes.

The view of the Muslim rulers in India was that the Hindus were their bitter enemies and were always scheming and organising instructions against them. Hence, they left no stone unturned to suppress them. The Hindus were made to pay high taxes and those were collected with great severity. Ala-ud-Din Khalji exacted 50% of their produce from the Hindus of the Doad. Most of the Hindus became poor and they had to struggle very hard to make their both ends meet. Their standard of living fell. They got no job in the state. Very few opportunities were given 'to them for rise in life. Sir Jadunath Sarkar has criticised in very strong words the treatment meted to the Hindus during the Sultanate period. The circumstances were such that there was no scope for the development and progress of the Hindus. Dr. Ishwari Prasad does not agree with his view. He admits that the Hindus were very badly treated during the Sultanate period and they had to face many difficulties even to save their religion. It is also true that they had to pay high taxes and were also humiliated. However, Dr. Ishwari Prasad maintains that the Hindus did their best to oppose the Muslims in every way. Moreover, all the Muslim rulers were not bad. It was during this period that many Hindu philosophers, writers, poets, saints and warriors appeared. It was during this period that we bad saints like Ramananda, Chatanya Mahaprabhu and Guru Nanak. Many Hindu poets added to the literature of India during this period. In spite of the various invasions, the Hindu did not Use their spirit. In spite of Muslim victories, Hindu culture continued to flourish. Their religion and philosophy continued to develop and grow. The writings of the Hindu scholars and saints of that period are a part of the great literature of the Hindus.

The Sufis challenged the orthodoxy of the Sunni. They believed in attaining God through love and devotion. The Muslims did not like the Sufis on account of their views. Most of the Sufis set up their own orders under their Shaikhs or Pirs. They spent all their time in devotion and prayers. The view of the Sufis was that the Ulama had not interpreted the Quran correctly and had given tip the principle of brotherhood of Islam. The Sufis and Ulama opposed each other. The Ulama criticised the Sufis on account of their broadmindedness. The Sufis called the, Ulama as opportunists who ran after the Sultans to win over favours. The Sufis did not revolt. They believed that good days were coming. The Sufis Firs were respected by the Hindus.

There were many similarities between the Sufis and saints of the Bhakti movement. Both of them put emphasis on the oneness of God and the desirability of devotion to God. They put all the emphasis on love to meet God. They realised the necessity of a Guru or Pir to achieve God. However, the Bhakti saints did not believe in the mysticism of the Sufis. They did not believe in remaining away from society and the common man. They wanted to solve the problems of the people and improving their condition.

Before the coming of the Muslims, there were Hindus, Buddhists and Jains in India. They bad different ways of living, worship and action. During the period, the influence of Jainism had declined. It was confined to Rajasthan and North-West parts of India. During this period, many Jain scholars wrote many books on their religion. It is true that further decline of Jainism was stopped but they could not complete with Mahayanism, Saivism and Vaishnavism.

ECONOMIC CONDITION

During the Sultanate period, India was famous for her fabulous wealth and it was the story of her enormous riches which tempted Sultan Mahmud to invade India. There is truth in the statement of the contemporary writers of the vast plunder acquired by Mohammad Bin Qasim, in Sind and Multan and Sultan Mahmud of Ghazni in India proper in the form of coined and the uncoined money, precious stones of various kinds and various other things valued at crores of rupees. Not only this, the Sultans of Delhi also acquired enormous booty in their expeditions, both in Northern and Southern India. It was the wealth of India which enabled them to incur heavy expenses on their wars and also give a lot of money to their soldiers and courtiers and likewise spend huge amounts on their palaces, households and the Durbar. The general prosperity of the country is testified to not only by Indians but also by foreign writers. Marco Polo visited Southern India between 1288 and 1293. Ibn Batuta travelled in most parts of India between 1334 and 1342. Mahuan, a Chinese, visited Bengal in 1406. The accounts of all of them show that India was prosperous both industrially and economically and there was "a great abundance of all the necessaries of life."

The main source of the wealth of India was agriculture. In most parts of India, the soil was fertile. There was copious rainfall and irrigation facilities were provided since early times and were systematically reinforced.

The economic outlook of the peasantry was determined neither by the state, nor by the intermediaries, nor by the village community, but by tradition. They produced and consumed practically in the same way as their ancestors had done. The economic measures of Ala-ud-Din Khalji disturbed the old equilibrium for a few years and that also for a limited area but the status quo was restored after his death. Agricultural produce was intended mainly for local consumption although a part of its made its way to the cities and even abroad. Prices were generally determined by local factors such as abundance or scarcity of rain. Cultivation was a family enterprise and all the members of the family participated in it.

During the Sultanate period, there was probably more than enough land for cultivation. To quote Moreland. "There was fertile land to spare, waiting for men with the resources needed to bring it under the plough". The state was anxious to encourage people to bring more land under cultivation but without much success. The irrigation projects of Firuz Tughlaq benefited only a limited area in the neighbourhood of Delhi. The people of the Doab were penalized by Ala-ud-Din Khalji for their industry and the fertility of their land. In one way, the state actually injured agricultural production. That happened when the royal troops marched from one place to another and that was very often.-Amir Khusrau has described in these words the destruction brought about by the royal troops, "The earth was denuded of all grass and the river dried of water and thanks to the compulsory requisitions of the royal party, the people were left without any food for themselves or grass and fodder for their animals."

In the Punjab, there was a widespread extension of cultivation in the 15th century as a result of the use of the Persian wheel. Malik Muhammad Jaisi refers to the use of the Persian wheel in Avadh under the name of Rahat. Ibn Batuta mentions the use of Persian wheels on the river Meghna in East Bengal. Babar has mentioned the use of Dhenkli for a constant supply of water. The cultivators tilled the soil in the same way ai their ancestors had done for centuries using primitive ploughs and bullocks and crying for rains during the dry season.

There are references to the extensive cultivation of foodgrains and other crops, nurture of fruit trees and rearing of domestic animals. Ibn Batuta refers to the fertility of the land and production of two crops per year. The crops mentioned by him are millet, peas, beans, wheat, barley, chick-peas and lentils. Sesame and sugarcane were cultivated with the autumn crops. Rice was sown three times a year. There was an abundance of fine rice at Sirsuti, sugar at Kanauj, wheat and betel-leaf at Dhar and wheat at Marh near Gwalior. He mentions fruits like mangoes, jack fruits, black berries and three varieties of oranges. Mahuan gives a long list of cereals and vegetables including rice, millet, sesamum and beans, ginger, mustard, onions and garlic, cucumber and egg-plant. He also mentions coconut, betel-nut, banana, jack fruit, pomegranate, sugarcane and honey. Barbosa found in Bengal cotton fields and sugarcane fields, ginger, and pepper plantations, gardens of fruit trees like oranges and lemon etc. White sugar was produced in Bengal from sugarcane. There was an abundance of horses, cows, sheep and domestic fowls.

Firuz Tughlaq laid gardens in the neighbourhood of Delhi and at some other places. That promoted a general improvement in quality of fruits. Improved methods of gardening and fruit cultivation were adopted in parts of Central India and Rajasthan. Importance was attached to horticulture. There are references to various kinds of flowers in the works of Amir Khusrau and Malik Mohammad Jaisi, Fragrant wood like sandal wood and aloes were grown in different parts of the country.

There are scattered references to prices of agricultural commodities. Fluctuations in prices were caused by natural calamities, administrative and political changes, difficulties of communication and transport and the general economic forces. In the time of Balban, baked bread was sold at two sers a Jital. In the reign of Jalal-ud-Din Khalji, corn sold at one Jital per ser on account of famine. Under Ala-ud-Din Khalji, prices per maund were wheat 7½ Jitals, barley 4 Jitals, paddy 5 Jitals, pulses 5 Jitals, lentils 3 Jitals, sugar (white) 100 Jitals, mutton 10 Jitals, ghee 16 Jitals etc.

Prices were higher during the reign of Mohammad Tughlaq, Under Firuz Tughlaq prices of commodities came down. Wheat was 8 Jitals per maund, barley 4 Jitals per maund, pulses 4 Jitals per maund and lentils

4 Jitals per maund. Prices rose when rainfall was scarce. When Firuz Tughlaq invaded Sind, the price of corn varied between 3.2 and 2 Jitals per ser. Prices were exceptionally low in the reign of Ibrahim Lodi. One Bahloli which was 1.6 Jital in value could buy 10 maunds of corn. 5 sers of oil and 10 yards of coarse cloth. All other commodities were also cheap.

In the outlaying provinces, the prices were determined by local conditions rather than by fluctuations in the upper Ganges valley and the Delhi region. Ibn Batuta tells us that the prices of commodities in Bengal were cheaper than in any other country visited by him. He was told by an inhabitant of Bengal that he could maintain himself with his wife and servant for full one year at a cost of 8 Dirhams (small silver coins), Bengal was known as "a paradise of plenty" in the mid-14th century. A Chinese writer of the 14th century tells us that 46 baskets of rice could be bought for one cowrie in Orissa.

Centuries before the advent of the Turks, India was industrially well organised. There were guilds and crafts in the villages and towns which carried on widespread commerce. Even without the help of the state, those institutions survived the shocks of foreign invasions and internal revolutions. There were two kinds of industries—those under state patronage and those which were, purely private. The Sultans had their own Karkhanas or workshops in Delhi which employed thousands of weavers of silk and other stuffs.

The Karkhanas were maintained by the Sultans for the manufacture of articles for use in the royal household. The number of Karkhanas probably varied in the different reigns. They were placed in-charge of a noble of high rank who was assigned by superintendents appointed directly by the Sultans. It is said about the Karkhanas of Mohammad Tughlaq that the manufactured robes of honour numbering two lacs every year to be distributed among the nobles and fine Muslim and other articles to be sent as gifts to other monarchs.

About 500 workers in gold brocade and silk were employed for the manufacture of golden tissues for brocades to be used by the ladies of the royal harem or given away as presents to the Amirs and their wives. Other articles to be used in the royal household like caps, shoes, curtains, tapestry, waistbands, saddles, embroideries etc. were also prepared in the Karkhanas. Arif tells us that there were 36 Karkhanas in the reign of Firuz Tughlaq.

The Sultan attached great importance to them and said, "Just as lakhs of revenue are collected in the provinces, similarly lakhs are collected in the Karkhanas. The turnover of a Karkhana is not less than the turn-over of the city of Multan." Afif's father and uncle were incharge of two Karkhanas and Afif himself worked with them. According to Afif, the Karkhanas were divided into two categories. Ratibi Karkhanas provided daily food for men and animals. Ghair-i-Ratibi Karkhanas dealt with commodities produced by human labour. The monthly expenditure of the Ratibi Karkhanas was 160,000 Tankas exclusive of salaries. Karkhanas were incharge of water supply department, departments for provision of lights and scents, departments for looking after stables, breeding of horses and looking after elephants, oxen, mules, camels etc. The Ghair-i-Ratibi Karkhanas looked after wardrobes, baths, standards library, furniture and tents, armour and war material, jewels etc. Some of the Karkhanas were factories in the literal sense while others purchasing agencies. Greatest attention was paid to luxury goods and war materials.

ECONOMIC CONDITION IN SULTANS PERIOD

As regards private industries, the Sultans followed the policy of laissez faire. The only exception was made by Ala-ud-Din Khalji who imposed prohibition on the sale of brocade and gold cloth, finer varieties of silk of Delhi and Cambay and certain varieties of cloth. His purpose was to control the use of luxuries by the nobility, The most important industries were the textile industry, including the manufacture of cotton, woollen and silk cloth, dyeing industry, printing industry, calico printing industry etc. The other industries were sugar industry, metal work industry, paper industry, stone and brick works industries and industries such as inlay of stone work, enamelling etc. There were minor industries like shoemaking, manufacture of liquors, brass and other metal and clay industries.

In the manufacture and export of textile goods, Bengal and Gujarat were in the forefront. They had the advantage of harbour facilities and the old tradition of commercial relations with foreign countries. Mahuan tells us that ocean-going ships which carried goods to foreign countries were made in Bengal. Chittagong was a great port but Satgaon was a small port. Cambay was a great industrial city and also a great port. There is a lot of evidence regarding the abundance, variety and high quality of the textiles of Bengal Amir Khusrau was impressed by the stuffs presented by Bughra Khan, the father of Kaiqubad, who was the Governor of Bengal.

Khusrau "describes a piece of cloth the texture of which was so fine that the body was visible through it; one could fold a whole piece of this cloth inside one's nail, yet it was large enough to cover the world when unfolded". The exaggeration in the language of the poet cannot be doubted but the fact remains that Bengal produced the finest varieties of cloth. In the 14th century, Ibn Batuta found cotton fabrics of the finest texture, 15 yards in length, selling at 2 silver coins (Dinars). Mahuan found several varieties of fine cotton fabrics and silk handkerchiefs and gold-embroidered caps, He also refers to mulberry trees and silk worms. The excellence of Bengal textiles is also praised by other writers. Barbosa tells us that the high quality of Bengal textiles secured for them a good market in Malacca and Ormuz.

Varthema tells us that Cambay in Gujarat contributed about half the total textile exports of India. Barbosa says that Cambay had skilled craftsmen of many kinds who manufactured coarse and find varieties of woven white cotton fabrics, printed cotton stuffs, silk cloth, coloured velvets, satins, thick carpets, beautiful quilts, quilted articles of clothing etc. Cambay textiles found an extensive market in Western Europe, South Africa and South Asia (Burma, Malaya and Indonesia).

There were industries based on metal work. There were iron, mercury and lead mines but their output was not adequate. The industry of sword-making was well established. There were several varieties of Indian swords. Mahuan refers to the manufacture of steel guns, knives scissors, basins and cups in Bengal. Ornaments of gold and silver were often decorated with excellent inlay work and they were used by the richer classes. Barbosa tells us that there were expert goldsmiths at Cambay who did very fine work. There as also the manufacture of jewellery, coral work and ivory work.

Building industry was developed by the workers in stone, brick and wood. They were patronised by the state. It is said that Ala-ud-Din Khalji employed 70,000 such workers. Firuz Tughlaq trained 4000 slaves as skilled masons. Babar employed 2000 stone-cutters in the construction of buildings at Agra and other places. Wood-work of high quality was required for the construction of oceans going vessels, boats, doors of houses, seats and bedsteads of the rich people. There was also the paper industry but its production was not adequate and the quality of paper produced was not of a high order. In Bengal, white paper of the Chinese variety was made from the bark of a tree. Nicolo Conti refers to the use of paper in Gujarat. Sugarcane was cultivated in different parts of Northern India for the production of sugar of which there were several varieties. Soft sugar was used by the rich and unrefined sugar (Gur) was used by the poor. Bengal produced sugar not only for its own consumption but also for export. Mahuan refers to the export of sugar from Bengal.

Leather was used for saddles and bridles of horses, scabbards of swords, covers of manuscripts, shoes, water buckets and for packing of sugar for the export etc. Dressed skins of different kinds of animals were exported in larger quantities to other countries from Gujarat. Workers in leather industry formed a separate caste known as Chamars.

During the Sultante period, the volume of trade, both internal and external, carried on by Indians, was enormous. India had commercial relations with the outside world. The value of her exports was much greater than that of her imports and the balance of trade was always in her favour. That is the reason why it was generally believed that "Merchants of all countries never ceased to carry pure gold into India, and to bring back in exchange commodities of herbs and gums".

There was a large volume of internal trade. Among the important centres of trade in Gujarat, Barbosa mentions the town of Limodara and the sea port of Rander. Multan and Lahore were clearing houses for trade in the North-Western region. There were good roads which were constructed mainly for the use of the army but were also used by the traders for the transport of commercial goods. There was a road from Delhi to Daulatabad which covered a distance of 40 days' journey. Travel was often insecure and that hindered trade.

In villages and small towns, petty business was in the hands of shop-keepers, itinerant dealers, pedlars and middlemen who were professionals. Large scale business was in the hands of special groups or particular communities. The Multanis and the Banias of Gujarat were the most important business communities of Northern and Western India. Internal trade was almost entirely in the hands of Hindu merchants while foreign trade was mostly in the hands of Muslim merchants and some in the hands of Hindus. When Ibn Batuta visited Cambay, he found foreign merchants forming the majority of the population of that city. Barbosa tells us that at Cannanore Hindu and Muslim merchants sailed in their own ships as far as Ormuz. The Hindu Chettis of Coromandel traded with Burma and joined the colony of foreign merchants engaged in wholesale business at Malacca. Orissa had a prosperous overseas trade with South-East Asia till the 15th century. The Muslim traders had certain advantages in foreign trade. Most of the foreign countries were ruled by Muslims and they patronised the Muslim merchants. Muslim merchants were required to pay only 50% of the import duties levied on Hindu merchants. The Hindus themselves were responsible for the loss of their share in foreign trade. Foreign travel was prohibited for the Hindus and those who violtated that rule were punished. The result was that the Hindus developed a sort of aversion towards sea voyages and thus were eliminated from overseas trade. However, the Hindu merchants of Malabar and Coromandel did not care for those prohibitions and carried on foreign trade.

The Banjaras of Rajasthan played an important part in transporting agricultural and other products from one part of the country to another. Their operations were on a large scale. They employed hundreds and thousands of oxen in their carts and wagons. On those roads which were insecure, their caravans were guided and guarded by the Bhats of Rajasthan.

Brokers played an important role in commercial transactions. They charged their commission from both the sellers and the purchasers. The bankers provided capital in the form loans and they also accepted deposits. Money-lenders also played their part. They lent money on interest through bonds. It appears that the rate of interest varied between 10% and 20%. Both the Hindus and Muslims did the work of lending on interest although the Shariat did not allow the Muslims to charge interest.

Foreign trade was carried on both through land routes and sea routes. Land route was interrupted for some time on account of the Mongol invasions but after their invasions were over, trade flourished in musk, furs, arms, falcons, camels and horses. Horses were imported from foreign countries in large numbers. In the time of Mohammad Tughlaq, a fixed tax of 7 Tankas per horse had to be paid on the border of Sind. Another amount had to be paid at Multan. It is mentioned in the Adi Granth that the Nawab of Sultanpur was thinking of purchasing horses in Kabul.

As regards foreign trade by sea, two routes were used on the West. Goods were carried either along the Persian Gulf and from there to Mesopotamia to the Mediterranean or by sea routes to the ports of the Red Sea and from there to the Mediterranean through Egypt. From Alexandria, Indian goods were taken by Italian merchants and they distributed them in Europe. Ormuz was the principal centre of trade by the first sea route. It was the entrepot of trade of Hind and Sind. Aden and Jiddha occupied the same position in the trade by the second route.

The ports of Malabar were the principal clearing houses for the Indian goods and Cambay occupied an important position. Goods were taken from Cambay to Ormuz and Aden and vice-versa. The principal exports were cotton and linen cloth, carpets, drugs, gems, seed pearls and carnelians. The principal imports were copper, quicksilver, vermillion, rose water, gold, silver, woollens, coloured velvets, coral, lead, alum, saffron etc. Cambay had trade relations with East Africa. Barbosa tells us that ships from Cambay visited Makdashau with cloths and spices and they brought gold, ivory and wax. Cambay cloth and beads were exported to the ports of Melinde, Mombasa and Kilwa and from there they were taken by local Muslim merchants to other places in Africa. Cambay cloth was sold at the African ports and African ivory was sold in Gujarat.

TRADE CONDITION IN DEVELOPMENT COUNTRY

There was a regular trade between India and China. Chinese ships visited the Malabar ports in the 14th century. Malacca was the most important international port in South-East Asia. The next was Pegu. Cambay and Rander in Gujarat participated in the trade with Burma and the Islands of South-East Asia. The merchants of India were known for their honesty and were welcomed and respected everywhere.

It is worthy of notice that to begin with the Sultans of Delhi did not pay much attention to economic matters as they were very busy in the work of conquest. Balban was the first Sultan who was able to establish law and order in the country. He was also the first to think of economic matters. Kampil and Patiali regions were cleared of robbers and thieves. That helped agriculture and trade. Merchants were able to go from one place to another without fear. Many changes in the economic field were made during the reign of Ala-ud-Din Khalji. There was a terrible famine during the reign of Firuz Tughlaq as a result of which the prices of goods increased. The condition of the people in the Shivalik was so bad that the Hindus of those areas migrated to Delhi and about 20 or 30 persons committed suicide by drowning in the Jamuna river. It appears that the state did not perform its duty of saving the people.

Ala-ud-Din Khalji was an energetic Sultan and he understood the economic problems. In his ambition to conquer the world, he devised an economic plan. Land revenue was reorganised in his reign and fixed. His Naib Wazir-i-Mumalik followed the policy of crushing completely the Hindus and making them powerless. He succeeded in suppressing the Hindus of the Doab. He charged from them 50% of their produce as land revenue. In addition to that, he levied house tax, grazing tax etc. Most of the burden fell on the peasants and they were Hindus. Most of the Muslims were either in administration or in the army. An achievement of the economic reforms of Ala-ud-Din Khalji was the control of the prices in the market. That led to a fall in the prices of the goods to such an extent that one soldier along with his horse could live on 234 Tankas for the whole year. Corn was stocked in the granaries of the state and it was available at the time of famine. Ibn Batuta tells us that he himself saw with his own eyes heaps of rice collected by Ala-ud-Din Khalji. As the economic reform, of Ala-ud-Din Khalji were not based on any sound economic principle, they disappeared after his death and the merchants were happy because they could charge whatever price they liked.

The economic policy of Mohammad Tughlaq was not successful at all. His token currency failed. The economic condition of the country was satisfactory between 1351 and 1388 A.D. The irrigation projects of the state helped agriculture. The income of the state from land revenue increased. There was an increase of six crores and eighty five lacs of Tankas in the income of the state. From Doab alone, the state got an increase of 85 lacs of Tankas as income. As the prices of commodities were low, the rich were able to save a lot of money. Afif writes that when Malik Shahi Shahana died, 50 lacs of Tankas and many valuable things were found from his house. The rates were so low that the people could travel from one place to another without much expense. Labour was cheap at that time. Afif writes that there was no dearth of gold or silver for anybody. There was no woman who did not put on an ornament. Every house had its own good furniture. The view of Dr. Ishwari Prasad is that there in much exaggeration in the account of Afif.

Towards the end of the 14th century, India had to pass through a terrible economic crisis. The Tughlaq Empire began to disintegrate. In 1398, Timur attacked India and after defeating the Sultan of Delhi, he looted to his heart's satisfaction the people of Delhi and also the surrounding areas. He took away with him a lot of gold, silver and precious stones. As a result of his invasion, the city of Delhi was completely deserted. Timor took away so much of wealth from India that not much was left in Delhi and the adjoining areas. Wealth remained only in the outlying provinces. Writing about Bengal in 1406, Mahuan says that the rich people of Bengal built ships and carried on foreign trade through them. Many people were engaged in trade and many more in agriculture. The people had their own professions. The coin used was known as Tanka. It was equal to two Chinese coins in weight. He also says that the people produced two crops of rice in a year. The other commodities of common use such as wheat etc. were found in plenty. There were many kinds of fruits.

Thus trade and industry in India were directed primarily for the satisfaction of the demands of the upper, classes who had plenty of money to pay for them. They spent wrecklessly. Amir Khusrau wrote that the "stream of gold flows through the majestic city of Delhi". However, the poor people suffered. Amir Khusrau was right in saying: "Every pearl in the royal crown is but the crystallized drop of blood fallen from the tearful eyes of the poor peasant."

SELF RESPECT AND SOCIAL CONDITION IN MEDIEVAL SOCIETY

The Hindus hated the Muslims and called them Mlechchhas. They were not prepared to interdine with them or to have marriage relations. There was a feeling among the Hindus that by doing so they would fall in life. Most of the Hindus cared for their self-respect. Their superiority was undoubted. They were known for their love for justice and were not prepared to give it up in actual life. In their professions, they were known for honesty and worthy of confidence. In all spheres of life, Hindus were respected for their qualities of head and heart. It is true that the religious and intellectual leaders of the Hindus were not influenced by Muslim conquest of India and they maintained their standard of nobility and superiority, but the ordinary Hindu was affected by Muslim conquest. On account of lack of independence, there was a fall in Hindu society. The Sultans of Delhi and other Muslim rulers regarded the Hindus as their enemies. With a few exceptions, no Hindu was given any position of responsibility in the state by the Muslim rulers. Even the right to life was given to them if they agreed to pay Jizya. For political reasons, Ala-ud-Din Khalji treated the Hindus of the Doab with great severity. He humiliated the Khuts, Chaudharies and Muqaddams. No Hindu could raise his head.

There was no sign of any gold or silver coin or even Jital in their houses. They could not ride on horse. They had no arms or good clothes, Birani tells us that their lot bad become so bad that their wives were forced to work as maid servants in the houses of the Muslims. The Muslims state offered many concessions to convert the Hindus to Islam. Ibn-Batuta tells us that when a Hindu desired to become a Muslim, he was taken in the presence of the Sultan who gave him valuable clothes and articles of gold. The orthodox Muslims hated the Hindus. When the condition of Hindus improved a little during the reign of Khusrau, Birani wrote in sadness that the Hindus had again begun to live in comfort and had become happy. Brahamanas were not taxed to Jizya but Firuz Tughlaq imposed Jizya even on the Brahamanas. Sikandar Lodi also started persecuting the Hindus and their condition became miserable.

In Hindu society, there were four principal castes (Brahamanas, Kshatriyas, Vaisyas and Sudras) in order of rank and status, and indefinite number of so-called mixed castes of varying status and the despised castes who were placed at the bottom of society. The old position of the Brahamanas and Kshatriyas was materially affected by the Muslim conquest of India. The Brahamanas lost their royal patronage. They got no job in administration. They were no longer prosperous. They lost the opportunity of earning a lot of money by officiating as priests in sacrifices. The result was that the new Smritis laid down that they could pursue agriculture through hired labour. In times of special distress, they could themselves cultivate the fields. Both agriculture and trade were the occupations of the people of all castes. In view of the change, the rank and file among the Brahamanas could not devote the same time and attention to Vedic studies and spiritual and intellectual pursuits as they used to do in the past. The new commentaries on the Smritis allowed them to give less time to their original occupation and content themselves with the study of just a part of the Vedas in which they were interested and in some cases with that of the Puranas alone. This was an admission of the decline of the Vedic studies during the Sultanate period and the importance of the Brahamanas. There was also a change in the attitude of the Brahamanas towards the Sudras. The latter were allowed to listen to recitations of the Puranas. It was made permissible to eat the food of certain Sudra castes under some special circumstances. The Sudras were allowed to engage themselves in some of the prohibited articles of sale, including meat.

The Kshatriyas lost not only political power but also the opportunity of earning their livelihood as soldiers. Except in Rajasthan, Central India and the Himalayan region in the North, West, many of the Kshatriyas sank into the status of local landlords serving as intermediaries in the revenue system organised by the Muslim rulers. Guru Nanak has referred to the demoralisation of the Kshatriyas in these words: "The Kshatriyas have forsaken their religion and adopted the language of the Malechchas." This refers to the acceptance of service by the Kshatriyas under the Muslim rulers and their imitation of Muslim manners and customs. The changed position of the Kshatriyas had a direct impact on Hindu society as a whole. On account of the elimination of the normal rivalry of the Kshatriyas, the authority and personal influence of the Brahamanas increased among the Hindu masses. However, that is not wholly true because the Brahamanas themselves were weakened as they could not look upto political power for support and patronage. The Brahamans continued to be the unofficial guides of Hindu society.

The picture of the condition of the Vaisyas and Sudras and the untouchable given by Al-Biruni seems to be exaggerated. The Sudras were divided into two categories. Those of the lower category were looked down upon as interior, as the untouchables. The number of mixed castes had gone up to 64 and those were divided into two groups, Those belonging to the Anuloma group (born of higher caste males and lower caste females) were considered twice-born and were entitled to the sacred thread and other sacraments. Those belonging to the Pratiloma group (born of lower caste fathers and higher caste mothers) were considered as belonging to low castes. The lower orders of society were discriminated against and even despised, Detailed rules were prescribed to avoid contact with the despised castes. Purification by bathing with clothes on was prescribed for touching a Chandala. Different penances were to be undertaken by a Brahman for conversing, or sleeping on the same bed, or going in company with a Chandala, for looking at or touching a Chandala, for drawing water from a tank owned by Chandala, for drinking water from a well from which water had been drawn in a Chandala vessel, for eating the food of a Chandala or living for some time in the same house with a Chandala, for the entrance of a Chandala in the house of a Brahmana etc.

The caste rules and the rules governing the relations between the various castes as laid down in the Shastras were not strictly followed. Some Brahmans followed the occupation of the Kshatriyas and some Sudras, "in the teeth of the canonical rule forbidding the lower Varnas to take up the functions of the higher ones, assumed the Kshatriya's occupation of ruling and fighting." In the seventh century A.D Sind was ruled by a Sudra dynasty. There were some Sudra rulers in other parts of the country.

The common practice was to marry in one's own caste but inter-caste marriages were not unknown. It was laid down in the Shastras that the marriage of girls of inferior castes with the twice-born or higher caste males was forbidden in the Kaliyuga, but such marriages did take place, though they were considered inferior and undesirable. Although Al-Biruni does not mention the Kayastha caste, yet it had come into existence as an important caste in the later half of the 9th century A.D. The individuals of the caste had risen "to the highest public offices in different tracts" in the eleventh and following centuries.

It is true that the caste system was in many respects a cruel and immoral system but was so deeply rooted in Hindu society that it could not be shaken even by Medieval religious reformers. Guru Nanak condemned the caste system as "folly" but inspite of that it continued. Even the Sikh Gurus who were Khatris did not marry non-Khatri girls. Chaitanya stood for removing all distinctions based on caste and religion but be himself observed practices and after his death Bengal Vaishnavism developed on traditional Hindu lines.

The caste system was in a sense a disruptive force but it was also a cohesive force in so far as it assured every Hindu of a recognised professional or occupational status. It promoted social integration in a limited sense as it assigned rights and duties to every individual and ensured a working harmony between the socio-religious and economic structures.

The view of Dr. K.M. Ashraf is that the caste system was "a contributory factor in the establishment of the foreign Muslim rule." (Life and Conditions of the People of Hindustan, p. 108). The view of Habib and Nizami is that the social system of the Hindus and the invidious caste distinctions "rendered the whole military organisation rickety and weak" (Comprehensive History of India, Vol. V, pp. 185-86). This view is not accepted by Prof. A.C. Banerjee. He points out that the first Arab raid in Sind took place in or about 643 A.D. and the Kingdom of Dahir fell in 712. The Caliphs failed to extend their dominions beyond Sind. The invasions of Sabuktagin and Sultan Mahmud resulted only in the annexation of a part of the Punjab and that too in the eleventh century A.D. The Indian campaigns of Mohammad Ghori covered a period of over thirty years (1175-1206). It took the Khaljis and the Tughlaqs more than thirty years to accomplish the partial subjugation of South India. The Rajput princes successfully resisted the Muslims till the days of Akbar. The primary cause of the loss of independence by India was not the caste system but the lack of unity among the Hindu princes, it was due to their lack of political vision and the absence of the ideal of imperialism. They did not keep themselves breast of the developments in the art of warfare in Central Asia. The Hindus also suffered from their superiority complex which kept them isolated from other countries.

The position of women in the Sultanate period was not as high as it used to be in ancient India. No women was allowed to enjoy an independent status. Before marriage, she was under the strict supervision of her father. After marriage, she was under the supervision of her husband and after his death, she was under the supervision of her grown-up sons. However, it was laid down that a husband must honour his wife and provide her with gifts of ornaments and good food. If the husband went abroad, he was required to provide for the maintenance of his wife, during his absence. Even if a husband left his wife for some valid reason, he was required to make provision for her maintenance. Even if a wife was guilty of adultery, she had to be provided for. If a husband in-treated his wife, he was punished by the state. Inspite of this, the position of women worsened during the Sultanate period. On account of fear from Muslims and other kinds of high-handedness, new rules were made to enforce early marriage. It was laid down that girls should be married at the age of 7, 10 and at the most 12 years. A marriage at or after the age of puberty was considered a bad marriage and a matter of sin for her parents. The revocation of marriage was permitted in certain special circumstances.

The seclusion of Hindu women came in the wake of the Muslim conquest of Northern India. Child marriage and Purdah brought about the segregation of girls and a degradation in the condition of Hindu women during Medieval India.

Sati was common, but not compulsory. Al-Biruni tells us that a widow had to choose between two alternatives viz remaining a widow all her life or burning herself on the funeral pyre of her dead husband and she usually chose the latter alternative. Ibn Batuta who has given an eye witness account of Sati in Malwa, tell us that the custom was highly esteemed but not obligatory. According to him, under a law made by the Sultans of Delhi, permission had to be-obtained before burning a widow.

The institution of Devadasis in principal temples was in existence. A large number of beautiful maidens were maintained for music and song in important temples in most parts of the country. Al-Biruni writes that while the priests were opposed to the institution of Devadasis, the kings maintained them for the sake of revenue. Women were allowed to possess certain kinds of property, besides their Stridhana. Contrary to the Smriti rule of the perpetual dependence of women, princesses and queens wielded great political authority. There were instances of Hindu women who ruled over, certain parts of the country at that time, particularly in Kashmir and South India. Queen Rudramba successfully ruled the Kakatiya kingdom for forty years. Polygamy was permitted. Rulers and princes were allowed to have many wives but the common people were monogamous.

The birth of a daughter was not considered to be auspicious. It is stated that when a daughter was born to Amir Khusrau, the great poet, it was considered to be an unfortunate occasion.

The Hindus celebrated many festivals such as Holi, Dussehra, Raksha-Bandhan, Vasant etc. The Muslim rulers put many restrictions on their celebration. Slavery was fairly common. Slaves were bought and sold. They were also distributed as ordinary gifts or presents among friends.

The customs of religious suicide by the Hindus prevailed during the Sultanate period. It was considered a great religious merit to commit suicide at certain sacred places such as Prayag and Kashi. Hindu devotees cut off their limbs or their necks with sharp swords in the fulfilment of their vows before their deities. Ibn-Batuta tells us that the Hindus committed suicide by drowning themselves voluntarily into the Ganges as an act of spiritual merit. The Hindus also went on religious pilgrimages to Prayag, Puri, Konarak, Gaya, Kashi, Dwarka and other holy places. Cow was worshipped by the Hindus all over India.

The Hindus had a high standard of honesty. The foreign travellers bear testimony to the high character of the Hindus. The people paid their debts without going to a court of law. If a debtor could not pay his debt during his life-time, he made it obligatory on his sons and grandsons to pay that amount. The people in general were superstitious. They had great faith in omens, lucky stars, auspicious and inauspicious moments and days. On the whole, the Hindus were honest and just. They were true to their word and their engagements. This is confirmed by Idrisi, Al-Biruni and Marco Polo.

The people were fond of music, dance and drama. The common musical instruments were flute, Vina and drums. Stringed instruments and trumpets were common. Boys and girls played with balls and enjoyed the swing. Indoor games like chess, were common.

The people in general were vegetarian. That was due to the influence of Buddhism, Jainism and Vaishnavism. The killing of an animal was considered sinful. Slowly and slowly, the custom of meat-eating became popular with the Kshatriyas. The Sudras took meat openly. The Tantrikas and the Shaktas also encouraged the use of meat and fish. There were some people among the Hindus who ate the meat of the dead animals. They were considered to be very low in society and were forced to live outside the villages and cities. Slowly, the use of wine and opium became popular among the higher castes. People put great emphasis on the preparation of food. Special dishes were prepared on the occasion of festivals and other auspicious occasions. The common food was rice, wheat, barley, gram etc. Great emphasis was put on the use of milk, butter, ghee and sugar in eating. Both the Hindus and Muslims were known for their treatment of guests.

People took great interest in decoration. People of all types and classes put on ornaments which were of different metals and qualities. Jewels were inland in ornaments. Sometimes holes were made in the ears and nose to put on ornaments. People used various kinds of clothes. Those were made of cotton, wool and silk. The rich put on costly clothes while the poor used ordinary clothes.

The Muslim population of Northern India consisted of many elements. Mohammad Ghori came with Turkish adventurers and they were followed by other foreigners who came for employment. The army of Qutub-ud-Din Aibak was composed of Turks, Ghurids, Khorasanis and Khaljis. The Afghans served in the armies of Sultan Mahmud and Mohammad Ghori. Balban employed Afghans in suppressing the people of Mewat. A large number of foreigners came to India on account of Mongol invasions. The Mongol converts were called "New Muslims". The Abyssinians also came to India. Jamaluddin Yaqut who was liked by Queen Raziya, was an Abyssinian. The Abyssinians also seized the throne of Bengal in the late 15th century A.D. Mohammad Tughlaq gave facilities to those who came from outside India. Barani tells us that people from different parts of the world came to India such as Khorasan, Iraq, Khwarizm, Seistan, Herat and Damascus. Barbosa tells us that foreigners from many lands such as Arabs, Mameluks, Persians and Khorasanis lived in the coastal towns, particularly in Gujarat. Many Arab traders settled in Chittagong. Men of learning from Arabia, Persia and Bukhara took up their residence at Agra during the reign of Sikandar Lodi. These various elements were united by the single faith of Islam. There were also inter-marriages among them. Social intercourse and the identity of political interests also united them and they permanently settled in India.

The Turks, the Persians, the Arabs, the Abyssinians and the Egyptians constituted an exclusive ruling oligarchy. The Turk was the most jealous guardians of the foreign aristocrats. He monopolised power in Hindustan and played the role of the leader of the Muslims in Asia. He believed in the policy of racialism and rigidly excluded the Indian Muslim community from a share in power and employment in the state. Balban openly despised "low-born non-Turks". As a very large number of persons migrated into India from Central Asia, there was a mixing up of the Muslims of different races and nationalities. During the reign of Alauddin Khalji, the policy of associating Indian converts with the administration was adopted. Alauddin Khalji appointed Malik Kafur as his Deputy. Firuz Tughlaq's Prime Minister was Khan-i-Jahan Maqbul who was a convert from Hinduism to Islam.

To begin with, the number of converts to Islam must have been small but with the passage of time their number increased. Most of the Hindus who were converted to Islam came from low castes and they were not admitted to the aristocracy of the Muslim conquerors. They were also not given any social and economic privileges.

There was a great deal of antipathy among the Muslims on account of their religious differences, particularly among the Sunnis and Shias. This rivalry and enmity continued throughout the medieval period. The Afghans were known as the sworn enemies of the Mughals and they looked upon them as usurpers. Foreign settlers in India preferred urban areas where military and civil employment was available to them. Some of them settled in rural areas to look after the lands assigned to them. However, the vast majority of the Muslims in rural areas were converts from Hinduism. Most of them belonged to lower castes and they continued to pursue their old occupations. They were not admitted to the social and political privileges of foreigners who were affiliated to the ruling class and had more money.

As regards social divisions among the Muslims, Barani refers to persons of low birth and high birth and contempt for the low-born. He refers to artists, merchants, clerks, soldiers, cultivators, Bazaris and Darveshes. In Fatawa-i-Jahandari, there are references to religious scholars, mystics, physicians, astrologers, artisans, shopkeepers, merchants, caravan workers, courtesans, musicians, dancers, buffoons, tavern-keepers, jugglers, story tellers, jokers and wrestlers. Tarikh-i-Mubarak Shahi refers to Amirs, Maliks. Ulama, Sadat, Mashaikh, beggars, artisans, money-lenders and cultivators. Khavand Mir's Humayun Nama refers to Ahi-i-Daulat comprising the royal family, nobility and the army, Ahl-i-Saadat comprising the Ulama, Qazis, the Sayyids, men of learning and men of letters and Ahl-i-Murad consisting of those-who catered for pleasures comprising musicians, minstrels and dancers.

There was a privileged class in Muslim society consisting of the Umara or the nobility and the Ulama or the theologians together with other religious groups. The nobles (Ahl-i-Suyuf or "men of the sword") were mostly of foreign origin. They derived their nobility not from birth but from the favour of the Sultan. In the 13th century, many of them were initially slaves. The sons and relatives of the Sultan formed a special section of the nobility. They stood at the top of the hierarchy and enjoyed exceptional prestige and privileges. The men of the sword constituted a military aristocracy. The title of Khan was the privilege of those who belonged to the highest grade. Some of them were given the title of Ulugh Khan-i-Azam. The nobles of the second grade were given the title of Malik and those of the third grade were designated as Amir. The term Amir was also used in a generic sense to indicate all the holders of important military and civil posts. Military officers of lower ranks were called Sarkhails and Sipahsalars but they were not recognised as nobles. On paper, there was a descending hierarchy from Khan downwards but in actual practice, it began to disrupt quite early. In the 14th and 15th centuries, it lost all its significance.

The highest posts and large revenue assignments were monopolised by the nobles and that enabled them to live in luxury. Those at the top copied their royal masters. They lived in palatial houses, richly decorated and furnished. They used costly tapestries and carpets imported from foreign countries, gold and silver dishes, exquisite glass and china etc. They maintained in their stables fine horses. Many of them maintained elephants. A Fil-Khan-was a familiar adjunct to the palaces of the big nobles. A large number of slaves and domestic servants, both males and femaales, were maintained by them. They were known for their lavish hospitality and charity. In theory, neither the office nor the revenue assignment to any noble was permanent or hereditary. There was no scope for the development of a hereditary nobility.

The Ahl-i-Qalam or "men of the pen" formed the second privileged class. The term Ulama covered various groups such as theologians, ascetics, Sayids, Pirs and their descendants. They did belong to the nobility but they enjoyed wealth and influence in varying degrees. Theologians were collectively known as Dastar-Bandan. They were shown a lot of respect although many of them did not deserve it. Barani puts the Ulama into two categories. Ulama-i-Akhirat (those who kept themselves aloof from wordly temptations and Ulama-i-Dunya (those who coveted worldly prizes). The people did not enquire whether a particular theologian belonged to the first category or the second category. They respected every Ulama. The Ulama were regarded as the heirs of the Prophet. The laws of the Shariat were enforced by them and things illegal and not sanctioned by the Shariat were suppressed by them. The religion of God stood firm due to them. The best kings and the best nobles were those who visited the doors of the Ulama and the worst Ulama were those who visited the doors of the kings and the nobles. The Ulama were much superior in dignity and status to others. The Sayyids claimed descent from the Prophet through his daughter Fatima. They commanded special respect in Muslim society. Even Timur protected the lives of Sayyids during his invasion of India although his policy was one of general slaughter. A Sayyid accused of misappropriating state revenue was discharged by Sikandar Lodi and was allowed to keep to himself his dishonest gains. The Sayyids put on a pointed cap (Kulah) and they were known as Kulah-Daran.

There was a widely prevalent belief in Pirs and Shaikhs as spiritual guides in Muslim society. Partly as a result of the decay of the spiritual and moral influence of the Ulama on account of their degeneration as a class, the Pirzadas (descendants of Pirs) and Mukhdumzadas (descendants of Shaikhs) took over to a large extent the spiritual guidance of Muslims. They were practically worshipped. Some nobles of King Bahlol Lodi offered their heads to the son of their Pir if he chose to sit on them.

Next to the two privileged classes, there was a middle class whose income was from small holdings of land and services in lower posts under the state of the nobles. Energetic and ambitious men of the middle class found opportunities for ascending to the highest class, the nobility. If fortune turned against them, they were reduced to the level of cultivators of land.

The lowest strata of Muslim society were composed mainly of artisans, shop-keepers, clerks and petty traders. At the bottom there were Qalandars and other beggars. Most of them were of Hindu origin. In most cases, the change of religion did not involve any change either in their occupation or in the place of their work. They continued their old religious and social ideas and prejudices. Converts from Hinduism were looked down upon and non-Indian extraction was a special claim to distinction in society. The result was that many Hindus who were converted to Islam and became rich or well-placed in life, claimed foreign origin in order to gain a higher social status.

The Muslims were essentially a city people. They dreaded village life Their main profession was in the army and in the offices of the state. Some of them were engaged in trade and commerce. A large number of them were engaged as shop keepers and teachers in primary schools. The Muslims of Indian origin followed handicrafts and petty trades in cities. A small number of them took to agriculture. There were also Muslim butchers, water carriers, corpse-washers engravers, painters, illuminators and physicians, some of them were calligraphists and copyists of the Quran, A large number of them were weavers, washermen, barbers, carpenters, blacksmiths, tailors and woodcutters.

Domestic servants and slaves were employed in the royal household and in every rich and respectable Muslim family. Barani writes that the royal slaves were supposed to confer power and dignity on the Sultan. They were employed rot only in domestic and menial work but also in war. Barani was aware of the danger of the use of slaves for military and political purposes. He wrote, "Most of the slaves are wreckless and shameless. There can be no permanent security against their revolt." Afif tells us that after the death of Firuz Tughlaq, his slaves "became so bold that they unhesitatingly severed the heads of the princes of his family and hung them at the Darbar Gate." In private households, there was practically no distinction between domestic servants and slaves. War was probably the most important source of the supply of slaves. Prisoners of war who were mostly Hindus, were reduced to slavery. Hasan Nizami tells us that after the victory of Kutbuddin Aibak at Kalinjar, 50,000 men were made slaves. Slaves were also imported from Africa and West and Central Asian countries. They were also procured from certain parts of India, Ibn-Batuta tells us that slaves from Assam were worth several times more than others. There were markets for the sale of slaves. Barani refers to such a market in Delhi. The regulations of Ala-ud-Din Khalji fixed the prices of slaves. The prices of male and female and handsome men and women slaves varied. Ibn Bututa found many slave girls in Bengal. A slave in the service of the Sultan was usually manumitted after some time and was provided with an honourable position. But that was not always so. Mohammad Ghori did not manumit either Qutb-uddin Aibak or any of his senior slaves. It is doubtful even if Balban was manumitted. Firuz Tughlaq had 180,000 slaves but it cannot be said how many were raised to high tank. The promotion of a slave so high office was usually a political device and not a generous recognition of the principle of social equality. Being dependent on his royal master, a talented slave could be used as a trustworthy agent and was, therefore, preferable to nobles.

A slave could be set free only when he and his master came to an agreement that the former would pay the latter an appropriate part of his earnings and the Qazi confirmed the agreement. The mere acceptance of Islam did not bring freedom to a non-Muslim slave although in theory a Muslim could not be enslaved. There was a custom among the Muslims that if a slave girl gave birth to a child from her master she ceased to be a slave and became the wife of the master and she also got a share in the property of her master. Slavery was not considered to be bad in Muslim society. Some slaves took pride in being the slaves of some big person. They got every opportunity to rise in life.

Slavery made very little contribution of the economic development of the country. The Indian slaves were engaged in domestic and menial work and contributed merely to the luxurious style of living of their masters.

Muslim women in India did not possess the privileged position which was occupied by Arab women. They occupied a subordinate position and were at the mercy of their husbands who could marry at least four wives at a time according to the Shariat. No women in a Muslim household could claim to be the mistress of her house. However, Muslim women were treated well as the honour of the family was supposed to depend upon the chastity of womenfolk. They observed strict Purdah. Muslim women of the upper class did not go out without a Burkah. Muslims were very jealous about their wives and they did not allow even their near relations to look at them. Women of the higher classes were taught the Quran and other religious books, There were a number of highly educated and talented women in medieval India.

Women of the lower classes assisted their husbands in the cultivation of land. They looked after cows and bullocks, poultry-keeping etc. They did not observe Purdah.

In one way, there was a fall in the morals of the Muslims in India. Drinking and gambling became very common among them, Balban imposed many restrictions on the use of intoxicants. The same was done by Ala-ud-Din Khalji. But inspite of that, the Muslims indulged in those evil habits in excess. There was some improvement during the reign of Mohammad Tughlaq but corruption became rampant during the reign of Firuz Tughlaq.

There were many causes for the decline of morals among the Muslims. One reason was that they acquired a lot of wealth without much effort. When the Muslims defeated the Hindu rulers, a lot of money fell into their hands. They got gold, silver, diamonds etc. in large quantities. The result was that the Muslims wasted their riches on beautiful women and drinking and that led to a decline in their morals.

Another reason was that the Sultans of Delhi did not possess high moral character. Many of them were really bad. They thought of nothing except beautiful women and drinking. Sultan Kaiqubad lived a licentious life. He required more beautiful women. The same was the case with Mubarak Shah (1316-20). He was also a man of no character. If such was the condition of the Sultans, their nobles tried to copy them and thereby lost their character.

Another cause was the system of among the Muslims. It is true that Qutb-ud-Din Aibak, Iltutmish, Balban etc. were slaves but they became Sultans on account of their high character and qualities of head and heart. In course of time, the slave system became a curse. It became a symbol of greatness to have more and more slaves in every household. The result was that the number of slaves, both males and females, multiplied. Barani tells as that in his time the price of a beautiful slave or eunuch ranged between, 1000 and 2000 Tankas. Ibn Batuta writes that he himself married four slave girls and also divorced them. Amir Khusrau also had many slave girls. As the Muslims kept in their households a large number of slave girls, that let to their decline in morals.

As a result of their permanent residence of India, the social life of the Muslims who came from foreign countries became Indianised in very many ways. There developed among the Muslim aristocrats something like the caste system, particularly in the matter of marriage. The Muslims borrowed from the Hindus the use of umbrellas and elephants as emblems of authority. They also borrowed from them the use of rings, necklaces and ear-ring. They started using rich spices for cooking food. They also borrowed from the Hindus the practice of chewing the betel-leaf. They borrowed headgears known as Chira and Pag from the Rajputs, The Muslims were accustomed to the use of coarse cloth in their original homelands but when they came to India they started using fine cotton and silk fabrics. The Muslim rulers and nobles started employing professional gesters after the fushion of the Hindus, The Muslims came to have belief in astrology as the Hindus did. Some of the marriage ceremonies and customs of the Hindus were adopted by the Muslims. Music is forbidden in Islam. It was banned by Iltutmish but it was patronised by Balban and Firuz Shah Tughlaq. It is said that when Firuz Shah Tughlaq ascended the throne, he entertained the public for three weeks with music. The Qawwali music became popular among the Muslims.

REFERENCES

Asher, Catherine: *Architecture of Mughal India*, Cambridge, New York, 1992.

Dutt, Sukumar : *Buddhist Monks and Monasteries of India*, George Allen and Unwin, London, 1962.

Kumar, Pradip : *Social Mobility and Caste Violence: A Study of the Gujarat Riots*, Delhi, Adjanta Publications, 1985.

Rao, M. S. A.: *Social Movement and Social Transformation: A Study of Backward Class Movement*, New Delhi, Macmillian Press, 1978.

Chapter 3

Bhakti Movement

The most effective Hindu protest against atrocities was registered by the Bhakti Movement in medieval India. Bhakti means devotion to God. A *Bhakt* may worship Him at home, in the temple, all by himself through meditation, or in congregations through *Bhajan* and *Kirtan* (chorus singing). He need not go out into the streets to organize a movement. But this is exactly what happened at the behest of the socio-religious reformers in the fifteenth-sixteenth century. And the movement triumphed insofar as it succeeded in saving India from total Islamization. The Bhakta saints who spearheaded this movement belonged to all classes, but essentially the protest was a middle class movement and it was a strange combination of Renaissance, Reformation and dissent.

The Hindus resented conversion of their co-religionists by invaders and rulers by force. Many such converts used to return to their original faith at the first opportunity as vouched by Arabic and Persian chroniclers writing about Mohammad bin Qasim's invasion of Sind and Mahmud of Ghazni's campaigns in Hindustan. As early as in the time of Sultan Iltutmish (1210-1236), soon after the establishment of the Delhi Sultanate in 1206, some Ulama suggested to him to confront the Hindus with a choice between Islam and death. The Wazir Nizamul Mulk Junaidi replied: 'But at the moment in India' the Muslims are so few that they are like salt (in a large dish). If such orders are to be enforced' the Hindus might combine' and the Muslims would be too few in number to suppress (them). However, after a few years when in the capital and in the regions and small towns, the Muslims are well established and the troops are larger, it will be possible to give Hindus, the choice of 'death' or 'Islam'.?

On the other hand, Hindu saints used to assuage the outraged feelings of Hindus and encourage them reconvert to Hinduism. For instance Harihar and Bukka, sons of the Raja of Kampil, converted to Islam by Mohammad bin Tughlaq, fled his court. At the instance of sage Vidyaranya they reverted to Hinduism and founded the Vijayanagar kingdom to resist the expansion of Muslim power in the South. Like Vidyaranya, there were scores of Bhakta saints who were helping people to resist injustice and retain their original religion.

In Maharashtra, Namdeva in the fourteenth century declared that people were blind in insisting upon worshipping in temples and mosques, while His worship needed neither temple nor mosque. Such courageous denunciations were infectious and these spread in Gujarat, Bengal, Punjab and Uttar Pradesh. Ramananda, Kabir, Nanak, Chaitanya, Raidas, Dhanna, Sain, Garibdas and Dadu Dayal and a host of others spoke out in the same idiom openly and repeatedly. They came from all classes of society-Raidas was a *chamar*, Sain was a barber while Pipa was a Raja, Raja of Gauranggarh-but they were all respected and listened to. Of these the three most important saints who turned Bhakti into a movement were Kabir, Nanak and Chaitanya.

Sant Kabir lived in U.P. from 1425 to about 1505, Guru Nanak in Punjab from 1469 to 1538 and Chaitanya Mahaprabhu in Bengal from 1486 to 1534. During this period, particularly after the invasion of Timur (1399 C.E.), northern India was broken up into a number of independent Muslim kingdoms like Gujarat, Malwa, Jaunpur and Bengal while the Sultanate of Delhi was ruled by the Saiyyads and Lodis. Sikandar Lodi (1489-1517) revived the strength of the Sultanate and was the strongest and most fanatical ruler of the dynasty. Babur conquered Hindustan from 1526 to 1530 and Akbar ascended the throne in 1556. Thus from the beginning of the fifteenth to the middle of the sixteenth century (1400-1556), India witnessed terrible political upheavals resulting in large-scale massacres and conversions. The division of the country into small kingdoms rendered the task of the Muslim rulers easy in pressurising their Hindu subjects in their micro units into accepting Islam. The local Sultans and nobles, in order to control and demoralize the subject people, not only demolished their temples and imposed 'legal' disabilities upon them but also confronted them with the choice between Islam and death-a phenomenon which had been going on since the days of Iltutmish in a rather haphazard manner. It is therefore necessary to cursorily go through this scenario to be able to make a correct appraisal of the services of these great saints, and their disciples and followers, in saving Hindu society from succumbing to Muslim proselytization.

Punjab was always the first to bear the brunt of Muslim invasions directed against India, and Muslim invaders were keenly interested in making converts. In the first half of the fifteenth century the successors of Timur were holding parts of Punjab to ransom. Under the Mongol invaders too conversions used to take place on a large scale. Rebellions of Muslim adventurers were also creating anarchical conditions. During this period and after, therefore, the Muslim population of the Punjab swelled considerably mainly due to proselytization. Added to this were the large number of Afghans whom the Saiyyads and Lodis had called from across the Indus with a view to consolidating their position. Like in Punjab, in Sind also the rule of the Turkish Sultans and the pressure of the Mongols had combined to Islamise the northern parts. In southern Sind the Summas became Muslims and Hindus by turns, but ultimately they seem to have 'adopted Islam, and propagated the religion in their dominions'. in Sind 'compulsory conversions to Mahometanism were not infrequent, the helpless Hindu being forcibly subjected to circumcision on slight or misconstructed profession, or the false testimony of abandoned Mahometans? When Humayun took refuge in Sind (1541), Muslim population in its cities had grown considerably.

There were Muslim kings in the Kashmir Valley from the middle of the fourteenth century. However, it was during the reign of Sikandar Butshikan (1394-1417) that the wind of Muslim proselytization blew the hardest. His bigotry prompted him to destroy all the most famous temples in Kashmir and offer the Kashmiris the usual choice between Islam and death. It is said that the fierce intolerance of Sikandar had left in Kashmir no more than eleven families of Brahmans. His contemporary, the Raja of Jammu, had been converted to Islam by Timur, by 'hopes, fears and threats'. The kingdom of Gujarat was founded by Wajih-ul-Mulk, a converted Rajput in 1396. One of its famous rulers, Ahmad Shah (1411-1442) was responsible for many conversions. In 1414 he introduced the *Jiziyah*, and collected it with such strictness, that it brought a number of converts to Islam. Mahmud Beghara's exertions (1458-1511) in the field of proselytization were more impressive. In Malwa there were large number of Muslims since the days of Khalji and Tughlaq sultans. These numbers went on growing during the rule of the independent Muslim rulers of Malwa, the Ghauris and Khaljis (1401-1562). The pattern of growth of Muslim population in Malwa was similar to that in the other regions but their harems were notoriously large, filled as they were with Hindu inmates.

About the conversions in Bengal three statements, one each from Wolseley Haig, Dr. Wise and Duarte Barbosa, should suffice to assess the situation. Haig writes that 'it is evident, from the numerical superiority in Eastern Bengal of the Muslims' that at some period an immense wave of proselytization must have swept over the country and it is most probable that the period was the period of Jalaluddin Mohammad (converted son of Hindu Raja Ganesh) during whose reign of seventeen years (1414-1431)' hosts of Hindus are said to have been forcibly converted to Islam'. With regard to these conversions, Dr. Wise writes that 'the only condition he offered were the Koran or death' many Hindus fled to Kamrup and the jungles of Assam, but it is nevertheless probable that more Mohammedans were added to Islam during these seventeen years (1414-31) than in the next three hundred years'. And Barbosa writes that 'It is obviously an advantage in the sixteenth century Bengal to be a Moor, in as much as the Hindus daily become Moors to gain the favour of their rulers'. The militant Mashaikh also found in Bengal a soil fertile for conversion, and worked hard to raise Muslim numbers. We may linger awhile in Bengal to have a clear picture of the spread of Islam through methods in which medieval Muslims took pleasure and pride while modern Muslims maintain a studied silence. The details of the conversion of Raja Ganesh bring out the importance of the role of force, of persuasion and of the Ulama and Sufis in proselytization. In 1409 Ra a Ganesh occupied the throne of Bengal and sought to establish his authority 'by getting rid of the prominent *ulama* and *Sufis'.* Qutb-ul-Alam Shaikh Nurul Haqq wrote to Sultan Ibrahim Sharqi to come and save the Muslims of Bengal.

Ibrahim Sharqi responded to the call, and Raja Ganesh, finding himself too weak to face the challenge, appealed to Shaikh Nurul Haqq for help. The latter promised to intercede on his behalf if he became a Musalman. The helpless Raja was willing, but his wife refused to agree. Ultimately a compromise was made by the Raja offering to retire from the world and permitting his son, Jadu, to be converted and ascend his throne. On Jadu being converted and enthroned as Jalaluddin Shah, Shaikh Nurul Haqq induced Sultan Ibrahim to withdraw his armies. If a Raja of the stature of Ganesh could not face up to the Ulama and the Sufis, other Rajas and Zamindars were still worse placed. Petty Rajas and Zamindars were converted to Islam, with their wives and children, if they could not pay land revenue or tribute in time. Such practice appears to be common throughout the whole country as instances of it are found from Gujarat to Bengal.

In Uttar Pradesh the region to the east and south of Delhi-Katehar, Doab, Bayana and Mewat-had become a problem tract in the fifteenth century, and there the Saiyyad and Lodi sultans contented themselves 'with the ignoble but customary satisfaction of plundering the people, and obtaining converts in the bargain.' Mohammad Bihamad Khani, the author of *Tarikh-i-Muhammadi*, gives a clear idea of the keenness of the Muslim sultans and their subtle methods in obtaining converts. He writes that sultan Mahmud while fighting Rai Sumer in the vicinity of Irich 'concluded that if he allowed his brave warriors to wage the war (outright), they would undoubtedly extirpate the infidels' but he deemed it fit to delay the operation (or advance slowly) in the hope that the infidels might accept Islam'.

Who could save the Hindus from extinction in such a scenario' Obviously, leaders of the society, the Brahmans. 'What the Brahmans as protectors of their culture achieved in those days,' writes Wilhelm von Pochhammer, 'has never been properly recorded, probably because a considerable number of people belonging precisely to this class had been slaughtered. If success was achieved in preserving Hindu culture in the hell of the first few centuries, the credit undoubtedly goes to the Brahmans. They saw to it that not too many chose the cowardly way of getting converted and that the masses remained true to the holy traditions on which culture rested' ?

Muslim kings knew this and treated the Brahmans sternly, restricting their sphere of activity. The Muslim Mashaikh were as keen on conversions as the Ulama, and contrary to general belief, in place of being kind to the Hindus as saints would, they too wished the Hindus to be accorded a second class citizenship if they were not converted. Only one instance, that of Shaikh Abdul Quddus Gangoh, need be cited because he belonged to the Chishtia *Silsila* considered to be the most tolerant of all Sufi groups. He wrote letters to Sultan Sikandar Lodi, Babur and Humayun to re-invigorate the Shariat and reduce the Hindus to payers of land tax and *Jiziyah*.

To Babur he wrote, 'Extend utmost patronage and protection to theologians and mystics' that they should be maintained and subsidized by the state' No non-Muslim should be given any office or employment in the Diwan of Islam. Posts of Amirs and *Amils* should be barred to them. Furthermore, in confirmity with the principles of the Shariat they should be subjected to all types of indignities and humiliations.

The non-Muslims should be made to pay *Jiziyah*, and *Zakat* on goods be levied as prescribed by the law. They should be disallowed from donning the dress of the Muslims and should be forced to keep their *Kufr* concealed and not to perform the ceremonies of their *Kufr* openly and freely? They should not be allowed to consider themselves equal to the Muslims.' He went from Shahabad to Nakhna where Sultan Sikandar was encamping. His mission was to personally remind the Sultan of the kingly duties and exert his influence over him and his nobles. He also wrote letters to Mir Mohammad, Mir Tardi, Ibrahim Khan Sherwani, Said Khan Sherwani, Khawas Khan and Dilawar Khan, making frantic appeals to them to live up to the ideals of Islam, to zealously uphold and strictly enforce the Shariat and extend patronage to the Ulama and the Mashaikh. Such communications and advices did not go in vain. Contemporary and later chroniclers relate how Sikandar Lodi destroyed idols of Hindu gods and goddesses, and gave their pieces to Muslim butchers for use as meat-weights. Even as a prince he had expressed a desire to put an end to the Hindu bathing festival at Kurukshetra (Thanesar). Subsequently, he ordered that the Hindus, who had assembled there on the occasion of the solar eclipse be massacred in cold blood, but later on stayed his hand. In Mathura 'and other places' he turned temples into mosques, and established Muslim *sarais*, colleges and *bazars* in the Hindu places of worship. The list of his atrocities is endless. 'Babur inherited his religious policy from the Lodis. Sikandar Lodi's fanaticism must have been still remembered by some of the officials who continued to serve under Babur' (who) was content to govern India in the orthodox fashion.'

The task of redeeming Hindu society, besides Brahmans, devolved on the Bhakta saints and they performed their obligation with a dedication that evokes our admiration and reverence. Their task was by no means an easy one. How to stop erosion in the Hindu society through. Muslim proselytization' If the trend was allowed to continue unabated, it would pose danger to the entire complex of the Hindu social structure. To check the penetration of Islam, particularly in the rural areas, the Hindu saints after Ramanand began to make Hinduism simple, straightforward and intelligible. They showed that there was nothing superior or inferior about one religion or the other, and there was no reason why Hindus should embrace a religion, implanted from abroad, when their own ancestral religion gave scope for infinite variety of worship and contained a philosophy and a message which could satisfy their social and spiritual needs. But their exhortations were devoid of ill-will towards any other religion or sect.

Kabir was more than sixty years of age when Sikandar Lodi ascended the throne and Nanak was twenty. Both saw the world around them and were dissatisfied with the unjust social and political order in which they lived. Not far from Nanak's home town of Talwandi, at Shahabad in the Ambala district, resided Shaikh Abdul Quddus Gangoh. Nanak must have heard about him and his fundamentalism which was shared by the Lodi monarch in equal measure, and it were the activities of Mashaikh like Abdul Quddus and Sultans like Sikandar Lodi which provoked the Bhakta saints to stand equal to them and confront and encounter them. Kabir openly declared: 'I have come to save the devotee. I was sent because the world was in misery? The Almighty sent me to show clearly the beginning and the end.' Similarly Guru Nanak 'regarded himself as' (having) received from His door-step the signs (*aitan*), the chapters (*surahs*) and the tradition (*hadis*) of the prophet'. He taught that 'there is one God in the world and no other, and that Nanak the Caliph (or son) of God speaks the truth'. In language, sometimes soft and sometimes hard, they challenged the onslaught of Islam by claiming to have received message from God Himself. Kabir was conscious of his apostolic mission and challenged the concept that Islam was superior to Hinduism. There had been times under Muslim rule when, if one as much as said that Hinduism was as good as Islam, he was summarily executed. Now Bhakta Kabir openly reiterated that 'Mecca has verily become Kashi, and Ram has become Rahim'. So also asserted Guru Nanak when he declared that 'There is no Hindu, there is no Musalman'.

Most Hindu saints travelled widely and so did Guru Nanak, acquainting himself with different systems, orders and philosophies. He freely borrowed from Hindu classics and Muslim orders. He established the *Sangat* and the *Langar* after the way in the Muslim *Khanqahs*.

The Bhakta saints attempted to resist Islamism in two ways-by removing internal weaknesses of Hindu society and resisting proselytization. Both Kabir and Nanak denounced the caste system which was responsible for many evils in Hindu society. Nanak declared himself to be 'with those who are low-born among the lowly,' But like other Bhakta saints Kabir's 'denunication of the caste system was as much an inspiration of Muslim example as response to its pull of conversion.' When Kabir denounced caste and ritual of the Hindus, he also denounced the superstitions and rituals of the Muslims; or, conversely, the idea is best expressed in the words of his disciple Naudhan Pandit (whom Sikandar Lodi executed): 'Islam was true, but his own religion was also true'. This was an open challenge to Muslim propagandism and proselytization. No wonder that Bhakti reformers were disliked by some Sufi Mashaikh, who looked upon them as competitors. If a Muslim changed his religion he was liable to be condemned to death for apostasy. But under the influence of these saints many Muslims were converted to Bhakti Hinduism. Namdeva, Ramdas, Eknath, Ramanand, Kabir, Nanak and Chaitanya and several other saints had Muslim disciples, Chaitanya openly converted Muslims to Bhakti Hinduism. The *Bhaktamala* relates many instances of conversions that Pipa effected.

They also infused in the Mughal Emperors a spirit of tolerance. Babur appreciated the teachings of Guru Nanak, and 'on learning how much the people of the country prized their institutions, Akbar began to look upon them with affection.' But the influence of Bhaktas on Muslim royalty and nobility should not be overrated; the influence of Sufis like Gangoh on them was much more. There is a tendency to seek and find influence of Sufism on the Bhakti movement. But there is no evidence of such impulsion. Muslim Mashaikh were as keen on the spread of Islam as the Ulama. No Sufi could say with Kabir that 'Mecca has verily become Kashi and Ram has become Rahim', or with Naudhan that Hinduism is as true as Islam. The Bhakti movement was an entirely Hindu reformist and resistance endeavour. All the Bhakta saints were Hindus. There is some controversy about Kabir's parentage, but 'the whole background of Kabir's thought is Hindu.' If these Bhakta saints sometimes spoke in terms of Ram-Rahim, Krishna-Karim, Allah-Govind and Kashi-Kaba, it was to bring about Hindu-Muslim unity and to impress upon the neo-Muslims the futility of conversion. Else, they drew their inspiration from ancient Hindu philosophy and scriptures instilled into them by their Gurus or gained through intuitive consciousness.

Some Bhaktas confined themselves to purely Hindu language and lore with equal if not greater success. Such an one was Tulsidas. Through his *Ramcharitmanas*, he 'slakes the thirst of those who are weary and heavy laden with the sorrow of the world.' Sometimes directly and at others symbolically he brings into focus contemporary problems of Hindu society, like the excruciating experience of exile in the forests, the relentless struggle of the righteous against *rakshasas*, the unflinching loyalty of the mace-warrior Hanuman (missing in contemporary scenario), the profound love among brothers (lacking in Mughal royalty), and above all the ultimate victory of truth over treachery (personified in Ravan). Tulsidasa's impulsion has been immense and lasting. His *Ramayan* is widely read with emotion. Ram, Hanuman and Anjaneya temples are spread all over the country and thronged with devotees.

So, from the very beginning of Muslim rule, from the thirteenth century onwards, from Namdeva in Maharashtra to Ramanand, Kabir, Nanak, Chaitanya and Tulsidas in North India, right upto the seventeenth century and thereafter, a galaxy of middle class socio-religious reformers tried to help Indian society through sermon and song. They showed the futility of religious conflicts.

They helped check excessive proselytization by attacking the caste system and reaching out to their audience in the languages of the common people throughout the country. Early Bhakta saints adhered to peaceful methods, but not all their disciples in later years. Kabir's followers spread out throughout North India and the Deccan.

Jiwan Das was the founder of the Satnami sect which took up arms against the Mughals. The Sikh disciples of Nanak's successor Gurus, for varied reasons, fought against the Mughals and many times converted people by force. So did the Marathas. According to Abdul Majid Khan it is because of Chaitanya's influence that large-scale conversions to Hinduism took place at the end of the eighteenth and beginning of the nineteenth century. Hindu saint reformers continued to appear in a chain in the succeeding centuries of medieval India, infusing courage and confidence among the people. The present day strife for Ramjanmabhumi shrine is another legacy of *Hindu Bhakti* resistance to Muslim political and religious vandalism in the medieval age.

EMERGENCE OF BHAKTI IN BRAHMANISM

Brahmanism had to accept the growing importance of new gods like Siva and Vishnu side by side with Vedic gods like Indra and Varuna. It also assimilated many other popular deities like Vasudeva, Skanda and so on. All these led to the growth of the Bhakti cult. Around the fourth century B.C. the cult of Vasudeva was becoming popular. This is suggested by reference to it by classical authors like Megasthenes who came to the court of Chandgragupta Maurya.

The worshippers of Vasudeva submitted to Bhakti as the proper religious approach and called themselves Bhagavatas. Several epigraphs of the early Christian era bear testimony to the prevalence of the Vasudeva cult in central India and the Deccan.

Simultaneously with the cult of Vasudeva arose the sect of Pasupatas, devotees of Pasupati or Siva, a fertility deity. This cult was kept alive in non-brahmanic circles from the days of the Harappan culture.

The popularity of these new gods increased during the Sunga and Kanvaa periods. Patanjali, who lived in the Sunga period, in his Mahabhashya refers to the exhibition and sale of the images of Siva, Skanda and Vishakha. These gods appear on the coins of the Kushana kings, especially Huvishka. An important characteristic of later Brahmanism was its capacity to adopt new trends.

This became necessary to meet the challenge of the 'hentical sects' which were opposed to Brahmanism. Besides adopting new gods, Brahmanism gradually shifted its emphasis from Vedic ritual to Bhakti, which implied the cultivation and development of a personal relationship between God and the devotee. Thus a monotheistic concept of God,, with either Siva or Vishnu as his manifestation and Bhskti (loyalty and devotion) to him was gaining strength. Soon Bhakti became the dynamic force of later Brahmanism also called Hinduism.

Adaptation of Tribal Rituals

Yet another important feature of later Brahmanism was its adaptation of the tribal rituals keeping the Vedic Yajna rites supreme only in theory. In course of time the merit derived out of these new rituals were equated with the merit of the Vedic Yajna. Further, the sacred spots of the tribals were included as new places of pilgrimage (Tirtha) with suitable myths to make them respectable. The Ithihasas and Puranas are full of such material or stories which inspire bhakti (devotion) to a personal god.

Syncretism of Deities

An important characteristic of the new Brahmanism was its genius to syncretise many local deities and to evolve a monotheistic great God. Syncretism in this context will mean that deities worshipped at different places and by different people were recognised as identical and were worshipped as manifestation of the same supreme deity. Thus Vasudeva was identified with Vishnu, a minor Vedic god and Narayana, a god of obscure origin mentioned in the Brahmana literature.

Then Vishnu was closely connected with the name of Krishna, who represented the fusion between martial hero and a flute-playing pastoral deity. Vishnu could assimilate many other cults-the cult of the 'divine boar' which prevailed among some of the tribes of Malwa, the cult of Parasurama, a Brahamna hero; and Rama, the great hero of the Ramayana. Then Vishnu rose to the status of the Universal God in the Bhagavad Gita.

Similarly, Siva came to be syncretised with the Vedic Rudra and Bhairava, a tribal god and was worshipped in the form of the phallic emblem or linga. With Siva were later associated certain other deities such as Skanda and the elephant-headed Ganesa.

These theistic cults stressed the merit of worship rather than the performance of Vedic sacrifice.

Royal Support to Temples and Theism

The Puranas highlighted the merits acquired by visiting great cult centres like Mathura and Varanasi which were major places of pilgrimage. This gave a stimulus to the institution of the temple. In fact, the Puranas and other texts of the period list numerous places of pilgrimage (tirthas) which drew devotees in large numbers because visiting tirthas would ensure merit.

The temple which housed the deity, became a place of worship and thus drew devotees away from home to an institution which became a public centre. The Gupta age marked the beginning of temple construction. It laid the foundation of the typical styles of Indian temple architecture. Among the few Gupta temples which survive, the Dasavatara temple of Devagarh, the Vishnu temple at Tigawa, and the Siva temple at Bhumara are known for their beauty.

The epic and Puranic stories relating to Rama and Krishna were represented in the temple sculptures. Excellent specimens of them are still found in the Devagarh temple. The Gupta emperors patronised both Shaivism and Vaishnavism. However, the personal religion of most of the Gupta rulers was Vaishnavism which led to the creation of a number of important Vaishnava centres and Vaishnava sculptures in the Gupta period. The idea of the awataras or incarnations of Vishnu in which Vishnu is born on earth as a boar, a fish, or a human being for rescuing earth from a crisis, also seems to have been systematised in the Gupta period.

In the sixth and seventh centuries A.D. Shaivism seems to have replaced Vaishnavism as recipient of royal patronage in northern India. Shaivism counted among its followers supreme plers, foreign as well as indigenous, such as Mihirakula, Yashodharman, Sasanka and Harsha. Pasupata or Shaiva acharyas are frequently mentioned in contemporary records which include inscriptions, and many literary works like those of Varahamihira, Bana and Hiuen Tsang.

SPREAD OF BHAKTI TO THE SOUTH

All the major north Indian religions-Brahmanism, Jainism and Buddhism-travelled southwards. The Brahmanas brought with them the Vedic Yajna cult and the two theistic cults, Vaishnavism and Shaivism. The kings were in favour of the Vedic rituals as they conferred ritual status on them. The theistic cults struck root among the people. However, eventually the devotional theistic cults were to prove stronger than any other religious force in the south, and this was recognized even by royal patrons who extended support to Vaishnavism, Shaivism and their sects.

Among the early chalukya kings of Vatapi some professed Bhagavatism and others, the Pasupata cult. The famous bas-reliefs of Badami testify to the popularity of the theistic cults in the Deccan in the sixth-seventh centuries A.D. Similarly, the Pallavas of Kanchi patronised the two theistic cults as shown by the monolithic rathas (chariots) at Mahabalipuram and many bas-reliefs on them.

Bhakti, centring around the worship of specific deities, began to spread fast in the south through the brahmana settlements and temple centres where the exposition of the epics and the Puranas was institutionalized by means of munificent land grants. Thus Bhakti was popularised among the common people. It is to be noted that the way in which the Brahmanas transformed the earlier religious forms into temple-centred theistic culture in the north was repeated in the south also.

Bhakti Movement in South India

The final form of theistic Bhakti was largely the result of the influence of the Tamil devotionalism. This devotionalism was a product of the fusion between ecstatic local tribal cults (e.g. Velan Veriyadal) and northern theistic schools. This cross fertilization started at Tiruppati and Kalahasti, which then constituted the northern door of the Tamil country.

Then it developed around Kanchipuram, the Pallava capital and soon reached the region of Madurai, the Pandyan capital. The Tiru Murugu Arruppadai, a famous devotional work on Muruga, the local tribal god who was syncretised with Skanda in this work, is the earliest example of this cross fertilization. Soon this Tamil devotionalism developed into a great movement when it was adapted to the two theistic cults, Shaivism and Vaishnavism. Then Tamil Bhakti movement was characterized not only by intense ecstatic piety for the deity, but also an aggressive militancy against the heterodox cults which were growing in popularity among the people with royal support.

This movement was spearheaded in the sixth century A.D. by gifted poet-saints who traversed the country many times with great missionary zeal. All their way they sang their hymns, danced and debated with the heterodox cults. Among these hymnal poet-saints the Shaiva saints are called Nayanmar and the Vaishnava saints as Alvars.

This great wave of religious enthusiasm attained its peak in the early seventh century and its triumph was largely achieved in the two centuries that followed. The hymns of the saints of this period are marked by an outspoken hatred against the Buddhists and the Jainas. As a result, public debates, competition in the performance of miracles and tests of the truth of I their doctrines by means of ordeal became the order of the day..I.

There were other reasons for the success and popularity of these hymnal saints. Unlike the Brahmanas who propagated Hinduism through theories and the use of Sanskrit, the hymnal saints sang in easily understood forms using only the popular language, Tamil. Their Bhakti was not a reverence for a transcendent deity, but ecstatic love for an imminent one. Being unable to stand before the force of this Bhakti wave which also attracted royal support, Jainism and Buddhism had to retreat from the South.

TRANSFORMATION OF THE BHAKTI MOVEMENT

Whereas the Brahmanas were obsessed with caste regulations, the Bhakti movement not only ignored caste but also included men and women of all castes. Among the Nayanar 'Karaikkal, Amrnai was a woman and Nandanar was a member of the depressed class. Among the Alvars, Andal was a woman and Timppan was a hymnist from a "low caste". Thus the whole movement carried elements of protest and reform. However, it soon became part of the establishment, lost its early character and got engulfed by brahrnanical orthodoxy.

The Bhakti movement grew first under the Pallavas and then under the cholas, Pandyas and the Cheras. Many rock temples were cut and structural temples were built for Siva and Vishnu throughout the Tamil land by almost all the reigning monarchs.

These temples were endowed with vast landed property, often tax-free. Extensive areas of land were donated to the Brahmanas as is evident from the thousands of inscriptions on the walls of the south Indian temples. A prince-priest axis soon emerged. The monarchs fervently welcomed the rich temple-centered bhakti (or unflinching loyalty) as it suited the monarchical ideology. The Brahmanas welcomed this as it enabled Brahmanism, with its institutional base in the temple centred agrarian settlements, to emerge as the most dynamic force in south India.

Everywhere the local temple was the nucleus of religious life and a new social formation. In these temples the two arms of the brahmanical religion-the ritualistic Vedic cult and the theistic devotional cult-could meet. The temple-centred Bhakti enabled the all-embracing caste system to attract all the origional tribes of south India within its fold and place them in the hierarchical caste order.

This order fixed the ritual and social status of the mbes with the Brahrnana as the fixed point of reference. The ideology of Bhakti could bring together kings, priests and the common people within a network of understandable social relations. With the increasing patronage of kings and landed magnates, the Bhakti movement soon became part of the establishment. Thus all trances of dissent, protest and reform were obliterated in the tenth century A.D. The Alvars and the Nayanars do not appear any more.

Their place was taken by Vaishnava acharyas, all of whom were Brahmanas or the Saivite acharyas who all came from the rich landed Vellala caste.

REFERENCES

Borchert, Bruno: *Mysticism: Its History and Challenge,* Samuel Wiser, York Beach, 1994.

Mandal, B.B.: *Industrialisation and Social Disorganisation:* Concept Publications: New Delhi, 1985.

Sharma, Sri Ram, *The Religious Policy of the Mughal Emperors*, Asia Publishing House, Bombay, 1962.

Sharma, K. L.: *Caste, Class and Social Movements*, Rawat Publications, Jaipur, 1986.

Chapter **4**

Sufi Cosmology and Philosophy

FANAA (SUFISM)

Fanaa is the Sufi term for extinction. It means to annihilate the self, while remaining physically alive. Persons having entered this state are said to have no existence outside of and unity with Allah. Fanaa is equivalent to the concept of nirvana in Buddhism or moksha in Hinduism which also aims for annihilation of the self.

Fana may be attained by constant meditation and by contemplation on the attributes of God, coupled with the denunciation of human attributes. It is a sort of mental, yet real, death. The man of the "Way" experiences it freely; it is the final passage which leads to the summit of the Stages. It liberates man from all contingency outside of his spiritual quest; his ultimate aim is the Truth. Three degrees may be distinguished here: fana' of acts, attributes and essence.

The Sufi fana' in its triple manifestation does not have an exclusively negative effect or action; it is the annihilation of everything contingent, whether this be in the form of action, attribute or essence; more precisely, it is the annihilation of everything that is not God, and God is the supreme object of all good, all beauty. Fana' thus conceived is an internal state which requires from the Sufi a sustained and permanent effort of concentration to break his fetters and take on the demands and calls of truth, by his acts, his moral virtues, his whole being. That implies perfect control of himself: in words, deeds and thoughts. It is at this price that he attains an interior spiritual state where he becomes the pure and clear mirror in which the lights of Truth are reflected in all their splendor.

There are three ways in man's journey towards God. The first is the way of ignorance, through which each must travel. It is like a person walking for miles in the sun while carrying a heavy load on his shoulder, who, when fatigued, throws away the load and falls asleep under the shade of a tree.

Such is the condition of the average person, who spends his life blindly under the influence of his senses and gathers the load of his evil actions; the agonies of his earthly longings creating a hell through which he must pass to reach the destination of his journey. With regard to him the Quran says, 'He who is blind in life, shall also be blind in the hereafter.'

The next way is that of devotion, which is for true lovers. Rumi says, 'Man may be the lover of man or the lover of God; after his perfection in either he is taken before the King of love.' Devotion is the heavenly wine, which intoxicates the devotee until his heart becomes purified from all infirmities and there remains the happy vision of the Beloved, which lasts to the end of the journey. 'Death is a bridge, which unites friend to friend' (Sayings of Mohammed).

The third is the way of wisdom, accomplished only by the few. The disciple disregards life's momentary comforts, unties himself from all earthly bondages and turns his eyes toward God, inspired with divine wisdom. He gains command over his body, his thoughts and feelings, and is thereby enabled to create his own heaven within himself, that he may rejoice until merged into the eternal goal. 'We have stripped the veil from thine eyes, and thy sight today is keen', says the Quran. All must journey along one of these three paths, but in the end they arrive at one and the same goal. As it is said in the Quran, 'It is He who multiplied you on the earth, and to Him you shall be gathered.'

BAQAA

Baqaa, with literal meaning of permanency, is a term which describes a particular state of life with God, through God, in God, and for God. It is the summit of the mystical manazil, that is, the destination or the abode. Baqaa comprises of three degrees, each one referring to a particular aspect of the divine thiophenes as principle of existence and its qualitative evolution, comprising of faith, knowledge, and grace.

First Aspect: the Level of Acts: The first aspect of the Sufi permanency is situated at the level of acts. The action of the Sufi is here united with the divine action acquiring its order, harmony and durability. This specific degree of Sufi "baqa"' is the result of the shooting forth of the divine theophany as existential principle and the lights of nature as source of knowledge.

Second Aspect: the Level of Qualities and Attributes: The second aspect of permanency is situated at the level of qualities and attributes.

Here human virtues are raised to the level of the divine Attributes, acquiring their perfection, dignity and durability: such that the man's heart attains to a spiritual abode where it is the pure and clear mirror on which the characteristics of the supreme Creator are engraved.

In its turn, the power of acts in the abode of permanence becomes a docile instrument by which the divine plans in the world and within the living person are realized. This particular form of "baqa'" is a reflection of the divine existential thiophenes at the level of the Attributes and Qualities, and the effect of the lights of the intellect as principle of knowledge.

Third Aspect: the Level of the Essence: The last degree of 'baqa' is permanency of the essence. In this domain the essence of the servant is raised to the height of the divine Essence in its Unity, Sublimity and Universality.

He is totally absorbed by the divine Life. It is through God that he sees, through Him that he hears, through Him that he expresses his will, through Him that he contemplates. This is the most perfect form of Sufi 'baqa', the final stage of the hero's quest. This particular abode is in its turn acquired by the effect of the thiophenes of the Essence on the existential plane and by the effect of the thiophenes of Light at the gnostic level.

YAQEEN

Yaqeen is generally translated as "certainty", and is considered the summit of the many stations by which the path of *walaya* (sometimes translated as Sainthood) is fully completed. This is the repository of liberating experience in Islam. In relation to the exoteric religious life Certainty is the sister of religious life in its perfection (*ehsn*), that is to say the adoration of Allah according to the visionary way; through this channel it is the pillar of Islam in the accomplishment of its external practices, as it is the foundation of faith (*imn*) in its internal dogma. It is in fact *ihsan* which gives the external religion its true meaning and the domain of faith its real values. Certainty (*al-yaqin*), comprises three degrees.

Stages

Ilm al-yaqin (the knowledge of Certainty): The first degree is referred to by the name *'ilm al-yaqin* (the knowledge of Certainty), which means that Certainty is the result of knowledge. At this degree the object of Certainty is knowledge just as the aim of knowledge is Certainty. Both together are in the soul uniquely, such that Certainty is the first degree of spiritual life and the last of speculative experience. This particular degree of mystical *yaqin* is the result of divine thiophenes in Act at the level of existence and also the result of thiophenes of lights of nature at the gnostic level.

Ayn al-yaqin (the Eye of Certainty): The second degree of *yaqin* is what one calls in Sufi terms *ayn al-yaqin* (the Eye of Certainty), that is,

Certainty as a consequence of contemplation and vision. At this level, the object of Certainty is present in front of the gnostic and is not only a speculative concept.

Here knowledge becomes what one calls 'ilm-e-huzuri" (Presence of knowledge), and that is the second aspect of Certainty in the spiritual way and in liberating experience. By this kind of knowledge, the man of the Way is distinguished from philosophers and learned men. This particular degree of spiritual Certainty is the result of divine thiophenes of Attributes at the level of existence, just as it is the result of thiophenes of lights of the intellect at the level of gnosis.

Haqq al-yaqin (the total reality of Certainty): Finally, the last degree of *yaqin* is called *haqq a1-yaqin* (the total reality of Certainty), that is, Certainty as supreme truth. Here, Certainty has a particular coloring: it is the fruit of an all-embracing experience because the object of Certainty is identical to the one who is experiencing it, knowledge being transformed into actual experience and actual experience into knowledge. At this stage, in fact, knowledge is not limited to the intellect, nor to the vision of the one who is contemplating it, it becomes one with the human being. This is the final phase of *yaqin*, the apotheosis of the spiritual and intellectual journey. This high degree of Sufi Certainty is the effect of the Emanation of the divine. Thiophenes in Essence at its existential level and that of the diffusion of the Light of lights (Dazzling Irradiations) at the level of the theophanies of the gnostic.

IHSAN

Ihsan (or Ehsan or Ahsan) is an Arabic term meaning "perfection" or "excellence." In Islam, Ihsan is the Muslim responsibility to obtain perfection, or excellence, in worship, such that Muslims try to worship God (Arabic Allah) as if they see Him, and although they cannot see Him, they undoubtedly believe he is constantly watching over them. That definition comes from the hadith in which Muhammad states, It (Ihsan) is to worship Allah as if you see Him, and if you cannot achieve this state then you must remember that He is seeing you." (Al-Bukhari and Al-Muslim).

The concept of Ihsan has been understood differently by various Islamic scholars. For example, some scholars explain Ihsan as being the "inner-dimension" of Islam whereas shariah is often described as the "outer-dimension". Ihsan is excellence in worship, work, and in social interactions. For example, ihsan includes sincerity during Muslim prayers and being grateful to parents, family, and God.

Sufis have divided Ihsan into two parts

- Muraqaba i.e. to worship with the thought that The God is seeing us.

- Mushahada i.e. to worship The God as if we see him

NOOR

Noor or Nur may refer to:

- An Arabic name, common among royalty
- The Arabic term for light
- Queen Noor of Jordan
- Noor Jahan, a Mughal Empress
- Noor Jehan, Pakistani actress/singer
- Noor Actress, actress
- Princess Noor Inyat Khan, secret agent and a descendant of Tipu Sultan
- Noor, Iran a city in northern Iran
- Noor, a champion racehorse in the 1950s
- Noor a concept in Sufism
- Surah of Wilaya and Nurayn
- *Dhun Nurayn* or the "Possessor of Two Lights", a Sunni nickname for Uthman, the third Sunni Caliph

Maqaam: Maqaam (the station) is one's spiritual station or developmental level, as distinct from one's hal, or state of consciousness. This is seen as the outcome of one's effort to transform oneself, whereas the haal is a gift. "Maqam" is also terms for "scale". These are the topmost foundations of "walaya:" the moral distinctions and spiritual degrees accorded to the men of the Way. They constitute the stabilizing element of liberating experience. According to Ibn 'Arabi, "al-yaqn " (certainty) the apex of the maqamaat.

Haal: Haal (Lit, "state" or "condition.", plural *ahwal*) is a special-purpose, temporary state of consciousness, generally a product of spiritual practices, recognised in Sufism.

A *haal* is by nature gratuitous and one should not attempt to prolong it. It results from psychological or spiritual influences which effect the man of the Way during his progress towards the God-King. Related concepts are Ecstasy *(wajad)*, Annihilation *(istilam)*, Happiness *(bast)*, Despondency *(qabd)*, Awakening *(sahu)* Drunkenness *(sukr)*, etc. They arise like flashes on the horizon, blinding flashes of lightning which disappear immediately. However, these stages are necessary for the liberating experience of Man; thanks to them He may distinguish the contingent from the consciousness anything except that which is destined to endure. According to Ibn Arabi, "al-fan" (extinction) is the apex of the *ahwal*.

Manzil: Manzil (plural manazil) is the Arabic name for one of seven parts of roughly equal length into which the Quran is divided for the purpose of reciting the entire text in one week. Another meaning is parts of the Quran which help in curing or preventing jadoo (witchcraft).

DHIKR

Dhikr, (zikr in Urdu and Persian) (Arabic "pronouncement", "invocation" or "remembrance") is the remembrance of God commanded in the Quran for all Muslims. To engage in dhikr is to have awareness of God according to Islam. Dhikr as a devotional act includes the repetition of divine names, supplications and aphorisms from hadith literature, and sections of the Quran. More generally, any activity in which the Muslim maintains awareness of God is considered dhikr. Dhikr is also spelled zikr based on its pronunciation in Turkish, Persian, and Urdu.

Dhikr Beads: Known also as tasbih are usually beads upon a string, 99 or 100 in number, which corresponds to the 99 names of Allah and other recitations. The beads are used to keep track of the number of recitations that make up the dhikr. A popular dhikr (Subhanallah (33x) al Hamduallah (33x) Laa ilaaha illa Allah (33x) Allahu Akbar) was prescribed by the Prophet and is still practiced by many muslims worldwide after each of the daily five prayers. Even muslim inmates are allowed to utilize their beads for therapeutic effects see, [1] This is a successful action brought pursuant to 28 USC @ 1983 (by Imam Hamzah S. Alameen in the State of New York against Thomas A. Coughlin III, the Deparment of Corrections) arguing that prisoners have a First Amendment Constitutional right to use dhikr beads. Many islamic clerics argue that using the beads are fobidden, however the practice is contiguous with approved islamic traditions. It should be said that use of the fingers instead of the beads is better, since it was the practice of the Prophet. Nevertheless the beads are allowed, as long as no extra religious significance is placed upon the beads themselves, and that they are not viewed as articles of worship. At best the beads are a crude form of calculator. The Prophet's companion Abu Hurayrah had a string with 1,000 knots that he used to dhikr with before bead; one of the Prophet's wives used to count her dihkr with date palm shells (see Sunan Abu Dawud, Kitabul Dhikr) and the we have nothing from the Prophet that forbids the use of the beads and therefore dhikr beads are "halal" or "allowed" in most Islamic religious traditions. Many of the Muslim scholars of the past 1400 years, whom muslims consider foremost in knowledge, used dhikr beads.

The Sufi orders engage in ritualized dhikr ceremonies. Each order or lineage within an order has one or more forms for group dhikr, the liturgy of which may include recitation, singing, instrumental music, dance, costumes, incense, meditation, ecstasy, and trance (Touma 1996, p.162).

Dhikr in a group is most often done on Thursday and/or Sunday nights as part of the institutional practice of the orders.

A group dhikr ceremony in Arabic countries is usually called the hadrah ("presence", referring not to God's presence but to that of the spirit of the Prophet Muhammad and to the awareness of each participant). The hadrah marks the climax of the Sufi's gathering regardless of any teaching or formal structure. Musically this structure includes several secular Arab genres and can last for hours. (Ibid, p.165)

The hadrah section consists of the ostinato-like repetition of the name of God over which the soloist performs a richly ornamented song. Often the climax is reached through cries of "Allah! Allah!" or "hu hu" ("He! He!"), with the participants bending forward while exhaling and stand straight while inhaling. The articulation of the name of God progresses as follows, with upward beams indicating inhalation and downward beams indicating exhalation: The hadrah is directed by a shaykh of the tariqa or one of his representatives; monitoring the intensity, depth and duration of the phases of the hadrah, the shaykh aims to draw the circle into deep awareness of God. Dhikr ceremonies may have a ritually determined length or may last as long as the shaykh deems his murids require.

Modes of Dhikr: Depending upon the mode of Dhikr, it has been divided into 3 kinds

- Dhikr-e-Jalli—Dhikr with tongue loudly
- Dhikr-e-Khaffi—Dhikr in heart (hidden dhikr-i.e. not from tongue)

Sufis further divide the mode of meditative Dhikr according to the Latifa in which they are done. These include:

- Dhikr-e-nafsi
- Dhikr-e-Qalbi
- Dhikr-e-Ruhi
- Dhikr-e-Sirri
- Dhikr-e-Khafi
- Dhikr-e-Akfha

Forms of Dhikr: Different Sufi Orders have different syllabus of dhikr. Most common ones are as follows:

- Ya-Hayyu-Ya-Qayyum (O Living & Giver of life)
- La illaha illallah (There is no god but God)
- Allah Hu (He is God)
- 99 Names of God
- Verses from Quran

- Darud Sharif (Asking God to send peace & blessings upon Prophet Muhammad)
- Istaghfar (Asking forgiveness from God)

MURAQABA

Muraqaba is the Sufi word for meditation. Literally it means "to watch over", "to take care of", or "to keep an eye". Metaphorically, it implies that with meditation, a person watches over or takes care of his spiritual heart (or soul), and acquires knowledge about it, its surroundings, and its creator.

Stages of Muraqaba: Following are the *maqamat* (stages) in which sufis have broadly categorised their journey of ascension. This categorization is an arbitrary one, and each level is generally further divided into several sub-levels. During the process of enlightenment, some stages can merge or overlap each other.

TAJALLI

Tajalliat (plural of tajalli) or theophanies in the realm of being are manifestations of the divine Truth with regard to infinite perfection and eternal glory. The divine theophanies are essentially the outpouring of His Beauty, His Perfection and His Love which are expressed in the immense theatre of the universe. The Existential Theophanies taken as a whole comprise three levels which the Ibn Arabi calls *hadarat* (Presences or Dignities).

First Level: Pure Essence: These are called existential theophanies of the Essence. They are the determinations of God in Himself, for Himself in His Essence transcending all manifestation and form. The world from which these theophanies and their radiance spring is called Unity *alam al-ahadiyya* (Realm of Unity). In this universe, the divine Essence appears as beyond all description, name or qualification. It is the world of pure Essence considered as Mystery of Mysteries and Secret of Secrets from which the theophanies of the Essence originate, the mirror in which the absolute existential Reality is reflected.

Second Level: the Attributes: These are the existential theophanies of divine qualities. The existential theophanies of divine Attributes are the determinations of God in Himself for Himself under the aspect of His intrinsic Names and Attributes. The world specified for this type of theophany is *alam al-wahda* (*Realm of Unicity* of the Essence with Its Attributes). God-Truth manifests both in His Essence and in His intrinsic Perfection after his concealment as "Hidden Treasure. This appearance arises by the mediation of what Ibn Arabi calls the most holy emanation *(al-fayd al-aqdas)*. In this particular world of theophanies the beings destined to incarnate appear in the form of immutable realities.

Third Level: Acts: These are the active existential theophanies since the nature of God or the divinity as such is Essence, Attributes and Action, personified by His Divine Names. The existential theophanies of divine Action are the extrinsic effects of divine Power in the manifest world. The world where these theophanies are exercised and revealed is called *alam al-Wahdaniyya, The Unification* in its three aspects: Essence-Attribute-Action. It appears by the way of the holy emanation (al-fayd al-Muqaddas): a universe where God manifests Himself in the form of eternal realities encompassing species and individuals, sensible forms and abstractions.

GNOSIS OF SELF

Ghanood (Somnolence): This is the starting level of meditation. When a person starts meditation, he enters into a somnolent or sleep state often. With the passage of time, the person goes into a state between sleep and wakefulness. So the person can remember that he saw something, but not specifically what it is.

Adraak (experience): With continuous practice of meditation, the sleepiness from meditation decreases. When the conscious mind is not suppressed by sleep and is able to focus, the person can receive the spiritual knowledge from his subconscious mind. At this stage, the person is unable to see or hear anything, but he is able to experience or perceive it.

Warood (coming, beginning): When *adraak* (experience) becomes deep, it is exhibited as sight. The stage of *warood* starts when mental concentration is sustained and somnolence is at its minimum. As soon as the mind is focused, the spiritual eye is activated. The conscious mind is not used to see through the spiritual eye, so concentration comes and goes. Gradually, the mind gets used to this kind of visions and the mental focus is sustained. With practice, the visions/experience becomes so deep that the person starts considering himself a part of the experience rather than considering himself an observer.

GNOSIS OF THE UNIVERSE

Kashaf/Ilhaam (unveiling of arcane knowledge): *Kashaf*, or *Ilhaam* is the stage where man starts getting information that most people are unable to observe. In the beginning, this condition occurs suddenly without personal control. With practice, the mind gets so energized that it can get this knowledge by will.

Shahood (evidence): When a person can get any information about any event/person with his will, this condition is called Shahood. This stage is broadly categorized according to activation of the senses:

1. The person can see things anywhere in the universe
2. The person can hear things anywhere in the universe

3. The person can smell things anywhere in the universe
4. The person can touch things anywhere in the universe (hadith)

Fatah (opening, victory): The peak of Shahood is called Fatah. At this stage, the person doesn't need to close his eyes for meditation. Here the person is freed from both space and time. He can see/hear/taste/touch anything that are present anywhere in time and space.

GNOSIS OF THE CREATOR

Fanaa (extinction, annihilation): Through a series of stages (*maqamat*) and subjective experiences (*ahwal*), this process of absorbation develops until complete annihilation of the self (*fana*) takes place and the person becomes *al-insanul-kamil*, the "perfect man". It is the disintegration of a person's narrow self-concept, social self- and limited intellect (feeling like a drop of water aware of being part of the ocean). The stage is also called *Fana fit tawheed* ("extinction with the unity"), and *Fana fil Haq* (Extinction in the reality). This stage may be equated with the concept of nirvana in Buddhism, which aims for the same goal using a similar practice.

Sair Illallah (journey towards the God): Here the person starts his spiritual journey towards the ultimate reality of the universe, i.e. God. Also called *Safr-e-Urooji*.

Fana Fillah (Extinction of the self in God): One of the important phases of mystical experience which is attained by the grace of God by a traveller on the mystical path is the state of *fana fi Allah*, "extinction of the self in God". This is the state where the person becomes extinct in the will of God. It is important to mention that this is not incarnation or union. Most Sufis, while passing through this experience, have preferred to live in the greatest depth of silence which transcends all forms and sounds, and enjoy their union with the beloved.

- The highest stage of *fana* is reached when even the consciousness of having attained *fana* disappears. This is what the Sufis call "the passing-away of passing-away" (*fana al-fana*). The mystic is now wrapped in contemplation of the divine essence.
- Since it is a state of complete annihilation of carnal self, absorbation or intoxication in God, the pilgrim is unable to participate in worldly affairs, he is made to pass into another state known as *Fana-al-Fana* (forgetfulness of annihilation). It is a sort of oblivion of unconsciousness. Since two negatives make one positive, the pilgrim at this stage regains his individuality as he was when he started the journey. The only difference is that in the beginning he was self-conscious, but after having reposed in the Divine Being, he regains that sort of individuality which is God-consciousness or absorbation in God. This state is known as *Baqa-bi-Allah* — living

or subsisting with God. (Alhaj W.B.S. Rabbani, *Gems of Sufi Gnosticism) [1]*

This stage has sometimes been equated with realization of Brahman of the Hindus.

Sair Min Allah (journey from the God): Here the person comes back to his existence. Also called *Safr-e-Nuzooli*.

Baqaa Billah (eternal life in union with God): This is the state where man comes back to his existence and God appoints him to guide the humans. This is a state in which the individual is part of the world, but unconcerned about his or her rewards or position in it. This doctrine is further explained in an authentic tradition of the prophet which states that God said:

And the most beloved things with which My slave comes nearer to Me, is what I have enjoined upon him; and My slave keeps on coming closer to Me through performing Nawafil (praying or doing extra deeds besides what is obligatory) till I love him, so I become his sense of hearing with which he hears, and his sense of sight with which he sees, and his hand with which he grips, and his leg with which he walks.

There is another verse from Quran, that is used to explain this concept.

We (Allah) are nearer to him (man) than his jugular vein.(50:6)

When Sufis have come out of the *Fana fillah* state and enter *Baqa billah*, many of them have produced works of unsurpassed glory, especially in the fields of philosophy, literature, and music. These works have crowned the culture of the entire Islamic world and inspired Sufis and non-Sufis for generations. As the great Persian Sufi poet, Hafiz of Shiraz, who is fondly remembered as the "tongue of the unseen", said centuries ago: "He whose heart is alive with love, never dies.". Allah says about these people in the *Quran*: "Lo, indeed, the friends of God have no fear, nor are they grieved."

There are many different kinds of *muraqaba* that are practiced in various Sufi schools in different parts of the world. Following is a list of the ones commonly practiced.

Beginner Level Muraqabas

1. *Muraqaba of light*

These are usually used for beginners, or for cure of various diseases.

- Violet
- Indigo
- Blue
- Torquise
- Green

- Yellow
- Orange
- Pink
- Red

1. Ehsan
2. Noor (Invisible Light)
3. Haatif-e-Ghabi (Unhearable sound of Cosmos)
4. Names of God — For getting acquaintance with attributes of God
5. Allah (Proper name of God) — Final level of Muraqaba of names of God

Middle Level Muraqabas

1. Moat (Death) — Forgetting acquaintance with life after Death
2. Qalb (Heart) — Forgetting acquaintance with Spiritual Heart
3. Wahdat (Unity) — Forgetting acquaintance with the reason behind cosmic unity i.e. God's will
4. La (Nothingness) — Forgetting acquaintance with material lessness, or non-material universe

   Adam (Preexistence) — Next level of Muraqaba of Nothingness.
5. Fana (Annihilation) — Annihilation of Self, getting acquaintance with the alpha and omega of universe.

High Level Muraqabas

1. Tasawwur-e-Sheikh (Focussing mind on master)— To facilate the transfer of spiritual knowledge from master to student.
2. Tasawwur-e-Rasool (Focussing mind on prophet)— To facilate the transfer of Faiz (arcane spiritual knowledge) from prophet to student. For Muslims, this focussing of mind is done on Muhammad. For people following other religions, their particular holy figures are used to focus mind upon.
3. Tasawwur-e-zat-e-Ilaahi (Focussing Mind on God)— With the help of this Muraqaba, the student experiences the Tajalli-e-Zaat of God.

SAMA

- Sama, a character of the Mahabharata.
- Shamash, the Assyrian and Babylonian sun god.
- Sema, form of Sufi ritual ceremony
- SAMA, the Saudi Arabian Monetary Agency
- *Sama* (Øi) in Japanese is an honorific suffix. See also: Japanese titles

CHISHTI ORDER

The Chishti Order was founded by Khawaja Abu Ishaq Shami ("the

Syrian") (d. 941) who brought sufism to the town of Chisht, some 95 miles east of Herat in present-day Afghanistan. Before returning to the Levant, Shami initiated, trained, and deputized the son of the local Amir, Khwaja Abu Ahmad Abdal (d. 966). Under the leadership of Khwaja Abu Ahmad's descendants, the *Chishtiyya* as they are also known flourished as a regional mystical order. Sema or Kawali is devotional music to enhance the remembrance of Allah and is not part of Worship or prayer. At its founding, the Chishti Order was known for its renunciation of worldly power, but this would change later when Chishti saints would ally with emperors, most notably the Mughale Emperor Akbar.

The most famous of the Chishti saints is Hazrat Khawaja Moinuddin Chishti (R.A) (also known as Khwaja Baba) who settled in Ajmer, India. Khwaja Baba (R.A) oversaw the growth of the order in the 13th century as religious laws were canonized. He saw the Prophet in a dream and then set off on a journey of discovery.

Other famous saints of the Chishti Order are Nizamuddin Auliya (R.A) of Delhi, Fariduddin Ganjshakar (R.A) of Pak Pattan, and Qutubuddin Bakhtiar Kaki (R.A). Hazrat Inayat Khan was the first to bring the Chishtia Order to North America. The Saint Kabir is also thought to have been part of the Chishti order.

The Chishti Order is famous for its emphasis on love, tolerance, openness, and ecstasy. The Order traces its origins through various saints all the way to the Prophet's Companion 'Hazrat Ali and to the Prophet Muhammad (PBUH).

The Chishti Order is also known for its nine principles. These include: Obedience to shaykh or pir, Renunciation of material world, Distance from worldly powers, Sama (or musical assemblies), Extreme prayers and fasting, Dependence on voluntary offerings, Disapproval of miraculous feats, Service to humanity and Respect for other devotional traditions.

The Golden Chain (Shijrah) Chistiya-Mujarradiya

1. Prophet Mohammad
2. Hazrat Ali ibn Abu Talib
3. Hazrat Hasan al-Basri
4. Hazrat Abdul Wahid ibn Zaid
5. Hazrat Fuzail ibn Ayaz
6. Hazrat Ibrahim ibn Adam of Balaq
7. Hazrat Khawaja Sadiyuddin Muraishi
8. Hazrat Khawaja Aminuddin Basri
9. Hazrat Khawaja Khawaja Karimuddin Mumshaad
10. Hazrat Khawaja Khawaja Abul Ishak Shami

11. Hazrat Khawaja Abu Ahmed Abdaal
12. Hazrat Khawaja Mohammad Abi Ahmed
13. Hazrat Khawaja Nasihuddin Abu Mohammad
14. Hazrat Khawaja Abu Yusuf Jamal
15. Hazrat Khawaja Nasiruddin Moudud Chisti
16. Hazrat Khawaja Haji Sharif Zindana
17. Hazrat Khawaja Usmaan Haruni
18. Hazrat Khawaja Moinuddin Chisti
19. Hazrat Khawaja Kutubuddin Baktiyaar Kaki
20. Hazrat Khawaja Kalimuddin Chisti
21. Hazrat Khawaja Sirajuddin
22. Hazrat Khawaja Alimuddin
23. Hazrat Khawaja Mehmood Chisti
24. Hazrat Khawaja Jamaluddin Chisti
25. Hazrat Khawaja Mohammad Hassan
26. Hazrat Khawaja Mohammad Sani
27. Hazrat Khawaja Yuhaiya Madni
28. Hazrat Khawaja Kalimullah
29. Hazrat Khawaja Nizamuddin Auliya
30. Hazrat Khawaja Fakruddin
31. Hazrat Khawaja Noor Mohammad
32. Hazrat Khawaja Suleiman Bande Nawaz
33. Hazrat Khawaja Allah Baksh
34. Hazrat Khawaja Shah Khairuddin Mujjarrad
35. Hazrat Khawaja Al-Haaj Abdul Rehman Sailani
36. Hazrat Mohammad Masoom Armaan
37. Hazrat Shah Sharfuddin Abdul Gafoor Abdaal
38. Hazrat Mohammed Aainuddin Arif Ali
39. Hazrat Mohammad Sadique Armani
40. Hazrat Mohammad Malang Masoom Naqshbandi

JERRAHI

The Jerrahi are a Sufi order (Tarika) derived from the Halveti (Khalwati) order. Their founder is Pir Nureddin al-Jerrahi, who died in Istanbul and is buried at the site of his tekke in Istanbul. During the late Ottoman period, the tarika was widespread throughout the Balkans, particularly Macedonia and southern Greece (Morea).

Founded in the 17th century by Hadrat Pir Muhammed Nureddin Al-

Jerrahi, the Halveti-Jerrahi Order of Dervishes is an Islamic Sufi path of Love: Worship the Creator with Love and serve His Creation with Love. Halveti-Jerrahi Order of Dervishes is a cultural, educational, and social relief organization with diverse professional, ethnic and national backgrounds. Besides the material connection, established by the fact that Hadrat Pir Muhammed Nureddin Al-Jerrahi is a direct descendant of Prophet Muhammed both from his mother and father, the path he has founded is dedicated to the teachings and traditions through an unbroken chain of spiritual transmission that goes directly back to the Prophet Muhammed.

The head dergah (sufi convention) of the Halveti-Jerrahi Dervishes is in Istanbul. It has branches in most of the European Countries, Australia, South Africa, South America and North America including Chicago.

The Branch of the Halveti Jerrahi Order of Dervishes in Chicago conduct mountly gatherings where the dervishes perform sufi remembrance ceremony (zikrullah), practise sufi music, serve dinner, pray together and listen to the discourse of Sheikh Ilhan Al-Jerrahi, the sufi guide.

One prominent member of the tarika was Muzaffer Ozak (also known as *Muzaffer Efendi*), the 19th Sheikh, who died in 1985. He brought the Jerrahi order into the western countries.

MEVLEVI

The Mevlevi Order or the Mevleviye are a Sufi order founded by the followers of Jalal al-Din Muhammad Rumi in 1273 in Konya, in present day Turkey. They are also known as the Whirling Dervishes due to their famous practice of whirling as a form of dhikr (remembrance of Allah). Dervishes are members of Sufi ascetic religious Tarika or "confraternities", known for their extreme poverty and austerity.

The Mevlevi, or Mevleviye, one of the most well-known of the Sufi orders, was founded in 1273 by Rumi's followers after his death, particularly his son, Sultan Veled Celebi (or *Celebi*, *Chelebi*). The Mevlevi, or "The Whirling Dervishes", believe in performing their dhikr in the form of a "dance" and music ceremony called the sema.

The Sema represents a mystical journey of man's spiritual ascent through mind and love to "Perfect." Turning towards the truth, the follower grows through love, deserts his ego, finds the truth and arrives to the "Perfect." He then returns from this spiritual journey as a man who has reached maturity and a greater perfection, so as to love and to be of service to the whole of creation.

The Mevlevi were a well established Sufi Order in the Ottoman Empire, and many of the members of the order served in various official positions of the Caliphate. The centre for the Mevlevi order was in Konya, where Rumi is buried. There is also a Mevlevi monastery or *dergah* in Istanbul, near the Galata Tower, where the sema ceremony is performed and accessible to the public.

During Ottoman Empire era, the Mevlevi order produced a number of famous poets and musicians such as Sheikh Ghalib, Ismail Ankaravi (both buried at the Galata Mevlevi-Hane) and Abdullah Sari. Music, especially the ney, play an important part in the Mevelevi order and thus much of the traditional "oriental" music that Westerners associate with Turkey originates with the Mevlevi order. Indeed, if one buys a CD of Turkish Sufi music, chances are it will be Mevlevi religious music.

During the Ottoman period, the Mevlevi order spread into the Balkans, Syria, and Egypt (and is still practiced in both countries where they are known as the *Mawlawi order*). The Bosnian writer Mesa Selimoviæ wrote the book *Death and the Dervish* about a Mevlevi *dergah* in Sarajevo. The Mevlevi Order is also linked to other Dervish orders such as the Qadiri (founded in 1165), the Rifa'i (founded in 1182), and the Kalenderis.

The Mevlevi Order was outlawed in Turkey at the dawn of the secular revolution by Kemal Atatürk in 1923. In the 1950s, the Turkish government, realizing that The Whirling Dervishes had value as a tourist attraction, began allowing the Whirling Dervishes to perform annually in Konya on the *Urs of Mevlana*, December 17, the anniversary of Rumi's death. In 1974, they were allowed to come to the West. They performed in France, for Pope Paul VI, and at the Brooklyn Academy of Music and other venues in the United States and Canada-under the direction of the late Mevlevi Shaikh Suleyman Hayati Dede.

SUFI WHIRLING

The practice of Sufi whirling (or Sufi spinning) is a twirling meditation that originated among the Turkish Sufis, which is still practiced by the Dervishes of the Mevlevi order.

Following a recommended fast of several hours, Sufi whirlers begin with hands crossed onto shoulders and may return their hands to this position if they feel dizzy. They rotate on their left feet in short twists, using the right foot to drive their bodies around the left foot. The left foot is like an anchor to the ground, so that if the whirler loses his or her balance, he or she can think of their left foot, direct attention towards it and regain balance.

The whirling is done on the spot in an anticlockwise direction, with the right arm held high, palm upwards, and the left arm held low, palm downwards. People who feel discomfort from whirling anti-clockwise can change to clockwise. The body of the whirler is meant to be soft with eyes open, but unfocused so that images become blurred and flowing. A 15 minute period of slow rotation is followed by a gradual build up of speed over the next 30 minutes. Then the whirling takes over. When the whirler is whirling so fast that he or she cannot remain upright, his or her body will fall by itself. The whirler does not consciously make the fall a decision or attempt to arrange the landing in advance; if his or her body is soft he or she should land softly—and the earth will absorb the energy. If the idea of letting oneself fall is too much for the practitioner then the whirler should allow his or herself to slow down very slowly. If the whirler has been whirling for an hour then the process of slowing down might take some time—even 10 minutes or more.

Once the whirler has fallen, the second part of the meditation starts—the unwhirling. The whirler rolls onto his or her stomach immediately so that his or her bare navel is in contact with the earth. If anybody feels strong discomfort lying this way, he should lie on his back. The practitioner feels his or her body blending into the earth, like a small child pressed to his mother's breasts. Eyes remain closed and the whirler remains passive and silent for at least 15 minutes. After the meditation whirlers try to be as quiet and inactive as possible.

Hadhra: Hadhra is the term given to a sacred dance performed by Sufi Muslims accompanied by dhikr recitations invoking the name of Allah. The term in Arabic literally means "presence". It is practiced primarily in the Arab world, but can also be found in some non-Arab Muslim countries such as Indonesia.

NAQSHBANDI

Naqshbandi (Naqshbandiyya) is one of four major Sufi orders (tariqa) of Islam. Formed in 1380, the order is considered by some to be a "sober" order which believes in silent dhikr (remembrance of God) and suhbat (an intimate relationship between student and master).

The order began with Abu Bakr a constant companion of Prophet Muhammad and father-in-law, whereas most other turuq (Chishtia, Suhrawardiyya and Qadiriyyah) trace their lineage from the Prophet Muhammad through Ali ibn Abu Talib.

The word *Naqshbandi* is Persian, taken from the name of the founder of the order, Baha-ud-Din Naqshband Bukhari. Some have said that the translation means "related to the image-maker," some also consider it to mean "Pattern Maker" rather than "image maker," and interpret "Naqshbandi" to mean "Reformer of Patterns", and others consider it to mean "Way of the Chain" or "Golden Chain."

Naqshbandi Hijazi Sufi Order

1. The Beloved of Allah, Prophet Muhammad (saws)
2. Hazrat Abu Bakr Siddiqi (ra)

3. Hazrat Salman al-Farsi (ra)
4. Hazrat Qassim ibn Abu Bakr (ra)
5. Hazrat Jafar as-Saddiq (ra)
6. Hazrat Bayazid al-Bistami (ra)
7. Hazrat Abul Hassan Ali al-Harqani (ra)
8. Hazrat Bue Ali al-Farmadi
9. Hazrat Yaqub Yusaf al-Hamadani (ra)
10. Hazrat Khawaja Abdul Khaliq Ajdwani (ra)
11. Hazrat Abul Abbas al-Khadr (ra)
12. Hazrat Arif al-Rewgani (ra)
13. Hazrat Khawaja Mahmood al-Injir al-Faghnawi (ra)
14. Hazrat Azizan Ali- Ar-Ramitani (ra)
15. Hazrat Muhammad Baba as-Samasi (ra)
16. Hazrat Sayyid Amir Kulal (ra)
17. Hazrat Mohammad Bahauddin Naqshband (ra)
18. Hazrat Alauddin al-Bukhari al-Attar (ra)
19. Hazrat Yaqub al-Charkhi (ra)
20. Hazrat Ubaydullah al-Ahrar (ra)
21. Hazrat Muhammad Az-Zahid Wali (ra)
22. Hazrat Mohammad Darwish (ra)
23. Hazrat Khawaja al-Akmangi (ra)
24. Hazrat Muhammad al-Baqi Billah (ra)
25. Hazrat Ahmad al-Faruqi as-Sirhindi, mujadid alf-at'thani (ra)
26. Hazrat Khawaja Muhammad Masoom (ra)
27. Hazrat Khawaja Saifuddin (ra)
28. Hazrat Syed Noor Muhammad Badayoori (ra)
29. Hazrat Mirza Jaane Janaan (ra)
30. Hazrat Shah Ghulam Ali Dehlvi (ra)
31. Hazrat Muhammmad Abdul Rasool Qusoori (ra)
32 Hazrat Muhammad Rasool Qusoori (ra)
33. Hazrat Khawaja Ghulam Dastigir (ra)
34. Munazir-e-Azam Maulana Mohammad Umar Icharvi (ra)
35. Hazrat Mujadid Abdul Wahab Siddiqi (ra)
36. Hazrat Allama Pir Shaykh Faiz-ul-Aqtab Siddiqi Hijazi

MUJADDIDIYA BRANCH

1. The mercy for the worlds Rasulullah [Holy City of Madinah Munawwarah].

2. Sayyedina Hadrat Abu Bakr Siddiq (radiallahu anhu) [Holy City of Madinah Munawwarah].
3. Hadrat Salman Farsi (radiallahu anhu) [Madain].
4. Hadrat Qasim bin Muhammad bin Abi Bakr (rahmatullahi alaihi) [Holy City of Madinah Munawwarah].
5. Hadrat Imam Jafar Sadiq (rahmatullahi alaihi) [Holy City of Madinah Munawwarah].
6. Hadrat Khuwaja Bayazeed Bustami (rahmatullahi alaihi) [Bastam].
7. Hadrat Khuwaja Abul Hasan Kharkani (rahmatullahi alaihi) [Kharkhan].
8. Hadrat Khuwaja Abul Qasim Gorgani (rahmatullahi alaihi) [Jarjan].
9. Hadrat Khuwaja Abu Ali Farmadi (rahmatullahi alaihi) [Mashad].
10. Hadrat Khuwaja Yusuf Hamdani (rahmatullahi alaihi) [Turkistan].
11. Hadrat Khuwaja Abdul Khaliq Gajadwani (rahmatullahi alaihi) [Bukhara].
12. Hadrat Khuwaja Muhammad Arif Riogri (rahmatullahi alaihi) [Tajikistan].
13. Hadrat Khuwaja Mehmood Injir Faghnavi (rahmatullahi alaihi) [Bukhara].
14. Hadrat Khuwaja Azizane Ali Raamitni (rahmatullahi alaihi) [Bukhara].
15. Hadrat Khuwaja Muhammad Baba Samasi (rahmatullahi alaihi) [Bukhara].
16. Hadrat Khuwaja Sayyed Amir Kalal (rahmatullahi alaihi) [Bukhara].
17. Hadrat Khuwaja Bahauddin Naqshband Bukhari (rahmatullahi alaihi) [Bukhara].
18. Hadrat Khuwaja Ala'uddin Attar (rahmatullahi alaihi) [Hassar].
19. Hadrat Khuwaja Yaqoob Charkhi (rahmatullahi alaihi) [Dushanbe].
20. Hadrat Khuwaja Ubaidullah Ahrar (rahmatullahi alaihi) [Samarqand].
21. Hadrat Khuwaja Maulana Muhammad Zahid (rahmatullahi alaihi) [Hassar].
22. Hadrat Khuwaja Darvish Muhammad (rahmatullahi alaihi) [Sher Sabz].
23. Hadrat Khuwaja Muhammad Amkangi (rahmatullahi alaihi) [Bukhara].
24. Hadrat Khuwaja Muhammad Baqibillah (rahmatullahi alaihi) [Delhi]
25. Hadrat Khuwaja Mujaddid Alf-Thani (rahmatullahi alaihi) [Sirhind Sharif].

26. Hadrat Khuwaja Muhammad Masoom (rahmatullahi alaihi) [Sirhind Sharif].
27. Hadrat Khuwaja Saifuddin (rahmatullahi alaihi) [Sirhind Sharif].
28. Hadrat Khuwaja Hafiz Muhammad Muhsin (rahmatullahi alaihi) [Delhi].
29. Hadrat Khuwaja Sayed Nur Muhammad Badaiooni (rahmatullahi alaihi) [Delhi].
30. Hadrat Mirza Mazhar Janejana (rahmatullahi alaihi) [Delhi].
31. Hadrat Shah Ghulam Ali Mujaddidi (rahmatullahi alaihi) [Delhi].
32. Hadrat Khuwaja Shah Abu Sa'eed (rahmatullahi alaihi) [Delhi].
33. Hadrat Khuwaja Shah Ahmed Sa'eed Dehlvi (rahmatullahi alaihi) [Holy City of Madinah Munawwarah].
34. Hadrat Haji Dost Muhammad Kandhari (rahmatullahi alaihi) [Musazai Sharif].
35. Hadrat Khuwaja Muhammad Usman Damani (rahmatullahi alaihi) [Musazai Sharif].
36. Hadrat Khuwaja Sirajuddin (rahmatullahi alaihi) [Musazai Sharif].
37. Hadrat Khuwaja Muhammad Fazal Ali Qureshi (rahmatullahi alaihi) [Miskeenpur Sharif].
38. Hadrat Khuwaja Muhammad Abdul Malik Siddiqui (rahmatullahi alaihi) [Khanewal].
39. Murshid-e-Alam Hadrat Khuwaja Ghulam Habib (rahmatullahi alaihi) [Chakwal].
40. Hadrat Maulana Hafiz Zulfiqar Ahmad Naqshbandi Mujaddidi (damat barakatuhu) [Jhang Sharif].

Naksi-Bendi Hakkani Golden Chain

1. Sayyidina Wa Mevlana Muhammad Mustafa (S.w.s)
2. Seyyid-ul Awliya Abu Bakr As Siddiq (R.a.)
3. Salman-i Farisi (R.a.)
4. Imam Kasim Bin Muhammed (R.a.)
5. Imam-i Jafer-i Siddiq Bin Imam Muhammed El-bakir (R.a.)
6. Sultan-ul Arifin Bayezid-i Bestami (K.s.)
7. Ebul Hasan Harkani (K.s.)
8. Ebu Ali Ahmed Farmedi (K.s.)
9. Haje Yusuf-ul Hamedani (K.s.)
10. Ebul Abbas (Hizir A.s.)
11. Imam-ul Hatim Abdul Halik Gujdevani(k.s.)
12. Haje Arif Rigveri (K.s.)

13. Haje Mahmud Injir-i Faghnevi (K.s.)
14. Haje Aziz ali Ramitani (K.s.)
15. Haje Muhammed Baba Semmasi (K.s.)
16. Haje Seyyid Emir Kulal (K.s.)
17. Imam-i Tariqa Wa Ghaus-ul Halika Haje Muhammed Bahauddin Nakshibendiy-yil Uwaysil Buhari (K.s.)
18. Haje Alauddin Muhammed-il Attar (K.s.)
19. Haje Yakub-ul Cherhi (K.s.)
20. Haje Ubeydullah-il Ahrar Semerkandi (K.s.)
21. Muhammed-uz Zahid (K.s.)
22. Dervish Muhammed-il Buhari (K.s.)
23. Hajegi-l Emkineki-l Semerkandi (K.s.)
24. Muhammed-il Bakibillah Semerkandi (K.s.)
25. Imam Rabbani Ahmed Faruki Serhendi (K.s.)
26. Muhammed Masum-urrabbani (K.s.)
27. Haje Seyfuddin-irrabbani (K.s.)
28. Nur Muhammed-il Bedvani (K.s.)
29. Habibullah Mirza Jan-u Janan-ul Mazhar (K.s.)
30. Gulam Ali Abdullah-ud Dehlevi (K.s.)
31. Ziya-uddin Halid Al Baghdadi Al-shami (K.s.)
32. Sheykh Ismail Enerani (K.s.)
33. Has Muhammed Shirvani (K.s.)
34. Sheykh Muhammed Efendi Yeraghi (K.s.)
35. Seyyid Jemaleddin Gumukiyyil Huseyni (K.s.)
36. Ebu Ahmed-is Sughuri (K.s.)
37. Ebu Muhammed-ul Medeni (K.s.)
38. Seyyid Sherafuddin Daghestan-i (K.s.)
39. Sultan-ul Awliya Abdullah Al-faizi Daghestan-i (K.s.)
40. Seyyid-ud Taife, Hatim-us Saadet, Kiblet-ul Islam, Sahib-uz Zaman, Sheykh-ul Islam, Sultan Ul Awliya, Hazreti Shah Sultan Mevlana Muhammed Nazim Adil Al-kibrisi Al-hakkani An-naksh-i bendi (K.s.)

The Golden Chain (Shijrah) of Naqshbandiya Mujaddadiya Mujarradiya

1. Prophet Huzoor Muhammad-ur-Rasoolullah s.a. (d. 12 Rabbiyul Awwal 11AH) -Medina
2. Hadhrat Abu Bakr Siddique r.a. (d. 22 Jama'dil A'lhar 13AH)-Medina

3. Hadhrat Salman al-faris r.a. (d. 10 Rajjab 35AH)-Madain
4. Hadhrat Imaam Qasim bin Muhammad bin Abu Bakr r.a. (d. 24 Jama'dil (Awwal/A'khar) 107AH)-Medina
5. Hadhrat Imaam Ja'far al-Sadiq r.a. (d. 15 Rajjab Murajjab 148AH)-Medina
6. Hadhrat Bayazid Bastami r.a. (d. 14/17 Sha'ba'n 261AH)-Bastam
7. Hadhrat Abul Hassan Khurqaani r.a. (d. 15 Ramda'n 425AH)-Khurqan
8. Hadhrat Abu Ali Farmadi r.a. (d. 4 Rabbiyul Awwal 477AH)-Mashad
9. Hadhrat Yusuf Hamdani r.a. (d. 27 Rajjab 535AH)-Turkistan
10. Hadhrat Abdul Khaliq Gajadwani r.a. (d. 12 Rabbiyul Awwal 575AH)-Bukhara
11. Hadhrat Muhammad Arif Riogri r.a. (d. 1 Shawwa'l 615AH)-Tajikistan
12. Hadhrat Mehmood Injir Faghnavi r.a. (d. 17 Rabbiyul Awwal 715AH)-Bukhara
13. Hadhrat Azizane Ali Raamitni r.a. (d. 718/721AH)-Bukhara
14. Hadhrat Muhammad Baba Samasi r.a. (d. 755AH)-Bukhara
15. Hadhrat Sayyed Amir Kulaal r.a. (d. 772AH)-Bukhara
16. Hadhrat Kwajah Bahauddin Naqshband r.a. (d. 2 Rajab al-Murajjab, 791AH)-Qasr-e-Aarifan (Bukhara)
17. Hadhrat Alaa'uddin Attaar r.a. (d. 20 Rajab 802AH)-Jafaaniyan (Mawralnahar)
18. Hadhrat Ya'qoob Charkhi r.a. (d. 5 Safar, 851AH)-Charkh (Bukhara)
19. Hadhrat Ubeydullah Ahraar r.a. (d. 20/29 Rabi al-Awwal, 895AH)-Samarqand (Mawralnahar)
20. Hadhrat Muhammad Zaahid r.a. (d. 1 Rabi al-Awwal, 936AH)-Wakhsh (Malk Hasaar)
21. Hadhrat Darwesh Muhammad r.a. (d. 19 Muharram, 970AH)-Samarqand (Mawralnahar)
22. Hadhrat Muhammad Waaqif Akangi r.a. (d. 21/22 Sha'baan, 1008AH)-Akang (Bukhara)
23. Hadhrat Khwaja Baaqi Billaah r.a. (d. 25 Jumaad al-Aakhar, 1012AH)-Delhi (India)
24. Huzoor Imam Rabbani, Mujaddid Alf Thani, Hadhrat Shaykh Ahmad Farooqui Sarhandi r.a. (d. 28 Safar, 1034AH)-Sarhand (India)
25. Hadhrat Muhammad Ma'soom Farooqui r.a. (d. 9 Rabi al-Awwal, 1079AH)-Sarhand (India)
26. Hadhrat Sayfuddeen Bin Ma'soom Farooqui r.a. (d. 19 Jumad al-Oola, 10951096AH)-Sarhand (India)
27. Hadhrat Noor Muhammad Badyooni r.a. (d. 11 Dhul Qa'dah, 1135AH)-Delhi (India)

28. Hadhrat Mirza Mazhar Jaan-I-Jaanan r.a. (d. 10 Muharram, 1195AH)-Khanqah Mazharia Dehli(India)
29. Hadhrat Abdullah Shah Naimullah r.a. (d. 22 Safar, 1240AH)-Behraich U.P.(India)
30. Hadhrat Mawla'na Muradullah r.a. (d. Dhul Qa'dah, 1248AH)-Lakhnow U.P.(India)
31. Hadhrat Sayyed Abul Hasan Saeed r.a. (d. Sha'ba'n, 1272)-Rai Bareli U.P.(India)
32. Hadhrat Niya'z Ali Shah r.a. (d. 2 Dhul Qa'dah, 1310AH)-Rai Bareli U.P.(India)
33. Hadhrat Sufi Wazeer r.a. (d. 1 Jama'dil Awwal, 1319AH)-Kasrawad Khargone M.P.(India)
34. Hadhrat Al-Haaj Abdullah r.a. (d. 6 Jama'dil Awwal, 13—AH)-Patkalyana, Samalkha, Karnaal, Haryaana, (India)
35. Hadhrat Shah Khairuddin Makhdoom Mujarrad r.a. (d. 12 Rabiyul Awwal, 1325AH)-Chopda, Jalgaon, Maharastra (India)
36. Hadhrat Al-Haaj Abdur Rehman Shah Sailaani r.a. (d. 22 Dhul Qa'dha 1326 AH)-Sailaani Gaon, 10 Miles From Chikli, Bultthana, Maharastra (India)
37. Hadhrat Mohd. Masoom Armaan r.a. (d. 5 Dhul Qa'dha 1378 AH)-Kasar Kheda, Balapur, Akola, Maharastra (India)
38. Hadhrat Shah Sharfuddin Abdul Gafoor Abda'l r.a. (d. 22 Safar 13—AH)-Kasali Muhalla, Motipura, Amalner, Maharastra (India)
39. Hadhrat Mohd. Ainuddin Arif Ali r.a. (d. 16 Sawwa'l 1410 AH)-Kasar Kheda, Balapur, Akola, Maharastra (India)
40. Hadhrat Salimuddin/Mohd. Sa'dique Armaani (Present Sajjadah Nashin)-Near Fort, Balapur, Akola, Maharastra (India)
41. Hadhrat Muhammad Malang Masoom Naqshbandi (Present Jaanashin & Sajjadah Nashin, Founder of D N F.
42. Hadhrat Nuseyreddin Rustem Fazilahovich Kovachi Mrahorovich Naqshbandi (Present Goranchich & Bretolich Gjakova, Founder of U C K)
43. Hazrat Allama Mufasir-Quran Mufaker-e-Islam PEER SYED RIAZ HUSSAIN SHAH Sahib Damat barakatum aalia (GENERAL SECTARY JAMAT-E-AHLE SUNNAT PAKISTAN)

OWAISIYA BRANCH

Naqshbandi Order has another famous branch called Naqshbandia Owaisiah Order. The method of spiritual instruction is quite close to Mujaddidya branch. However there are two main differences. First Naqshbandia Owaisiah order uses the "Pas Infas" method of zikr. Secondly, the method of spiritual instruction is "Owaisee", which means that the Shaikh can impart spiritual instruction regardless of physical distance and even difference of time period. Seekers of Naqshbandia Owaisiah can obtain spiritual blessing from their Shaikh regardless of their location in the world. Owaisiah connection is also useful in obtaining spiritual blessings from Sufies of the Past. Naqshbandia Owaisiah Order is based in Pakistan and its modern founder was Shaikh Allah Yar Khan (R.A). Current shaikhs are Hazrat Muhammad Ahsan Baig and Hazarat Syed Buniad Hussain Shah.

Owaisiya Chain of Transmission

1. Hazrat Muhammad S.A.W
2. Hazrat Abu Bakr Siddique Razi Allah Anho
3. Hazrat Imam Hasan Basri R.A
4. Hazrat Daud Tai R.A
5. Hazrat Junaid Baghdadi R.A
6. Hazrat Khwaja Ubaid Ullah Ahraar R.A
7. Hazrat Abdul Rahman Jami R.A
8. Hazrat Abu Ayub Muhammad Saleh R.A
9. Hazrat Khwaja Allah Din Madni R.A
10. Hazrat Maulana Abdul Raheem R.A
11. Hazrat Maulana Allah Yar Khan R.A
12. Hazrat Maulana Muhammad Akram Awan (Present)

Some Famous Naqshbandis

- Imam Rabbani,Mujaddid Alf Thani, Hadhrat Shaykh Ahmad Farooqui Sarhandi
- Bayazid Bastami
- Khwaja Mir Dard
- Imam Shamil
- Jami
- Shaykh Nazim al-Qubrusi
- Professor Sibghatullah Mojaddedi
- Huseyin Hilmi bin Said-i lstanboli
- Verdaro Krakov Muhamad Fihmi-Effendi bin Abu-Abdurehhmani al-Albani
- Ameer-e-Millat Pir Sayed Jamat Ali Shah
- Wali Muhammad Shah Chadar walli Sarkar
- Haji Soofi Masood Ahmad Siddiqui Lasani Sarkar
- Ahmet Kayhan Dede

SHADHILI

The Tariqa ash Shadhiliya is the Sufi order founded by Abu-l-Hassan ash-Shadhili. Followers, or *murids* (Arabic: seekers), of the Shadhiliya, are often known as Shadhilis.

It is the most popular Sufi order in North Africa and many of its followers have made great contributions to Arab and Islamic literature, most notably Sheikh Ibn 'Ata Allah, author of the 'Hikam' amongst other works, Sheikh Ahmed Zarruq, who died in Libya, who was the author of a commentary upon the Risala of al-Qayrawani (a standard work in Maliki Islamic jurisprudence) and a commentary upon the Hikam, he also wrote extensively on religion (Sufism) and law. Sheikh ibn Ajibah who wrote a commentary upon the Quran. Many of the sheikhs of al-Azhar University in Egypt have also been followers of the Shadhili tariqa.

The Swedish impressionist painter and Sufi scholar Sheikh Abd Al-Hadi Aqhili (1869-1917) was the first official Moqaddam (representative) of the Shadhili Order in Western Europe.

The Hamadiyya Shadhili branch is most popular. The Darqawi Shadhili branch is found mostly in Morocco and the Alawiyya (no connection to the Turkish or Syrian Alawi or Alevi groups) is found mostly in Algeria but now also in Syria, Jordan, and France amongst French North-Africans. The British Muslim convert Martin Lings wrote an extensive biography of the founding Sheikh of this branch, Sheikh Ahmad al-Alawi, entitled 'A Sufi Saint of the 20th century'.

FAMOUS SUFIS

Hasan al-Basri: Hasan al-Basri (Abu Sa'id al-Hasan ibn Abi-l-Hasan Yasar al-Basri), (642-728 or 737), was a well-known Arab theologian and scholar of Islam who was born at Medina.

His father was a freedman of Zayd ibn Thabit, one of the Ansar (Helpers of the Prophet), his mother a client of Umm Salama, a wife of the Prophet Muhammad (d.632). Tradition says that Umm Salama often nursed Hasan in his infancy. He was thus one of the *Tabi'een* (i.e. of the generation that succeeded the *Sahabah*). He became a teacher of Basra (Iraq) and founded a *madrasa* (school) there. Among his many pupils were Amr Ibn Ubayd (d.761) and Wasil ibn Ata (d.749), the founder of the Mu'tazilites.

He himself was a great supporter of orthodoxy and the most important representative of asceticism in the time of its first development. According to him, fear is the basis of morality, and sadness the characteristic of his religion. Life is only a pilgrimage, and comfort must be denied to subdue the passions. Al-Basri is also held in high regard by the Sufis, for his asceticism and subtle directions relating to the science of practical religion (*ilm-i mu'amalat*).

Many writers testify to the purity of his life and to his excelling in the virtues of Muhammad's own companions. He was "as if he were in the other world." In politics, too, he adhered to the earliest principles of Islam, being strictly opposed to the inherited caliphate of the Umayyads (r.661-750) and a believer in the election of the caliph. However, despite his critical position concerning the Umayyads, he did not approve of rebellion against tyrannical rule. His sermons contain some of the earliest and best examples of Arabic linguistic prose style.

Rabia: Rabia al-Adawiyya (717-801 C.E.) was a female Sufi saint from Basra in modern-day Iraq, who first set forth the doctrine of mystical love and who is widely considered to be the most important of the early Sufi poets. The defining work on her life and writing was written over 50 years ago by Margaret Smith, a small treatise written as a Master's Thesis.

Also known as Rabia al-Qaysiyya or Rabia of Basrah, she was born in Basra, Iraq between the years 95 A.H. and 99 A.H. (about 717 C.E.). Much of the poetry that is attributed to her is of unknown origin. After a life of hardship she became spontaneously realized. When asked by Sheikh Hasan al-Basri how she discovered the secret, she responded by stating:

You know of the how, but I know of the how-less.

One of the many myths that swirl around her life, is that she was freed from slavery because her master saw her praying while surrounded by light, realized that she was a saint and feared for his life if he continued to keep her as a slave.

One day, she was seen running through the streets of Basra carrying a torch in one hand and a bucket of water in the other. When asked what she was doing, she said:

I want to put out the fires of Hell, and burn down the rewards of Paradise. They block the way to God. I do not want to worship from fear of punishment or for the promise of reward, but simply for the love of God.

While she apparently received many marriage offers (including a proposal from Hasan al-Basri himself), she remained celibate and died of old age, an ascetic, her only care from the disciples who followed her. She was the first in a long line of female Sufi mystics.

Her name is also transliterated as *Rabia* and *Rabia al-»Adawiyya al-Quaysiyya of Basra*.

Bayazid Bastami: Bayazid Bastami also known as Abu Yazid Bistami or Tayfur Abu Yazid al-Bustami, (804-874 CE) was a Persian Sufi born in Bostam (alternate spelling: Bastam), Iran. The name Bastami means "from the city of Bastam". Bayazid Bastami had great influence on Sufi mysticism and is considered to be one of the important early teachers of Sufi Islam. Bastmi's predecessor Zu al-Nun al-Misri (d. CE 859) had formulated the doctrine of ma'rifa (gnosis), presenting a system which helped the *murid* (initiate) and the *shaykh* (guide) to communicate. Bayazid Bastami took this another step and emphasized the importance of ecstasy, referred to in his words as *drunkenness*, a means of union with God. Before him, Sufism was mainly based on piety and obedience and he played a major role in placing the concept of divine love at the core of Sufism.

Bistami was the first to speak openly of "annihilation of the self in God" (fana fi 'Allah') and "subsistence through God" (baqa' bi 'Allah). His paradoxical sayings gained a wide circulation and soon exerted a captivating influence over the minds of students who aspired to understand the meaning of the wahdat al-wujud, *Unity of Being*.

When Bayazid died, he was over seventy years old. Before he died, someone asked him his age. He said: I am four years old. For seventy years I was veiled. I got rid of my veils only four years ago."

He died in 874CE and is buried either in the city of Bistam in north central Iran, or in Semnan, Iran. Interestingly enough, there is a shrine in Chittagong, Bangladesh that local people believe to be Bastami's tomb as well. This is unlikely to be true, as Bastami was never known to have visited Bangladesh. However, Sufi teachers were greatly influential in the spread of Islam in Bengal and this might explain the belief. The Islamic scholars of Bangladesh usually regard the tomb at Chittagong attributed to him as a *jawab*, or imitation.

Bayazid lived a century before Abul Hassan Kharaqani. Attar Neishapouri has mentioned in his book Tazkiratul Awliya that Bayazid had spoken about the personality and state of Shaikh Abul Hassan Kharaqani with his disciples while passing from the village of Kharaqan, almost 100 years before the birth of Shaikh Abul Hassan.

Some of his words quoted from Tazkeratol-owlya by Attar:

- I never saw any lamp shining more brilliantly than the lamp of silence.
- I went to a wilderness, love had rained and had covered earth, as feet penetrate snow, I found my feet covered with love.
- I stood with the pious and I didn't find any progress with them. I stood with the warriors in the cause and I didn't find a single step of progress with them. Then I said, 'O Allah, what is the way to You?' and Allah said, 'Leave yourself and come.'

Al-Ghazali : Abu Hamid Muhammad ibn Muhammad al-Ghazali (born 1058 in Us, Khorasan province of Persia, modern day Iran, died 1111, Us) was a Persian Muslim theologian and philosopher, known as Algazel to the western medieval world. Abu Hamid Al-Ghazali, or al-Ghazzali as he is written sometimes, contributed significantly to the development of a systematic view of and acceptance in mainstream Islam. Al-Ghazali was both a Sufi and a scholar of orthodox Islam, belonging to the Shafi'i school of legal thought of Sunnite Islam. Imam Ghazali received many titles: Sharaful A'emma, Zainud din (Arabic), Hujjatul Islam.

Al-Ghazali remains one of the most celebrated scholars in the history of Islamic thought. He lectured at the Nizamiyyah school of Baghdad (the highest ranked academy of the golden era of Islamic civilization) between 1091 and 1096. He was the scholar par excellence in the Islamic world. He had literally hundreds of scholars attending his lectures at the Nizamiyyah. His audience included scholars from other schools of jurisprudence. This position won him prestige, wealth and respect that even princes and viziers could not match.

After some years he distributed his wealth and left Baghdad to begin a spiritual journey that lasted over a decade. He went to Damascus, Jerusalem, Hebron, Madinah, Mecca and back to Baghdad where he stopped briefly. He then left for us to spend the next several years in seclusion. He ended his seclusion for a short lecturing period at the Nizamiyyah of Nishapur in 1106. Later he returned to Us where he remained until his death in December.

He is also viewed as the key member of the influential Asharite school of early Muslim philosophy and the most important refuter of Mutazilites. His 11th century book the *"Incoherence of the Philosophers"* marks a major turn in Islamic epistemology, as Ghazali effectively discovered philosophical skepticism that would not be commonly seen in the West until George Berkeley and David Hume in the 18th century. The encounter with skepticism led Ghazali to embrace a form of theological occasionalism, or the belief that all causal events and interactions are not the product of material conjunctions but rather the immediate and present will of God. The logical consequence of this belief in practice, and an outcome that has developed in part from it over the subsequent centuries, is a turn towards fundamentalism in many Islamic societies.

The *Incoherence* also marked a turning point in Islamic philosophy in its vehement rejections of Aristotle and Plato. The book took aim at the *falasifa*, a loosely defined group of Islamic philosophers from the 8th through the 11th centuries (most notable among them Avicenna) who drew intellectually upon the Ancient Greeks. Ghazali bitterly denounced Aristotle, Socrates and other Greek writers as non-believers and labelled those who employed their methods and ideas as corrupters of the Islamic faith.

In the next century, Averroes drafted a lengthy rebuttal of Ghazali's *Incoherence* entitled the *Incoherence of the Incoherence*; however, the epistemological course of Islamic thought had already been set. Ghazali's influence has been compared to the works of St. Thomas Aquinas in

Christian theology (he has been called the "Thomas Aquinas of Islam" by some), but the two differed greatly in methods and beliefs. Whereas Ghazali rejected non-Islamic philosophers such as Aristotle and saw it fit to discard their teachings on the basis of their "unbelief," Aquinas embraced them and incorporated ancient Greek and Latin thought into his own philosophical writings.

Ghazali wrote two of his works in Persian: Kimyayé Saadat (The Alchemy of Happiness) and Nasihatul Mulook (Counseling Kings). Abdul Qadir Jelani Sheikh.

Abdul Qadir Jelani was a noted Hanbali preacher, Sufi sheikh and the eponymous founder of the Qadiri Sufi order (*selsela*). He was born in Ramadan 470 A.H (About 1077 AD) in the Persian province of Jilan (Iran) south of the Caspian sea. His contribution and renown in the sciences of Sufism and Sharia was so immense that he became known as the spiritual pole of his time, *al-Gauth al Azam* (the "Supreme Helper" or the "Mightiest Succor"). His writings were similar to those of al-Ghazali in that they dealt with both the fundamentals of Islam and the mystical experience of Sufism.

Abdul Qadir Jilani was a Sufi master and Syed (descendant of the Prophet Muhammad) from both his father and mother. His father Abu Saleh Jangidost, was an illustrious and God-fearing man. Once while engrossed in meditation by the bank of a river he saw an apple floating down the river. He picked it up and ate it. It struck to him that he ate the apple without paying for it so he set out in search of the owner, on the bank of the river and at last reached the owner of the apple orchard "Abdullah Somai" whom he requested to tell him the price of the apple, Abdullah Somai replied that it was an expensive thing. Syed Abu Saleh replied that he had not much by way of worldly material but he, could serve him for compensation. Abdullah Somai then asked him to work for a year in the orchard. In course of time the duration was extended several times. In the end Abdullah Somai admitted that he had served him in excess of the price and desired to reward him. Abu Saleh hesitated in accepting it but when Abdullah Somai persisted, he relented. He said he had a daughter, blind of eyes, handicapped of hands and feet and wanted to give her in marriage to him.

In this way Abu Saleh was married to Abdullah Somai's daughter, Syeda Fatimah. To his astonishment found her wondrously beautiful and wholesome. He complained to his father-in-law that he found her exactly the opposite to what he had described her. Abdullah Somai insisted on the truthfulness of his statement. She was blind because she had not seen any *Ghair Mehram* (a man who could marry her). She was mute because she had not uttered a word repugnant to the Shariah (Islamic law). She was deaf because she had not heard anything inconsistent with the Shariah. She was handicapped of hand and feet because she had never moved in the direction of evil.

Abdul Qadir Jilani's father died soon after and the young orphan was reared up by his mother and his grandfather, Abdullah Somai.

At the age of 18 he went to Baghdad on 488 Ah (1095 AD), where he pursued the study of Hanbalite law under several teachers. His mother sewed 40 gold coins in his quilt so that he might spend then when needed. The dacoits struck the caravan on the way, and looted all the travelers of their belongings. They asked him what he had. He replied that he had 40 gold coins. The dacoits took his reply for a joke and took him to their chief, who asked him the same question and he again replied that he had 40 gold coins. He demanded him to show, upon whom he tore away, the quilt and produced the gold coins. He was surprised and asked him why he had given the hidden gold coins when he could have kept them hidden. Young Abdul Qadir Jilani replied that he was travelling to Baghdad to receive education and his mother had instructed him to speak the truth. This left a deep effect on the chief of the dacoits and he gave up looting.

Abdul Qadir received lessons on Islamic Jurisprudence from Abu Said Ali al-Mukharrimi, Hadith from Abu-Bakra-bin-Muzaffar, and commentary (tafseer) from the renowned commentator, Abu Muhammad Jafar.

In Sufism, his spiritual instructor was Shaikh Abul-Khair Hammad. From him, he received his basic training, and with his help he set out on the spiritual journey. Abu Shuja' was also a disciple of Shaikh Hammad, once he said: "Shaikh Abdul Qadir was in the company of Shaikh Hammad, so he came and sat in front of him, observing the best of good manners, until he stood up and took his leave. I heard Shaikh Hammad say, as soon as Shaikh Abdul Qadir had left: 'This non-Arab has a foot that will be raised, when the proper time comes, and placed upon the necks of the saints of that time. He will surely be commanded to say: This foot of mine is upon the neck of every saint of Allah. He will surely say it, and the necks of all the saints of his age will surely be bent at his disposal.'" Hazrat Junayd Baghdadi (d. 910 A.D.), who died about 167 years before the birth of Shaikh Abdul Qadir Jilani, predicted about him on one occasion, when he was performing meditation & during that he said: "His foot will be over all Saints' necks." After finishing meditation, his disciples asked him about his words, he replied: "One Sufi would be born in the future, who would be greater than all saints." Thus, Shaikh Hammad proved the words of Hazrat Junayd as right. The historians says that, later Shaikh Abdul Qadir Jilani also repeated the same words on many occasion by himself.

After completion of education, Hazrat Abdul Qadir Jilani abandoned the city of Baghdad, and spent twenty-five years as a wanderer in the desert regions of Iraq as a recluse. He was over fifty years old by the time he returned to Baghdad, in 521 A.H. (1127 A.D), and began to preach in public. His hearers were profoundly affected by the style and content of his lectures, and his reputation grew and spread through all sections of society. Not only Muslims, but also Jews and Christians, not only caliphs and viziers but also farmers, merchants and traders allegedly altered their lives in response to Abdul Qadir's perorations. He moved into the school belonging to his old teacher al-Mukharrimii, there he engaged himself in teaching. Soon he became popular with his pupils. In the morning he taught *hadith* and *tafseer*, and in the afternoon held discourse on mysticism and the virtues of the Quran. The number of students increased so much that the seminary could no more contain them. He, therefore, decided to extend the premises of the seminary. The students and the people willingly came forward with their wholehearted contributions. The campus buildings were ready in 528 Hijri and thereafter it came to be known as *Madarsai-e-Qadriya*.

Hazrat Abdul Qadir Jilani was a Non-Arab (*ajami*), so he wasn't fluent in Arabic and was having some difficulties because of it. Once The Prophet Muhammad came to him in a dream, before the time of the midday prayer (Zuhr), and he said him: "O my dear son, why do you not speak out?" He replied: "O dear father, I am a Non-Arab man. How can I speak fluently in the classical Arabic language of Baghdad?" Holy Prophet said: "Just open your mouth!" He opened his mouth, and The Holy Prophet put his slavia seven times in his mouth. A few moments later, Hazrat Ali ibn Abi Talib also came & did the same to him six times. And from that time, Hazrat Abdul Qadir Jilani spoke classical Arabic language with fluency, his memory increased and he felt some great positive spiritual changes in him.

Once some one asked Shaikh Abdul Qadir Jilani about Mansur Al-Hallaj, he replied: "His claim extended too far, so the scissors of the Sacred Law (Shari'a) were empowered to clip it."

He busied himself for forty years in the service of the Islam from 521 to 561 Hijri During this period hundreds embraced Islam because of him and organized several teams to go abroad for the purpose. He arrived in Indian sub-continent in 1128 A.D., and stayed at Multan (Pakistan). He died in 561 A.H. (1166 A.D.) at the age of 91 years, and was buried in Baghdad.

Some of Abdul Qadirs major literary works include; *Al-Ghunya li-talibi tariq al-haqq* (Sufficient Provision for Seekers of the Path of Truth), *Al-Fath ar-Rabbani* (The Sublime Revelation), *Malfuzat* (Utterances), *Futuh al-Ghaib* (Revelations of the Unseen), and *Jala' al-Khatir* (The Removal of Care) or *Jala' al-Khawatir* (The Removal of Cares). As mentioned earlier, the Sheikh was a *seyyid*, which is considered a title of high regard in both Sunni and Shia Islam. Abdul Qadir's full name is Abu Muhammad Abd al-Qadir ibn Abi Salih Musa ibn Abdullah al-Jili ibn Yahya az-Zahid ibn

Muhammad ibn Daud ibn Musa ibn Abdullah ibn Musa ibn Abdullah al-Mahd ibn al-Hasan al Muthanna ibn al-Hasan ibn Ali ibn Abi Talib.

Ibn Arabi: Abu 'Abd Allah Muhammad. 'Ali b. Muhammad b. al-'Arabi al-Satimi al-la'i commonly known as Ibn Arabi, was an Islamic scholar. He was born 1165 in Murcia, Spain and died 1240 in Damascus.

Also known in the Islamic world by the titles of *Muhyi id-Din* ("Revivifier of religion") and *al-Shaykh al-Akbar* ("Great Master"), he is sometimes described as a mystical philosopher. Even in his lifetime he was acknowledged to be one of the most important spiritual teachers within Sufism, the mystical tradition of Islam. His name is usually confused with another scholar of Andalusia known as Ibn al-Arabi that was a master of Al-Maliki Jurisprudence.

A vastly prolific writer, Ibn Arabi is generally known as the prime exponent of the idea that would later be termed *wahdat al-wujud* ("unity of being"). His emphasis, as with any mystic, lay rather on the true potential of the human being and the path to realising that potential, which reaches its completion in the Perfect or Complete Man (al-insan al-kamil). Ibn Arabi wrote at least 300 works, ranging from minor treatises to the huge 37-volume Meccan Illuminations (al-Futuhat al-Makkiyya) and the quintessence of his teachings, The Bezels of Wisdom (Fusus al-hikam). Approximately 110 works are known to have survived in verifiable manuscripts, some 18 in Ibn Arabi's own hand. He exerted an unparalleled influence, not only upon his immediate circle of friends and disciples, many of whom were considered spiritual masters in their own right, but also on succeeding generations, affecting the whole course of subsequent spiritual thought and practice in the Arabic, Turkish and Persian-speaking worlds. In recent years his writings have also become increasingly the subject of interest and study in the West, leading to the establishment of an international academic Society in his name.

Ibn Arabi's life can be divided into three discrete phases: born in Medinat Mursiya the present day Murcia in south-eastern Spain in 560AH/ 1165AD, he spent the first thirty-five years of his life in the Maghreb, the western lands of Islam which stretched from al-Andalus to Tunis; then he embarked on pilgrimage and spent the next three years in or around Mecca, where a series of dramatic experiences initiated the writing of several works including his magnum opus, the Meccan Illuminations ; the final phase of his life was spent in the Levant and Anatolia, where he raised a family, and in addition to an unceasing literary output and instruction given to numerous disciples, he became adviser to kings and rulers. He settled in Damascus, where he lived for 17 years, dying in 638AH/1240AD, and his tomb is still an important place of pilgrimage. Many Wahabis reject the notion that Ibn Arabi was a Muslim, despite the fact that he openly accepted shahadat. Reasons for Ibn Arabi being branded a heretic were some of his statements in his books such as Fusoos Al-Hikam and Al-Ahkaam. One example is where Ibn Arabi said, "Al-`Abdu Rabbun Warrabbu `Abdun" meaning The slave (human) is the Lord/God and the Lord/God is the slave (human)." Sufis claim that such statements were always considered to be the most elevated exposition of mystical thought in Islam, and therefore unsuitable for the untrained mind.

A profound visionary capacity, coupled with a remarkable intellectual insight into human experience and a thorough comprehension of all the traditional sciences, marks out Ibn Arabi from comparable figures in Islam. It has been tempting for scholars to characterise him as a mystical philosopher, a formulation which is rather at odds with his own teachings on the limitations of philosophical thinking. He was as much at home with Quran and Hadith scholarship as with medieval philology and letter symbolism, philosophy, alchemy and cosmology. He could write with equal facility in prose or poetry, and utilised the polysemous ambiguity of the Arabic language to great effect. The characteristic resonances of rhymed prose (saj), which are to be found in the Quran, abound in his works.

In recent years Western scholars such as William Chittick and Michel Chodkiewicz have begun to explore the radical way in which Ibn Arabi's thought is underpinned and inspired by the infallible revelation of the Quran. He adopts the rich vocabulary of spiritual phenomenology which previous mystics had built up, and gives it both a scriptural basis and an ontological root.

This all-inclusiveness and flexibility equally make him one of the most demanding of authors, and one whose subtlety lesser minds have often struggled to comprehend, some falling into rejection and outright opposition. He combines a detailed architecture of spiritual experience, theory and practice, with descriptions of the attainments of other masters he met as well as his own personal visions, insights and dreams. It is his propensity to recount stories from his own direct experience, primarily in order to make a teaching point, that allows readers to gain such a detailed insight into the inner world of one of the greatest mystics the world has known, and also allows us to reconstruct his life and times with some accuracy.

Mawlana Rumi: Mawlana Jalal ad-Din Muhammad Rumi known as Mawlana Jalal ad-Din Muhammad Balkhi but known to the world simply as Rumi, was a 13th century Persian poet, jurist, theologian and teacher of Sufism.

Rumi was born in Balkh (then a city of Khorasan, now part of Afghanistan) and died in Konya (in present-day Turkey). His birthplace and native tongue indicate a Persian heritage. He also wrote his poetry in Persian and his works are widely read in Iran and Afghanistan where the language is spoken. He lived most of his life and produced his works under the Seljuk Empire.

Rumi's importance transcends national and ethnic borders. He has had a significant influence on both Persian and Turkish literature throughout the centuries. His poems have been translated into many of the world's languages and have appeared in various formats. He was also the founder of the Mevlevi order, better known as the "Whirling Dervishes", who believe in performing their worship in the form of dance and music ceremony called the sema.

Rumi's life is fully described in Shams ud-Din Ahmad Aflaki's *"Manakib ul-Arifin"* (written between 1318 and 1353). He is described as a descendant of the caliph Abu Bakr, and of the Khwrizm-Shh Sultan Ala ud-Din bin Takash (1199–1220), whose only daughter, Malika-e Jahan, had allegedly been married to Rumi's grandfather.

When the Mongols invaded Central Asia sometime between 1215 and 1220, his father (Bahauddin Walad, a theologian, jurist and a mystic of uncertain lineage) set out westwards with his whole family and a group of disciples. On the road to Anatolia, Rumi encountered one of the most famous mystic Persian poets, Attar, in the city of Nishapur, located in what is now the Iranian province of Khorsn. Attar immediately recognized Rumi's spiritual eminence. He saw the father walking ahead of the son and said, "Here comes a sea followed by an ocean." He gave the boy his Asrarnama, a book about the entanglement of the soul in the material world. This meeting had a deep impact on the eighteen-year-old Rumi's thoughts, which later on became the inspiration for Rumi's works.

From Nishapur, Walad and his entourage set out for Baghdad, meeting many of the scholars and Sufis of the city. From there they went to the Hejaz and performed the pilgrimage at Mecca. It was after this journey that most likely as a result of the invitation of Allah ud-Din Key-Qobad, ruler of Anatolia, Bahauddin came to Asia Minor and finally settled in Konya in Anatolia within the western most territories of Seljuk Empire.

Bahauddin became the head of a madrassa (religious school) and when he died Rumi succeeded him at the age of twenty-five. One of Bahauddin's students, Syed Burhanuddin Mahaqqiq, continued to train Rumi in the religious and mystical doctrines of Rumi's father. For nine years, Rumi practiced Sufism as a disciple of Burhanuddin until the latter died in 1240-1. During this period Rumi also travelled to Damascus and is said to have spent four years there.

It was his meeting with the dervish Shams Tabriz in the late fall of 1244 that changed his life completely. Shams had traveled throughout the Middle East searching and praying for someone who could "endure my company". A voice came, "What will you give in return?" "My head!" "The one you seek is Jelaluddin of Konya." On the night of December 5, 1248, as Rumi and Shams were talking, Shams was called to the back door. He went out, never to be seen again. It is believed that he was murdered with the connivance of Rumi's son, Allaedin; if so, Shams indeed gave his head for the privilege of mystical friendship.

Rumi's love and his bereavement for the death of Shams found their expression in an outpouring of music, dance and lyric poems, *Divani Shamsi Tabrizi*. He himself went out searching for Shams and journeyed again to Damascus. There, he realized:

Why should I seek? I am the same as

He. His essence speaks through me.

I have been looking for myself!

For more than ten years after meeting Shams, Mevlana had been spontaneously composing ghazals, and these had been collected in the *Divan-i Kabir*. Rumi found another companion in Saladin Zarkub, the goldsmith. After Saladin's death, Rumi's scribe and favorite student Husam Chelebi assumed the role. One day, the two of them were wandering through the Meram vineyards outside of Konya when Husam described an idea he had to Rumi: "If you were to write a book like the Ilahiname of Sanai or the Mantik'ut-Tayr'i of Attar it would become the companion of many troubadours. They would fill their hearts from your work and compose music to accompany it."

Rumi smiled and took out a piece of paper on which were written the opening eighteen lines of his Mathnawi, beginning with:

Listen to the reed and the tale it tells,

How it sings of separation...

Husam implored Rumi to write more. Rumi spent the next twelve years of his life in Anatolia dictating the six volumes of this masterwork, the *Mathnawi* to Husam. In December 1273, Rumi fell ill; he predicted his own death and composed the well-known ghazal, which begins with the verse:

How doest thou know what sort of king I have within me as companion?

Do not cast thy glance upon my golden face, for I have iron legs.

He died on December 17, 1273 in Konya; Rumi was laid to rest beside his father, and a splendid shrine, the *Ye°il Türbe* "Green Tomb", was erected over his tomb. His epitaph reads:

"When we are dead, seek not our tomb in the earth, but find it in the hearts of men."

The general theme of his thoughts, like that of the other mystic and

Sufi poets of the Persian literature, is essentially about the concept of Tawheed (unity) and union with his beloved (the primal root) from which/whom he has been cut and fallen aloof, and his longing and desire for reunity.

The "Mathnawi" weaves fables, scenes from everyday life, Qur'anic revelations and exegesis, and metaphysics, into a vast and intricate tapestry. Rumi is considered an example of *"insani kamil"* — the perfected or completed human being. In the East, it is said of him, that he was, "not a prophet — but surely, he has brought a scripture". Rumi believed passionately in the use of music, poetry and dancing as a path for reaching God. For Rumi, music helped devotees to focus their whole being on the divine, and to do this so intensely that the soul was both destroyed and resurrected.

It was from these ideas that the practice of Whirling Dervishes developed into a ritual form. He founded the order of the Mevlevi, the "whirling" dervishes, and created the "Sema", their "turning", sacred dance. In the Mevlevi tradition, Sema represents a mystical journey of spiritual ascent through mind and love to "Perfect." In this journey the seeker symbolically turns towards the truth, grows through love, abandons the ego, finds the truth, and arrives at the "Perfect"; then returns from this spiritual journey with greater maturity, so as to love and to be of service to the whole of creation without discrimination against beliefs, races, classes and nations.

According to Shahram Shiva, one reason for Rumi's popularity is that "Rumi is able to verbalize the highly personal and often confusing world of personal/spiritual growth and mysticism in a very forward and direct fashion. He does not offend anyone, and he includes everyone. The world of Rumi is neither exclusively the world of a Sufi, nor the world of a Hindu, nor a Jew, nor a Christian; it is the highest state of a human being— a fully evolved human. A complete human is not bound by cultural limitations; he touches every one of us. Today Rumi's poems can be heard in churches, synagogues, Zen monasteries, as well as in the downtown New York art/performance/music scene." In Divan-i Shams, Rumi says:

What is to be done, O Muslims? for I do not recognize myself.

I am neither Christian, nor Jew, nor Gabr, nor Muslim.

I am not of the East, nor of the West, nor of the land, nor of the sea;

I am not of Nature's mint, nor of the circling heaven.

I am not of earth, nor of water, nor of air, nor of fire;

I am not of the empyrean, nor of the dust, nor of existence, nor of entity.

I am not of India, nor of China, nor of Bulgaria, nor of Saqsin

I am not of the kingdom of 'Iraqian, nor of the country of Khorasan

I am not of the this world, nor of the next, nor of Paradise, nor of Hell

I am not of Adam, nor of Eve, nor of Eden and Rizwan.

My place is the Placeless, my trace is the Traceless.

According to Professor Majid Naini, one of the foremost international Rumi scholars who travels the world trying to spread Rumi's universal message of love, Rumi's life and transformation provide true testimony and proof that people of all religions and backgrounds can live together in peace and harmony throughout the world. At Rumi's grand funeral procession Jews, Christians, Muslims, Hindus, Buddhists, and Sufis cried and mourned in a manner that one would have thought that Rumi belonged to each one of them. Rumi's visions, words, and life teach us how to reach inner peace and happiness so we can finally stop the continual stream of hostility and hatred and achieve true global peace and harmony. In other beautiful verses in Mathnavi, Rumi describes in detail the universal message of love. For example, he states:

Love's nationality is separate from all other religions, The lover's religion and nationality is the Beloved (God).

The lover's cause is separate from all other causes Love is the astrolabe of God's mysteries.

Rumi's poetry is often divided into various categories: the quatrains (rubaiyat) and odes (ghazals) of the Divan, the six books of the Mathnawi, the discourses, the letters, and the almost unknown Six Sermons. Rumi's major work is Masnavi-ye Manavi (Spiritual Couplets), a six-volume poem regarded by many Sufis as second in importance only to the Quran. In fact, the Masnawi is often called the "Quran-e Parsi" (The Persian Quran). It is considered by many to be one of the greatest works of mystical poetry. Rumi's other major work is the Diwan-e Shams-e Tabriz-i (The Works of Shams of Tabriz-named in honor of Rumi's great friend and inspiration, the darvish Shams), comprising some 40,000 verses. Several reasons have been offered for Rumi's decision to name his masterpiece after Shams. Some argue that since Rumi would not have been a poet without Shams, it is apt that the collection be named after him. Others have suggested that at the end, Rumi became Shams, hence the collection is truly of Shams speaking through Rumi. Both works are among the most significant in all of Persian literature. Shams is believed to have been murdered by disciples of Rumi who were jealous of his relationship with Shams (also spelt Shems).

Fihi Ma Fih (*In It What's in It*) is composed of Rumi's speeches on different subjects. Rumi himself did not prepare or write these discourses. They were recorded by his son *Sultan Valad* or some other disciple of Rumi and put together as a book. The title may mean, "What's in the Mathnawi is in this too." Some of the discourses are addressed to *Muin al-Din Parvane*.

Some portions of it are commentary on Masnavi.

Majalis-i Sab'a (seven sessions) contains seven sermons (as the name implies) given in seven different assemblies. As *Aflaki* relates, after *Sham-i Tabrizi*, Rumi gave sermons at the request of notables, especially *Salah al-Din Zarqubi*.

The Mevlevi Sufi order was founded in 1273 by Rumi's followers after his death. His first successor in the rectorship of the order was Husam Chelebi himself, after whose death in 1284 Rumi's younger and only surviving son, Sultan Walad, favorably known as author of the mystical Mathnawi Rabbnma, or the Book of the Guitar (died 1312), was installed as grand master of the order. The leadership of the order has been kept in Jalaluddin's family in Iconium uninterruptedly for the last six hundred years. The Mevlevi, or "The Whirling Dervishes", believe in performing their dhikr in the form of sema. During the time of Rumi (as attested in the "Manakib ul Arifin" of Eflaki Dede), his followers gathered for musical and "turning" practices. Mevlana himself was a notable musician, who played the rebab although his favorite instrument was the ney. The music accompanying the traditional ritual consists of settings of poems from the "Mathnawi" and "Diwan-i-Kebir" or of his son Sultan Veled's poems. The Mevlevi were a well-established Sufi Order in the Ottoman Empire, and many of the members of the order served in various official positions of the Caliphate. The centre for the Mevlevi order was in Konya. There is also a Mevlevi monastery or dergah in Istanbul, near the Galata Tower, where the sema ceremony is performed and accessible to the public. Rumi's order issues invitation to people of all backgrounds:

"Come, come, whoever you are.

Wanderer, idolater, worshipper of fire,

"Come even though you have broken your vows a thousand times,

Come, and come yet again.

Ours is not a caravan of despair.

During Ottoman times, the Mevlevi order produced a number of famous poets and musicians such as Sheikh Ghalib, Ismail Ankaravi (both buried at the Galata Mevlevi-Hane) and Abdullah Sari. Music, especially the ney, play an important part in the Mevlevi order and thus much of the traditional 'oriental' music that Westerners associate with Turkey originates with the Mevlevi order. Indeed, if one buys a CD of Turkish Sufi music, chances are it will be Mevlevi religious music.

The Mevlevi Order was outlawed in Turkey at the dawn of the secular revolution by Kemal Atatrk in 1923. In the 1950s, the Turkish government, realizing that The Whirling Dervishes had value as a tourist attraction, began allowing the Whirling Dervishes to perform annually in Konya on the Urs of Mevlana, December 17, the anniversary of Rumi's death. In 1974, they were allowed to come to the West. The Mevlana annual festival is held every year in Konya in December. It lasts two weeks and its culminating point is the 17th December called *Sheb-i Arus* meaning 'Nuptial Night', the night of the union of Mevlana with God.

Rumi's importance transcends national and ethnic borders. Speakers of the Persian language in Iran, Afghanistan and Tajikistan see him as one of their most significant classical poets and an influence on many poets through history. He has also had a great influence on Turkish literature throughout the centuries. His poetry forms the basis of much classical Iranian and Afghan music. Contemporary classical interpretations of his poetry are made by Muhammad Reza Shajarian (Iran), Shahram Nazeri (Iran), Davood Azad (Iran) and Ustad Mohammad Hashem Cheshti (Afghanistan). To many modern Westerners, his teachings are one of the best introductions to the philosophy and practice of Sufism. Pakistan's National Poet, Muhammad Iqbal (November 9, 1877-April 21, 1938) was also inspired by Rumi's works and considered him to be his spiritual leader and addressed him as *Pir Rumi* in his poems (*pir* literally means *old*, but in sufi/mystic context, it means *guide*, *teacher*, *master*, *guru*.)

Rumi's work has been translated into many of the world's languages including Russian, German, French, Italian and Spanish, and is appearing in a growing number of formats including concerts, workshops, readings, dance performances and other artistic creations. Coleman Barks's translations of Rumi have sold more than a 250,000 copies in the United States. Recordings of Rumi poems have made it to Billboard's Top 20 list. A collection of Deepak Chopra's translations of Rumi's love poems has been sung by Hollywood personalities such as Madonna, Goldie Hawn and Demi Moore; also Shahram Shiva's CD, *Rumi: Lovedrunk* has been very popular on the Internet's music communities such as MySpace.com. The 13th-century poet of the Seljuk Empire is one of the most widely read poets in the United States.

Data Ganj Bakhsh: Syed Abul Hassan Bin Usman Bin Ali Al-Hajweri (sometimes spelled Hujwiri), also known as Shaikh Ali Hajweri, Data Ganj Bakhsh, or Data Sahib, was a scholar of Islam and a Sufi saint, and writer of the 11th century. His contribution in spreading of Islam in South Asia is huge.

He was born in Ghazna (in present day Afghanistan) and died in Lahore (in present day Punjab, Pakistan) in 1077 CE. His most famous work is Kashf al Mahjub ("Unveiling the Veiled"), which was the first Persian language treatise on Sufism. The work debates Sufi doctrines of the past. Hujwiri said that individuals should not claim to have attained "marifat" or gnosis because it meant that one was prideful. True understanding of God should be a silent understanding.

Hujwiri is also viewed as an important intercessor for many Sufis. His mausoleum, popularly known as Data Durbar, is located in Lahore, Punjab, Pakistan.

Amir Khusro: Abul Hasan Yaminuddin Khusro (1253-1325 CE), better known as Amir Khusro Dehlavi is one of the iconic figures in the cultural history of the Indian subcontinent. A Sufi mystic and a spiritual disciple of Nizamuddin Auliya of Delhi, Amir Khusro (or Khusrau or Khusraw) was not only one of India's greatest poets, he is also credited with being the founder of both Hindustani classical music and Qawwali (the devotional music of the Sufis). He was born of a Turkish father, Saif Ad-din, and an Indian mother, in India.

Major life events in chronological order

1. 1253 Khusro was born in Patiali near Etah in what is today the state of Uttar Pradesh in northern India. His father Amir Saifuddin came from Balkh in modern day Afghanistan and his mother hailed from Delhi.
2. 1260 After the death of his father, Khusro went to Delhi with his mother.
3. 1271 Khusro compiled his first divan of poetry, "Tuhfatus-Sighr".
4. 1272 Khusro got his first job as court poet with King Balban's nephew Malik Chhajju.
5. 1276 Khusro started working as a poet with Bughra Khan (Balban's son).
6. 1279 While writing his second divan, Wastul-Hayat, Khusrau visited Bengal.
7. 1281 Employed by Sultan Mohammad (Balban's second son) and went to Multan with him.
8. 1285 Khusro participated as a soldier in the war against the invading Mongols. He was taken prisoner, but escaped.
9. 1287 Khusro went to Awadh with Ameer Ali Hatim (another patron).
10. 1288 His first mathnavi, "Qiranus-Sa'dain" was completed.
11. 1290 When Jalal ud din Firuz Khilji came to power, Khusro's second mathnavi, "Miftahul Futooh" was ready.
12. 1294 His third divan "Ghurratul-Kamal" was complete.
13. 1295 Ala ud din Khilji (sometimes spelled "Khalji") came to power and invaded Devagiri and Gujarat.
14. 1298 Khusro completed his "Khamsa-e-Nizami".
15. 1301 Khilji attacked Ranthambhor, Chittor, Malwa and other places,

and Khusro remained with the king in order to write chronicles.

16. 1310 Khusro became close to Nizamuddin Aulia, and completed Khazain-ul-Futuh.
17. 1315 Alauddin Khilji died. Khusro completed the mathnavi "Duval Rani-Khizr Khan" (a romantic poem).
18. 1316 Qutb ud din Mubarak Shah became the king, and the fourth historical mathnavi "Noh-Sepehr" was completed.
19. 1321 Mubarak Khilji (sometimes spelled "Mubarak Khalji") was murdered and Ghiyath al-Din Tughluq Ghiassuddin Tughluq (Real Name in Arabic, Farsi and Urdu Languages)came to power. Khusro started to write the Tughluqnama.
20. 1325 Sultan Muhammad bin Tughluq came to power. Nizamuddin Aulia died, and six months later so did Khusro. Khusro's tomb is next to that of his master in the Nizamuddin Dargah of Delhi.

Khusro was a prolific classical poet associated with the royal courts of more than seven rulers of the Delhi Sultanate. He is popular in much of North India and Pakistan, because of many playful riddles, songs and legends attributed to him. Through his enormous literary output and the legendary folk personality, Khusro represents one of the first (recorded) Indian personages with a true multi-cultural or pluralistic identity. He wrote in both Persian and Hindustani. His poetry is still sung today at Sufi shrines throughout Pakistan and India. Amir Khusro was the author of a Khamsa which emulated that of the earlier Persian-language poet Nizami Ganjavi. His work was considered to be one of the great classics of Persian poetry during the Timurid period in Transoxiana. Amir Khusro is credited with fashioning the *tabla* as a split version of the traditional Indian drum, the *pakhawaj*.

Popular lore also credits him with inventing the *sitar*, the Indian grand lute, but it is more likely that the sitar was invented by a different Amir Khusro several centuries later.

QADIRIYYAH

Qadiriyyah (also transliterated Qadiri), is one of the oldest Sufi tariqas, derives its name from bdul Qadir Jilani (also transliterated as Gilani) (1077-1166), a native of the Iranian province of Gilan. In 1134 he was made principal of a Hanbalite school in Baghdad.

The order is one of the most widespread of the Sufi orders in the Islamic world and can be found in India, Pakistan, Turkey and the Balkans and much of East and West Africa. Some famous Qadiri Sheikhs include Sheikh Abd al-Qadir al-Jaza'iri who led the Algerian resistance to French colonialism and Sheikh Usman dan Fodio whose followers Islamized much of West Africa and established the Caliphate of Sokoto in Northern Nigeria. The

Chechen people are also mostly followers of the Qadiri Sufi order as was the famous traveller and writer Isabelle Eberhardt.

The Qadiriyyah has not developed any distinctive doctrines or teachings outside of mainstream Islam. They believe in the fundamental principles of Islam, but interpreted through mystical experience. As a result, even opponents to Sufism such as the Hanbali Sheikhs Ibn Taymiya, his student ibn al-Qayyim and ibn Rajb al-Hanbali were all followers of the Qadiri Sufi order and spoke highly of Sheikh Abdul Qadir Jilani.

Spiritual Chain

This is the spiritual chain (*silsila*) of the Qadiriyyah:

- The Prophet Muhammad
- The Caliph Ali ibn Abi Talib
- Imam Husain
- Imam Ali Zayn al-Abidin
- Imam Muhammad Baqir
- Imam Ja'far as-Sadiq
- Imam Musa al-Kazim
- Imam Ali Musa Rida
- Ma'ruf Karkhi
- Sari Saqati
- Junayd al-Baghdadi
- Sheikh Abu Bakr Shibli
- Sheikh Abdul Aziz al-Tamimi
- Abu al-Fadl Abu al-Wahid al-Tamimi
- Abu al-Farah Tartusi
- Abu al-Hasan Farshi
- Abu Said al-Mubarak Mukharrami
- Sheikh Abdul Qadir Jilani

SUHRAWARDIYYA

Suhrawardiyya is the name of a Sufi order founded by Diya al-din Abu 'n-Najib as-Suhrawardi (1097–1168).

Many Sufis from all over the islamic world joined the order under the founder's nephew Shihab ad-din Abu Hafs 'Umar (1145 – 1234). Later the Order spread into India.

A well known member of the order was Shihabuddin Yahya as-Suhrawardi (1153-1191).

BENGALI SUFIS AND HINDU THOUGHT

From the beginning of the Indo-Turkish encounter with Bengal, one section of Muslims sought to integrate into their religious lives elements of the esoteric practices of local yogis, together with the cosmologies that underpinned those practices. Contemporary Muslims perceived northern Bengal generally, and especially Kamrup, lying between the Brahmaputra River and the hills of Bhutan, as a fabulous and mysterious place inhabited by expert practitioners of the occult, of yoga, and of magic. During his visit to Sylhet, Ibn Battuta noted that "the inhabitants of these mountains are noted for their devotion to and practice of magic and witchcraft." Around 1595 the great Mughal administrative manual *Ain-i Akbari* described the inhabitants of Kamrup as "addicted to the practice of magic [*jadugari*]." Some twenty-five years later a Mughal officer serving in northern Bengal described the Khuntaghat region, in western Kamrup, as "notorious for magic and sorcery." And in 1662–63 another Mughal chronicler, referring to the entire Assam region, of which Kamrup is the western part, remarked that "the people of India have come to look upon the Assamese as sorcerers, and use the word 'Assam' in such formulas as dispel witchcraft."

Since Sufis were especially concerned with apprehending transcendent reality unmediated by priests or other worldly institutions, it is not surprising that they, among Muslims, were most attracted to the yogi traditions of Kamrup. Within the very first decade of the Turkish conquest, there began to circulate in the delta Persian and Arabic translations of a Sanskrit manual on tantric yoga entitled *Amritakunda* ("The Pool of Nectar"). According to the translated versions, the Sanskrit text had been composed by a Brahman yogi of Kamrup who had converted to Islam and presented the work to the chief, or judge, of Lakhnauti, Rukn al-Din Samarqandi (d. 1218). The latter, in turn, is said to have made the first translations of the work into Arabic and Persian. While this last point is uncertain, there is no doubt that for the following five hundred years the *Amritakunda*, through its repeated translations into Arabic and Persian, circulated widely among Sufis of Bengal, and even throughout India. The North Indian Sufi Shaikh 'Abd al-Quddus Gangohi (d. 1537) is known to have absorbed the yogic ideas of the *Amritakunda* and to have taught them to his own disciples. In the mid seventeenth century, the Kashmiri author Muhsin Fani recorded that he had seen a Persian translation of the *Amritakunda*, and in the same century the Anatolian Sufi scholar Mohammad al-Misri (d. 1694) cited the *Amritakunda* as an important book for the study of yogic practices, noting that in India such practices had become partly integrated with Sufism. In both its Persian and Arabic translations, the *Amritakunda* survives as a manual of tantric yoga, with the first of its ten chapters affirming the characteristically tantric correspondence between parts of the human body and parts of the macrocosm, "where all that is large in the world discovers itself in the small." In the mid sixteenth century, there appeared in Gujarat a Persian recension of the *Amritakunda* under the title, attributed to the great Shattari Shaikh Mohammad Ghauth of Gwalior (d. 1563). A prologue to this version, written by a disciple of the Shaikh, records how these yogic ideas were thought to have entered the Bengali Sufi tradition:

This wonderful and strange book is named in the Indian language [i.e., Sanskrit]. This means "Water of Life," and the reason for the appearance of this book among the Muslims is as follows. When Sultan 'Ala al-Din [i.e., 'Ali Mardan] conquered Bengal and Islam became manifest there, news of these events reached the ears of a certain gentleman of the esteemed learned class in Kamrup. His name was Kama, and he was a master of the science of yoga.

In order to debate with the Muslim [scholars] he arrived in the city of Lakhnauti, and on a Friday he entered the Congregational Mosque. A number of Muslims showed him to a group of, and they in turn pointed him to the assembly of Qazi Rukn al-Din Samarqandi. So he went to this group and asked: "Whom do you worship?" They replied, "We worship the Faultless God." To his question "Who is your leader?" they replied, "Mohammad, the Messenger of Allah." He said, "What has your leader said about the Spirit" They replied, "God the All-nourishing has commanded (that there be) the Spirit." He said, "In truth, I too have found this same thing in books that are subtle and committed to memory."

Then that man converted to Islam and busied himself in acquiring religious knowledge, and he soon thereafter became a scholar (*mufti*). After that he wrote and presented this book to Qazi Rukn al-Din Tamami [Samarqandi]. The latter translated it from the Indian language into Arabic in a book of thirty chapters, and somebody else translated it into Persian in a book of ten chapters....And when Hazrat Ghauth al-Din himself went to Kamrup he necessarily spent several years in studying this science....The name of this book is *Bahar al-hayat*.

The exchange between the yogi and the *ghazi* cited here appears to have been modelled on a passage in the Qur'an (17:85), in which God tells the Prophet Mohammad: "They [the Jews] will ask thee concerning the Spirit. Say: the Spirit is by command of my Lord." By putting into the mouth of a yogi words that in the Qur'an were those of the Jews of Mohammad's day, the author of this recension apparently intended to make the yogi's exchange comprehensible to a Muslim audience.

A second prologue to the *Bahar al-hayat* established a framework within which a text on yoga could be accommodated within the rich body of classical Sufi lore. In it, the translator tells of once being in a country whose king summoned him and ordered that he undertake a great journey to a distant but fabulous realm. The king reminded the traveller that they were joined together by a covenant and that they would meet again at the end of the traveller's voyage. Then the translator/traveller describes the hardships he endured while on his journey: the two seas (the soul and nature), the seven mountains, the four passes, the three stations filled with dangers, and the path narrower than the eye of an ant. Ultimately, he reached the promised land, where he found a Shaikh who mirrored or echoed each of his own moves and words. Realizing that the man was but his own reflection, the traveller remembered his covenant with his master, to whom he was now led. The story's climax is reached in the traveller's epiphanic self-discovery: "I found the king and minister in myself." The dominant motifs of this second prologue—the traveller, the arduous path with its temptations and dangers, and the ultimate realization that the goal is identified with the seeker—all show the influence of Sufi notions current in the thirteenth-century Perso-Islamic world. The placement of the yogic text immediately after this prologue suggests that the esoteric practices described therein constitute, in effect, the means to achieving the mystical goals stated in the second prologue.

Although some scholars have regarded the *Bahar* as a work of religious syncretism, this judgment is difficult to sustain if by syncretism one means the production of a new synthesis out of two or more antithetical elements. Rather, the work consists of two independent and self-contained worldviews placed alongside one another—a technical manual of yoga preceded by a Sufi allegory—with later editors or translators going to some lengths to stress their points of coincidence. Although Islamic terms and superhuman agencies are generously sprinkled through the main text, allusions to Islamic lore serve ultimately to buttress or illustrate thoroughly Indian concepts. Here, at least, yoga and Sufi ideas resisted true fusion.

Nonetheless the book's popularity illustrates the Sufis' considerable fascination with the esoteric practices of Bengal's indigenous culture. The renowned Shattari saint Shaikh Mohammad Ghauth even travelled from Gwalior in Upper India to Kamrup in order to study the esoteric knowledge that Muslims had identified with that region. In doing so he was following a tradition of Sufis of the Shattari order, whose founder, Shah 'Abd Allah Shattari (d. 1485), included Bengal on his journey from Central Asia through India. Although one cannot establish a continuous intellectual tradition between Bengali Muslims of the thirteenth century and the Shattari Sufis of the fifteenth and sixteenth centuries, the association of the *Bahar al-hayat* both with Rukn al-Din Samarqandi in the former century and with Shaikh Mohammad Ghauth in the latter century suggests the likelihood of its continued use in Bengal during the intervening period.

SUFIS OF THE CAPITAL

The principal carriers of the Islamic literary and intellectual tradition in the Bengal sultanate were groups of distinguished and influential Sufis who resided in the successive capital cities of Lakhnauti (from 1204), Pandua (from ca. 1342), and Gaur (from ca. 1432). Most of these men belonged to organized Sufi brotherhoods—especially the Suhrawardi, the Firdausi, and the Chishti orders—and what we know of them can be ascertained mainly from their extant letters and biographical accounts. The urban Sufis about whom we have the most information are clustered in the early sultanate period, from the founding of the independent Ilyas Shahi dynasty at Pandua in 1342 to the end of the Raja Ganesh revolution in 1415. The political roles played by Sufis in Bengal's capital were shaped by ideas of Sufi authority that had already evolved in the contemporary Persian-speaking world. We have already referred to the central place that Sufi traditions assigned to powerful saints, a sentiment captured in 'Ali Hujwiri's statement that God had "made the Saints the governors of the universe." Being in theory closer to God than warring princes could ever hope to be, Muslim saints staked a moral claim as God's representatives on earth. In this view, princely rulers possessed no natural right to earthly power, but had only been entrusted with a temporary lease on such power through the grace of some Muslim saint. This perspective perhaps explains why in Indo-Muslim history we so often find Sufis predicting who would attain political office, and for how long they would hold it. For behind the explicit act of "prediction" lay the implicit act of appointment—that is, of a Sufi's entrusting his *wilayat*, or earthly domain, to a prince. For example, the fourteenth-century historian Shams-i Siraj 'Afif recorded that before his rise to royal stature, the future Sultan Ghiyath al-Din Tughluq, founder of the Tughluq dynasty of Delhi (1321–1398), had been one of many local notables attracted to the spiritual power of the grandson of the famous Chishti Sufi Shaikh Farid al-Din Ganj-i Shakar (d. 1265). The governor made frequent visits to the holy man's lodge in the Punjab, and on one occasion brought along his son and nephew, the future sultans Mohammad bin Tughluq and Firuz Tughluq. All three were given turbans by the saint and told that each was destined to rule India. The length of each turban, moreover, exactly corresponded to the number of years each would reign. In this anecdote one may discern the seeds of the complex pattern of mutual patronage between Shaikhs of the Chishti order and one of the mightiest empires in India's history.

Similar traditions circulated in Bengal concerning the foundation of independent Muslim rule there. In 1243–44 the historian Minhaj al-Siraj visited Lakhnauti, where he recorded the following anecdote. Before embarking for India, the future sultan of Bengal Ghiyath al-Din 'Iwaz (1213–27) was once travelling with his laden donkey along a dusty road in

Afghanistan. There he came upon two dervishes clothed in ragged cloaks. When the two asked the future ruler whether he had any food, the latter replied that he did and took the load down from the donkey's back. Spreading his garments on the ground, he offered the dervishes whatever victuals he had. After they had eaten, the grateful dervishes remarked to each other that such kindness should not go unrewarded. Turning to their benefactor, they said, "Go thou to Hindustan, for that place, which is the extreme (point) of Muhammadanism, we have given unto thee." At once the future sultan gathered together his family and set out for India "in accord with the intimation of those two Darweshes." In the Perso-Islamic cultural universe of the thirteenth and fourteenth centuries, Bengal really did in some sense "belong" to those two dervishes, that they might "entrust" it to a kind stranger.

In Bengal as in North India, the connection between political fortune and spiritual blessing is most evident in the early history of the Chishti order, the order to which the most ascendant Shaikhs of early-fourteenth-century Delhi belonged. "Anybody who was anyone," as Simon Digby puts it, visited the lodge of Delhi's most eminent Shaikh of the time, Nizam al-Din Auliya (d. 1325). Indeed, the two principal Persian poets of the early fourteenth century, Amir Khusrau and Amir Hasan, together with the sultanate's leading contemporary historian, Zia al-Din Barani, were all spiritual disciples of this Shaikh. Since Delhi at this time happened to be the capital of a vital and expanding empire, it is not surprising that the literary, cultural, and institutional traditions of that city—together with the Shaikhs and institutions of its dominant Sufi order—expanded along with Khalaji and Tughluq arms to the far corners of India, including Bengal.

But there was a deeper reason why Indo-Muslim courts patronized Chishti Shaikhs. By the fourteenth century, when other Sufi orders in India still looked to Central Asia or the Middle East as their spiritual home, the Chishtis, with their major shrines located within the Indian subcontinent, had become thoroughly indigenized. Seeking to establish their legitimacy both as Muslims and as Indians, Indo-Muslim rulers therefore turned to prominent Shaikhs of this order for blessings and support. For the same reason, leading Chishti Shaikhs dispersed from Shaikh Nizam al-Din's lodge to all parts of the empire and often enjoyed the patronage of provincial rulers. Conversely, many young Indian-born Muslims journeyed from all over India to live in or near that Shaikh's lodge, later to return to their native lands, where they would establish daughter Chishti lodges and enjoy the patronage of local rulers. The first Bengal-born Muslim known to have studied with Shaikh Nizam al-Din was Akhi Siraj al-Din (d. 1357), who journeyed to Delhi as a young man. Having distinguished himself at the Sufi lodge of the renowned Shaikh, Siraj al-Din received a certificate of succession and so thoroughly associated himself with the North Indian

Chishti tradition that he was given the epithet "âyina-yi Hindûstân," or "Mirror of Hindustan." Returning to Bengal some time before 1325, when his master died, he inducted others into the Chishti discipline, his foremost pupil being another Bengal-born Muslim, Shaikh 'Ala al-Haq (d. 1398). But unlike his own teacher, who had no known dealings with royalty, Shaikh 'Ala al-Haq was destined to play a special role in the political history of Muslim Bengal. In fact, the earliest-known monument built by the founder of Bengal's longest-lived dynasty, the Ilyas Shahi line of kings (1342–1486), was dedicated to this Shaikh. On a mosque built in 1342 in what is now part of Calcutta, Shams al-Din Ilyas Shah praised the Sufi as "the benevolent and revered saint (Shaikh) whose acts of virtue are attractive and sublime, inspired by Allah, may He illuminate his heart with the light of divine perception and faith, and he is the guide to the religion of the Glorious, 'Alaul-Haqqmay...his piety last long."

The importance of this inscription derives from its political context. Shams al-Din Ilyas Shah, an ambitious and politically astute newcomer to the delta, was just then launching a bid for independence from Delhi, evidently using southwestern Bengal as his power base. The imperial governor of nearby Satgaon having recently died, Shams al-Din, aware that Delhi was convulsed by the various crises provoked by the eccentric Sultan Mohammad bin Tughluq, seized the moment to attain provincewide power. As his earliest-known coin was minted at Pandua in A.D. 1342–43 (A.H. 743), Shams al-Din's ascendancy exactly synchronizes with the dedication of this mosque and his patronage of Shaikh 'Ala al-Haq. Moreover, the patronage of the two men was mutual, since Shaikh 'Ala al-Haq, attaching himself to this rising political star, adopted Shams al-Din as a recipient of his teachings and blessings. This early connection cemented an alliance between government and prominent Chishti Shaikhs that would last for the duration of Muslim rule in Bengal.

Not all alliances between Sufis and sultans were initiated by would-be rulers seeking to broaden their political bases. Some Sufis were drawn to the court out of a fervent desire to advance the cause of Islam as they understood it, and to augment the welfare of Muslims in the realm. We see this in the correspondence between Muzaffar Shams Balkhi (d. 1400) and Sultan Ghiyath al-Din Azam Shah (r. 1389–1410). An immigrant from Central Asia, Muzaffar had left his native Balkh for Delhi, where he taught at the college of Firuz Shah Tughluq. But the man's restless spirit led him to Bihar city, where, after meeting and becoming the disciple of the great Firdausi Shaikh Sharaf al-Din Maneri (d. 1381), he experienced a major change in life-orientation. Abandoning his pride in scholarship, Muzaffar subjected himself to various austerities and distributed all his worldly possessions in charity. He also made several pilgrimages to Mecca, where he once stayed for four years, teaching lessons in *hadith* scholarship. His extant letters reveal him not as an ecstatic, quiescent, or contemplative sort, but as committed to imposing his understanding of the Prophet's religious vision on the here-and-now world, a man inclined to scrutinize human society by scriptural standards and, finding it wanting, to transform it so as to meet those standards. In the sultan of Bengal, the Sufi found an outlet for these impulses.

Muzaffar Shams first seems to have become concerned about tutoring Sultan Ghiyath al-Din while waiting in Pandua for official permission to embark on a trip from Chittagong to Mecca. "The four months of the ship season are ahead of us," he wrote; "there are eight months still left; during all this while I have spent my life as a guest in the auspicious threshold of your majesty, may not your exaltation lessen." Although the Sufi politely described himself as a mere "guest" of the sultan, it is evident that he felt himself entrusted with a higher calling. "In my opinion," he wrote the king, by the gifts of God, the cherisher of mankind, you have developed a capacity of looking at the inside of things of the pure faith and the understanding of things of manifold signification. It appears that my heart would be opened out to you. A pious inspired man, Abdul Malik, has been a recipient of my letters[,] which might form a volume. It may be at Pandua or at Muazzamabad, but I don't remember where it exactly is. Oh, my son, get the permission and go through its contents. Something of my inward part may be opened out to you. You are the second person on whom I have poured out my secret (mystic) thoughts. It behooves you not to disclose these to anyone else.

Who, here, is patronizing whom? The Sufi's reference to the sultan as his "son" signals a clear inversion of the usual relationship between a patrimonial king and his subjects. Nor would the Sufi give the king privileged access to his personal correspondence; to see it the monarch had first to secure permission from a third party. Muzaffar Balkhi also reminded the king that although Sultan Firuz Tughluq of Delhi had repeatedly requested letters and spiritual guidance from Muzaffar's own master, Shaikh Sharaf al-Din Maneri, the latter had refused to oblige him, choosing instead to correspond with Sultan Sikandar of Bengal, Ghiyath al-Din's father. "You," he noted pointedly, "have had the effects and legacy of those blessings on yourself." In short, Muzaffar felt that he and his own master had been doing the Bengal sultans a favour by bestowing their blessings and advice on them instead of on the sultans of Delhi.

In addition to his recommendations concerning Islamic piety—for example, on the need to suppress innovation not prescribed by the Sharia, or to enforce the payment of alms by Muslims —Muzaffar cautioned the king against placing non-Muslims in positions of authority. "The substance of what has come in the tradition and commentaries," wrote the Shaikh, "is this":

"Oh believers, don't make strangers, that is infidels, your confidential favourites and ministers of state." They say that they don't allow any to approach or come near to them and become favourite courtiers; but it was done evidently and for expedience and worldly exigency of the Sultanate that they are entrusted with some affairs. To this the reply is that according to God it is neither expediency nor exigency but the reverse of it, that is an evil and pernicious thing....Don't entrust a work into the hands of infidels by reason of which they would become a *wali* (Governor-ruler or superior) over the Musalmans, exercise their authority in their affairs, and impose their command over them. As God says in the Quran, "It is not proper for a believer to trust an infidel as his friend and *wali*, and those who do so have no place in the estimation of God." Hear God and be devout and pious; very severe warnings have come in the Kitab (holy book) and traditions against the appointment of infidels as a ruler over the believers.

The Sufi thus saw in Islamic Law a clear course of action the sultan should take in order to avert certain disaster. For in Bengal's affairs Muzaffar Shams discerned more than just a political crisis. Referring to Timur's recent sacking of Delhi (A.D. 1398, or A.H. 801), which marked the eclipse of the once-mighty Tughluq empire, he wrote: "The eighth century has passed out, and the signs of the coming Resurrection are increasingly visible. An Empire like that of Delhi with all its expanse and abundance, spiritual and physical comfort, peace and tranquility, has turned upside down (is in a topsy-turvy condition). Infidelity has now come to hold the field; the condition of other countries is no better. Now is the time, and this is the opportunity." His gaze riveted on scripture, Muzaffar saw a palpable link between worldly decay and the Day of Judgment, heralded by that decay. Only by removing infidelity could Muslims forestall an otherwise inevitable cosmic process. And since the sultan had the power to stamp out infidelity by suppressing non-Muslims in a kingdom originally established by Muslims, the Sufi saw the sultan as capable of playing a pivotal role in implementing what he understood as God's will in that process.

It was Shaikhs of the Chishti order, however, who by the early fifteenth century had emerged as the principal spokesmen for a Muslim communal perspective in Bengal. If Shaikh 'Ala al-Haq had risen to prominence with the ascending fortunes of the founder of the Ilyas Shahi dynasty, his son and successor, Nur Qutb-i 'Alam (d. 1459), presided over Bengal's Chishti tradition when Ilyas Shahi fortunes had sunk to their lowest point—the period of Raja Ganesh's domination over the Ilyas Shahi throne.

According to Sufi sources, Raja Ganesh even persecuted Chishti Shaikhs, banishing Nur Qutb-i 'Alam's own son, Shaikh Anwar, to Sonargaon, and plotting the death of the son of another Chishti Shaikh, Husain Dhukkarposh.

In these circumstances, the Shaikh implored Sultan Ibrahim Sharqi of Jaunpur to invade Bengal and remove the "menace" of Raja Ganesh.

The following passage shows the extent to which the Chishtis of Bengal had come to identify the fortunes of Islam with the political fortunes of the Ilyas Shahi dynasty. "After a period of three hundred years," wrote the Sufi, "the Islamic land of Bengal—the place of mortals, the kingdom of the end of the seven heavens—has been overwhelmed and put to the run by the darkness of infidels and the power of unbelievers." The Shaikh elaborated this point using the Sufi and Qur'anic metaphor of light:

The lamp of the Islamic religion and of true guidance

Which had [formerly] brightened every corner with its light,

Has been extinguished by the wind of unbelief blown by Raja Ganesh.

Splendor from envy of the victorious news,

The lamp of [the celebrated preacher, Abul-Husain] Nuri, and the candle of [the Shia martyr] Husain

Have all been extinguished by the might of swords and the power of this thing in view.

What does one call the lamp and candle of men

Whose nature is devoid of virility [lit., has eaten camphor]?

When the abode of faith and Islam has fallen into such a fate,

Why are you sitting happily on your throne?

Arise, come and defend the religion,

For it is incumbent upon you,

O king, possessed of power and capacity.

While publicly clamoring for military intervention, privately, in a letter to his exiled son, Nur Qutb-i 'Alam brooded over the theological implications of Raja Ganesh's appearance in Bengali history. To the anguished Sufi, it seemed that God had not been heeding the supplication of the very people to whom the Qur'an had promised divine favour and protection. "Infidelity," he wrote;

Has gained predominance and the kingdom of Islam has been spoiled....Neither the devotion and the worship of the votaries of God proved helpful to them nor the unbelief of the infidels fettered their steps. Neither worship and devotion does any good to His Holy Divine Majesty, nor does infidelity do any harm to Him. Alas! Alas! O, how painful! With one gesture and freak of independence he caused the consumption of so many souls, the destruction of so many lives, and shedding of so much of bitter tears. Alas, woe to

> *me, the sun of Islam has become obscured and the moon of religion has become eclipsed.*

But the fortunes of Bengali Muslims did not ebb as the Shaikh had feared. Once the stormy period of Raja Ganesh had subsided, his converted son resumed the patronage of the Chishti establishment, re-confirming the Chishti-court alliance that had been established between Nur Qutb-i 'Alam's father and the dynasty's founder. Both Sultan Jalal al-Din and his son and successor Ahmad (r. 1432–33) became disciples of Nur Qutb-i 'Alam himself, and twelve succeeding sultans down to the year 1532 enlisted themselves as disciples of the descendants of Shaikh 'Ala al-Haq. By the end of the fifteenth century, the tomb of Shaikh Nur Qutb-i 'Alam in Pandua had become in effect a state shrine to which Sultan 'Ala al-Din Husain Shah (r. 1493–1519) made annual pilgrimages. Despite the mutual patronage and even dependency between Bengal's Sufis and its rulers, one also detects an undercurrent of friction between the two. Occasionally erupting into open hostility, this friction derived from the radical distinction made in Islam between *din* and *dunya*, "religion" and "the world." Withdrawn from worldly affairs and living in a state of poverty, self-denial, and remembrance of God, the Sufi recluse was in theory dramatically opposed by the ruler-administrator, glittering in his wealth and utterly immersed in worldly affairs. Sufis who rejected the world made much of their refusal to consort with "worldly" people—including above all royalty. Conversely, rulers sometimes suspected their Sufi allies, or even feared having around them such popular, charismatic leaders who might conceivably stir up the mob to riot or rebellion.

Here we may consider an inscription of Sultan Sikandar Ilyas Shah, dated 1363, in which the king dedicated a dome he had built for the shrine of a saint named Maulana 'Ata. Although the Shaikh may have been the king's contemporary, Maulana 'Ata was more likely an earlier holy man whose shrine had become the focus of an important cult by the time the inscription was recorded. "In this dome," the inscription reads,

> *Which has been founded by 'Ata, may the sanctuary of both worlds remain. May the angels recite for its durability, till the day of resurrection:* "We have built over you seven solid heavens" *[Qur'an 78:12].*

By the grace of (the builder of) the seven wonderful porticos *"who hath created seven heavens, one above another"* [Qur'an 67:3], may His names be glorified; the building of this lofty dome was completed. (Verily it) is the copy of a vault (lit., shell) of the roof of Glory, (referred in this verse) *"And we have adorned the heaven of the world"* (lit., lamps) [Qur'an 67:5]. (This lofty dome) in the sacred shrine of the chief of the saints, the unequaled among enquirers, the lamp of Truth, Law and Faith, Maulana 'Ata, may the High Allah bless him with His favours in both worlds; (was built) by order of the lord of the age and the time, the causer of justice and benevolence, the defender of towns, the pastor of people, the just, learned and great monarch, the shadow of Allah on the world, distinguished by the grace of the Merciful, Abul Mujahid Sikandar Shah, son of Ilyas Shah, the Sultan, may Allah perpetuate his kingdom. The king of the world Sikandar Shah, in whose name the pearls of prayer have been strung; regarding him they have said, "May Allah illuminate his rank," and regarding him they have prayed "May Allah perpetuate his kingdom."

While outwardly acclaiming the greatness of Maulana 'Ata, Sultan Sikandar was also asserting his own claims to closeness to God, styling himself the one in whose name "the pearls of prayer have been strung," and "the Shadow of God on Earth." And by referring to this shrine as a copy (*nuskha*) of the heavens, the sultan drew attention to parallels between God's creative activity and his own. For if it had been God's creative act to adorn the seven heavens with lamps, that is, stars, it was Sultan Sikandar's creative act to adorn the earth with a tomb for the lamp (*Siraj*) of Truth, Law, and Faith, that is, Maulana 'Ata. Implicitly, then, had it not been for the munificence of Sultan Sikandar, Maulana 'Ata would have remained shrouded in obscurity.

Royal distrust of or aversion to Sufis, even those of the Chishti order, is seen in other ways. Although Shams al-Din Ilyas Shah had patronized a prominent Chishti Shaikh while establishing a new dynasty, the king's son and successor, Sultan Sikandar, was suspicious of the disciples of his father's saintly patron. He was especially suspicious of the most eminent of these, Shaikh 'Ala al-Haq, whose shrine complex had become in Sikandar's day a major nexus for economic transactions, redistributing amongst the city's poor large sums of money received in the form of pious donations. Alarmed at the Sufi's substantial expenditure on the urban populace, Sikandar declared: "My treasure is in the hands of your father [the kingdom's Treasurer]; [yet] you are giving away as much as he spends." Evidently jealous of the Shaikh's wealth and influence, the king banished the Sufi to Sonargaon.

Bengal's Sufis and sultans, then, were fatefully connected by ties of mutual attraction and repulsion. Generally, when they were first establishing themselves politically, and especially when launching new dynasties, rulers actively sought the legitimacy powerful saints might lend them. Sultan Ghiyath al-Din 'Iwaz's earliest chronicler situated the launching of Bengal's first independent dynasty (1213) in the context of the grace, or *baraka*, of two simple dervishes in Afghanistan. And in 1342, when Sultan Shams al-Din Ilyas Shah launched the longest-lived dynasty in Muslim Bengal, he did so with the blessings of a renowned scion of the prestigious Chishti line.

Struck by the awesome spiritual powers people attributed to charismatic Shaikhs, or believing that their own lease on power was somehow extended by such forceful men, new Muslim kings sought their favour, built lodges or mausolea for them, or made public pilgrimages to their tombs. Conversely, some Sufis sought royal patronage out of their own reformist impulses to bring "the world" (*dunya*) into proper alignment with their understanding of the dictates of normative "religion" (*din*).

ULAMA AND MASHEIKH

Muslim scholars and Sufi Sheikhs, though not all rich, also belonged to the upper classes because of the respect they enjoyed in society. Most of them were patronised by kings and nobles, many were actually in their employ. Some of them were very well-off.

The Ulama

Ulama (plural of alim or learned) used to be well-versed in the Muslim law. As such they assisted Muslim monarchs in administering their dominions according to the Shariat. That way they also helped the Muslims in organizing their lives according to the Shariat which comprehends not only beliefs and practices, public and personal law, and rules of behaviour but even includes dress and personal appearance. Acquiring knowledge for the sake of earning money was looked down upon; hence tradition classified the Ulama into two categories, *Ulama-i-Akhirat* (the pious) and *Ulama-i-su* (the worldly). Knowledge was an extremely valuable ornament in an age when the educated were few and the Ulama were respected for their learning and ability.

Naturally, there was hardly any secular approach to education. Great emphasis was laid on theological education (*manqulat*). The most important subjects taught were Hadis, Fiqh (jurisprudence) and Tafsir (exegesis). The institutions of higher learning, called *madrasas*, were essentially schools of theology, with auxiliaries of grammar, literature and logic. These *madrasas* were the strongholds of orthodoxy and were subsidised by the state. A high value is placed on Muslim orthodoxy everywhere, because it is claimed that it maintains the identity of the community as against other communities. In actual practice it has served as a force against an integrated living, even coexistence, with other communities.

In a word, the Ulama were an orthodox lot. Those who were denied the life of affluence usually took to teaching (as *mutawalli*) in some mosque or under the thatched roof of their own mud houses. Some other Ulama or *danishmands* became pious preachers and scholars. Very often they too had to work under indigent circumstances. Some outstanding scholars were appointed as teachers in *madrasas* established by the Sultans. It was the ambition of the Ulama to join government service. There were many offices which the establishment could offer to a scholar. In official hierarchy of such appointments the post of the Sadr-i-Jahan came at the top, then followed Qazis (judges), Muftis (interpreters of law) Muhtasibs (censors of public morals), Imams (who led prayers) and Khatibs (reciters of the Quran).

The Sadr-i-Jahan was the chief of the judicial department. He served as the Qazi-i-Mumalik (chief judge) and recommended to the king about the appointment of junior Qazis. The Sheikh-ul-Islam was in charge of the ecclesiastical affairs of the empire. All those saints, *faqirs* and indigent scholars who enjoyed state patronage were looked after by him. Normally, only well-read scholars were appointed as Khatibs and Imams. So also was the case with Muftis and Muhtasibs. Muslim public opinion did not approve of the appointment of less qualified persons to these posts.

The Ulama received salaries pertaining to the offices they held. Most of the Ulama dabbled in politics. They wielded influence with the kings and nobles as interpreters of Muslim law. Their presence was indispensable to a ruler who was generally uneducated. During the protracted struggle between the crown and the nobility which raged throughout the Sultanate period, they aligned themselves with one or the other of political groups. They always remained on the right side of the regime and forgot the community whom they were expected to help in times of economic distress and political oppression. In this way they encouraged political oppression on the one hand and on the other they preached the necessity of obedience and submission by the people even to an oppressor, taking shelter under the Quranic injunction: Obey God and obey the Prophet, and those in authority among you. Naturally, an unholy alliance with them smoothed the path of king's depotism. They themselves did not lag behind in obsequiousness.

Their collaboration with and integration into the state apparatus made them subservient to the regime, so much so that when Iltutmish nominated Raziya as his successor, there was not a single theologian in the Delhi Empire who could protest against this nomination on the grounds of Shariat. The way they encouraged Sultans like Ruknuddin Firoz and Muizuddin Kaiqubad not to offer prayers or keep fasts during the month of Ramzan, and live licentious lives, shows how servile they had become and how they were wallowing in the dirty welters of politics. Of course the Ulama were openly critical of one another and, for this they have been criticised by their contemporary writers like Amir Khusrau, Zia Barani, Abdul Haq Muhaddis and Abdul Qadir Badaoni. Kings like Iltutumish and Balban and prince Bughra Khan are also critical of them.

But in one thing they did not fail. They kept the rulers and the ruling class on the path of Islam and virtue by informing them correctly about their duty towards the non-Muslims. Some modern secularist historians blame the Ulama for making Muslim rulers intolerant through their orthodox advice. Such writers fail to realise that it was not safe for the Ulama to cheat the Sultans by giving wrong interpretation of their holy scriptures vis-a-vis the treatment of non-Muslims. I have not come across any instance where the Ulama deliberately gave a distorted version of their scriptures in this context. And why should they have done so They were as much interested in seeing the Muslim state being run according to the Shariat as the Sultans.

In short, they always interpreted their scriptures correctly and honestly when it came to the Hindus. So that a foreign visitor like Maulana Shamsuddin Turk, who is very critical of the Qazis of the day, condoned their faults for the reason that because of their right advice their king was prone to treating the Hindus terribly. The lifestyle of the Ulama did not come in the way of serving Islam. Like other Muslims of the higher classes, it was normal for the Ulama to keep harems, live luxuriously and drink wine.

Despite a few faults and a little criticism, therefore, the Ulama as a class were indispensable to the regime. They were advisers of the king and ran the establishment. It was from the Ulama class that the various officers of the government as well as religious institutions were chosen. It was through these people that the regime systematized the religious and social life of the Muslim community just as it organized the extension and administration of Muslim dominions in India through the nobility.

The Masheikh

Equally influential, if not more, were the Sufi Masheikh. In the early years of Muslim immigration, and more so with the establishment of Muslim rule in India, many Muslim *faqirs*, scholars and Sufi Masheikh arrived in India. They entered Hindustan on their own or came with the invading armies. Later on, the disturbed conditions in Central Asia, consequent upon the Mongol upheaval also encouraged them to leave their homes in search of security. Many came to settle in India where peace and plenty and the protective arm of Muslim rule promised them all they wished.

Sufism may be defined as Islamic mysticism. In its early years in Central and West Asia, it was deeply influenced by Neo-Platonism, the monastic tradition of Buddhism and Christianity and the Vedantist and Yogic philosophy of Hinduism. All these were Islamized by the Sufis in such a way as to make them virtually unidentifiable. Nawbahar was a great Buddhist monastry in Balkh.

The name of the city of Bokhara itself is derived from Vihar. Some Khurasan Sufis lived in caves like Buddhists. They were known as

Shikafatiyah from the word Shikafat (cave). When Hindu and Buddhist thinkers and saints converted to Islam in Central and West Asia during the eighth to eleventh centuries they carried their thought and philosophy to Sufism. Ibn al-Arabi (1165-1241) wrote in his Diwan that idol-worship, Chritian ways and Kaaba were all acceptable to him as he believed in the religion of love.

The Sufism that came to India in the twelfth century with the Muslim Masheikh did not, by and large, envisage direct communion with God without the intermedium of Islam. Just as the soul and body are one, in Islamic sufism *Tariqah* and *Shariah* are so interrelated. Some Sufis believed in the doctrine of Wahadat-ul-Wajud, or the Unity of Being which means There is nothing but God, nothing in existence other than He. This theory, propounded by Sheikh Ibn al-Arabi and akin to Hindu Vedantism, was developed later on in order to harmonise the doctrine of mysticism with the teachings of orthodox Islam.

There were a number of Sufi orders or *silsila* as they are called. Abul Fazl mentions as many as fourteen. But four orders-Chishti, Suhrawardi, Qadiri and Naqshabandi-became prominent in India. Of these only the first two became more popular, for the latter two were extremely orthodox and legalistic in their strictness. By the thirteenth century, northern India saw the flowering of two Sufi orders, Chishti and Suhrawardi, and we will concern ourselves with the Masheikh of only these two orders. The founder of the Suhrawardi order was Sheikh Bahauddin Zakariya. He was born near Multan in Sind in 578 H. (1182-83 C.E.). He and his disciples played a leading part in the north-west and symbolically asked the Chishtis not to dispute possession (of the region) with them. Sheikh Bahauddin Zakariya (and his successors) mixed freely with the Sultans, took part in political affairs, amassed wealth and accepted government honours.

The Chishtis established themselves at Ajmer in Rajasthan, some parts of the Punjab, Delhi, U.P. and Bihar and further east. They were probably the largest in number and represented what seems to be the most typical in the Sufi way of life. The first great Chishti Sheikh was Khwaja Muinuddin Chishti. He was born in Sijistan in eastern Persia in C.E. 1141. He came to India a little before or after the battle of Taraori or Tarain (1192) and settled down at Ajmer. There also he lies buried after his death in 1236. His mausoleum is a great centre of pilgrimage. He is known as Gharib Nawaz or Friend of the Poor and Nabi-ul-Hind or Prophet of India. Sheikh Saiyyad Muhammad Gesu Daraz (he of the long locks) said that if people were unable to make the pilgrimage to Mecca, a visit once in their lives to the mausoleum of Muinuddin Chishti would convey the same merit.

Sheikh Muinuddin is very famous today. But he was not known as such to his contemporaries. The three contemporary chronicler-Hasan Nizami,

Fakhr-i-Mudabbir and Minhaj do not refer to him at all. Early mystic records, the *Favaid-ul-Fuad* and *Khair-ul-Majalis* do not give any information about him. Barani makes no reference to him. Isami tells us only this much that Muhammad bin Tughlaq had once visited his grave. In all probability his fame spread from the time of emperor Akbar (1556-1605 C.E.) who held his memory in great reverence and often paid visit to his dargah in *Ajmer*. However, the legend and fame of Muinuddin rests, as of all other Sheikhs, on the magic-like miracles (*karamah*) he is supposed to have performed. It is difficult to say when the stories of the miracles of Sufis be an to be told but once this process had begun, it could not be stopped.

It became a criterion by which Sufis were judged, and the common reason why people believed in them. They credited them with supernatural powers and feared and respected them. P.M. Currie quotes Mohammad Habib to say that most of the mystic records and Diwans are forgeries, but regard for public opinion has prevented them (Indian scholars) from making a public declaration that these are forgeries. However, stories of miracles apart, he (Muinuddin Chishti) was Saiyid by descent. He did not depart in any way from Sunna, the Ulama could not fault him, and he performed the hajj.

Sheikh Muinuddin Chishti had a number of disciples two of whom, Sheikh Hamid and Qutbuddin, had earned reverence of great and small. Sheikh Hamiduddin Nagauri lived with his wife as a villager. Sheikh Qutbuddin Bakhtiyar Kaki came to Delhi in the reign of Iltutmish and lived in a *khanqah* outside the city. He was very fond of *sama* (devotional music). Once he was so overtaken by *wajd* (ecstasy) that he collapsed and breathed his last. One of his principal disciples was Sheikh Fariduddin Ganj-i-Shakar (1175-1265) popularly called Sheikh Farid. Sheikh Farid lived in extreme poverty bordering on starvation. He trained a large number of disciples, established many *khanqahs* and raised the prestige of the Chishti order. The greatest disciple of Sheikh Farid was Hazrat Nizamuddin Auliya (1236-1325). He was born at Badaun. In 1258 he settled at Ghayaspur near Delhi where his shrine exists and a railway station is named after him. The Sheikh had a large circle of disciples who hailed from all sections of society, rich and poor, noble and plebian. In his life of almost a century, Nizamuddin Auliya witnessed the reigns of seven Sultans, but he did not attend the darbar of any one of them. He was popularly known as *Mahbub-i-Ilahi* (Beloved of God). His popularity was due to his saintly virtues and service to humanity. His disciples included Amir Khusrau, Ziyauddin Barani and the renowned Sheikh Nasiruddin Chiragh-i-Delhi whom he appointed as his successor (Khalifa). Professor Mohammad Habib rightly calls Nasiruddin the last great saint of the Chishti *Silsilah* to have enjoyed an all India status. This was the best period in India for Sufism in general and the Chishti *Silsilah* in particular. To this famous line of Sufis belongs Sheikh

Salim Chishti, a contemporary of emperor Akbar, for whom the latter built a mausoleum in Fatehpur Sikri.

Many of the Sufi Masheikh lived in poverty. Sheikh Hamiduddin (d. 1276 C.E.) lived in a small mud house in the city of Nagaur in Rajasthan. He eked out his meagre subsistence by cultivating a single *bigha* of land. His wife spent her time in cooking and spinning like a peasant woman. He was a strict vegetarian. He refused to accept government gift of land and money from the muqta of Nagaur and Sultan of Delhi. Sheikh Muinuddin and Sheikh Qutbuddin Bakhtiyar never owned houses of their own. Sheikh Farid Ganj-i-Shakar built a small *kachcha* house only when his family had considerably increased For many years during his early life Sheikh Nizamuddin Auliya had to wander from one quarter of the city to another in search of a house Generally starvation conditions prevailed in the houses of the Chishti saints very often these saints did not possess sufficient clothes to cover their bodies.

This is one side of the coin. The other is that Sheikh Muinuddin's sons owned land, which may have been granted to them directly or accepted by the Sheikh for their sake. Sheikh Fariduddin was destitute to the end of his days, but gifts were received and distributed at his *khanqah*. The *khanqah* of Nizamuddin Auliya, probably after he received money from Sultan Nasiruddin Khusrau, became an institution in which money, food and goods circulated freely. However, the Sheikhs who lived in affluence were deemed to possess no less merit than those who elected to remain destitute.

The Sufi Masheikh are also reported to have shunned the company of the nobles and nearness to the court. But that too was not always so. On the contrary, the attractions of staying near the throne were compulsive. Sidi Maula was a disciple of Sheikh Farid at Ajodhan. He aspired for name and fame and shifted to Delhi. Once in the capital, Sidi Maula hurled himself headlong in the politics of the court and, after many vicissitudes paid with his life. But Sidi was not alone in this pursuit.

As K.A. Nizami has pointed out, Even Chisht the cradle-land of the *silsilah* looked to Delhi for guidance in spiritual matters. The Masheikh mostly lived in cities and towns where they were popular with kings and people and enjoyed the respectability of upper class elite. Sheikh Qutbuddin Bakhtiyar Kaki was much admired by the people of Delhi headed by Sultan Iltutmish himself.

Muinuddin Chishti was very much liked by the Muslims of Ajmer but he was suspected of dabbling in politics which prompted Prithviraj III to ask Ramdeva to expel him from Ajmer. Sheikh Nizamuddin Auliya used to hold his own *darbar* which was often more awe-inspiring than even the court of kings.

The Sheikh was so popular with the people that Sultan Alauddin Khalji began to entertain suspicions about his influence and authority in Muslim society. With a view to ascertain the real intentions of the Sheikh, and to find out to what extent he was interested in seeking political power, the Sultan sent him a note seeking his advice and guidance on certain political problems. The Sheikh immediately surmised Alauddin's motives in sending the letter, and replied that he had nothing to do with politics and so could render no advice on political matters: he kept busy with seeking God's grace for Muslim monarchs (*duagoee*). Only after this was the Sultan's mind set at rest. But to many he was popularly known as Sultan Nizamuddin and his resting place as Dargah Sultanji Saheb.

Alauddin greatly respected Nizamuddin Auliya for his supernatural powers and knack for correct predictions. But his son Sultan Qutbuddin Mubarak Khalji disliked him because of his political leanings.

He even declared a reward of a thousand *tankahs* for one who would cut off Nizamuddin's head. Once when they chanced to meet, the Sultan refused to acknowledge the salutations of the saint and even called Sheikh Ruknuddin from Multan to eclipse Nizamuddin's popularity. After Qutbuddin's death, Sultan Nasiruddin Khusrau ascended the throne at Delhi, but his authority was challenged by Ghazi Tughlaq. Khusrau Shah, to gain the support of the Sheikhs sent two or three lakhs of *tankahs* to each of them and five lakh *tankahs* to Nizamuddin Auliya. When Ghazi Tughlaq ascended the throne as Sultan Ghiyasuddin Tughlaq (1320 C.E.) he asked Nizamuddin to render the account of the amount he had received. The latter sent a reply, seemingly insolent, that the money belonged to the *Bait-ul-mal* (Public Treasury) and therefore he had given it to the poor.

The Sultan took umbrage at the Sheikh's answer. The relations between the two were sore also because of the Sultan's dislike of sama in which Nizamuddin freely indulged. In this scenario, Nizamuddin Auliya began to support Ghiyasuddin's son, Muhammad Tughlaq, who aspired for the throne. When Ghiyasuddin Tughlaq went on an expedition to Bengal, Nizamuddin Auliya prophesied that the Sultan would never come back from there.

When the news of his return was received in Delhi, a worried Prince Muhammad rushed to Nizamuddin with the tiding at which the Sheikh uttered the famous words, Delhi is still far off (*hanuz Delhi dur ast*). Nizamuddin Auliya was thus immersed in Delhi court politics, at least towards the end of his life (1320-25). But he was a Sufi. He had many disciples who were regular visitors to his *khanqah*. Such an one was Amir Khusrau. Abul Hasan, popularly known as Amir Khusrau, was the most favoured disciple of Nizamuddin Auliya. He was a historian, a musician, a poet, a litterateur, a Sufi Sheikh, and a full-fledged protege of Delhi Sultans.

His first patron was Prince Muhammad, son of Sultan Ghiyasuddin Balban. Thereafter for about forty years (1285-1325) he served a continuous succession of monarchs-Muizuddin Kaiqubad, Jalaluddin Khalji, Alauddin Khalji and Mubarak Shah Khalji-and his shrewdness was successful in keeping them all pleased. The Sultan (Kaiqubad) flattered him by calling him the seal of authors and promised to give him a big reward which would free him from all worldly cares ever afterwards. His genius, if not character, helped him spend the whole of his life in spinning yarn (or writing many untruths). Soon after, when Kaiqubad was murdered by Jalaluddin Khalji, he composed a new *masnavi, Miftah-ul-Futuh* in praise of his new patron.

Six years later Jalauddin was murdered by his nephew and son-in-law Alauddin Khalji who marched into Delhi with the late king's head held aloft on the point of a spear and, writes Dr. Wahid Mirza, our poet Khusrau was one of the first to offer his congratulations to the murderer whose hands were still red with the blood of his king, his uncle and his benefactor The poet changed with changing time and turned with shifting wind. No wonder, even Ghiya-suddin Tughlaq, who was hostile to Khusrau's *pir-o-murshid*, Nizamuddin Auliya, receives fulsome praise in Khusrau's *Tughlaq Nama*. Amir Khusrau was very shrewd. When he found the reign of Qutbuddin Mubarak Khalji nothing to boast about, he wrote *Nuh Sipehr*, praising all things Indian, including the beauty of Indian women. In *Nuh Sipehr* he also wrote: They have four books in that language (Sanskrit), which they are constantly in the habit of repeating. Their name is *Bed* (Vedas). They contain stories of their gods, but little advantage can be derived from their perusal. This betrays the one-track mind of Muslim elite in general. This weakness was shared by almost all Sufi Masheikh, debunking the belief that Sufi Masheikh treated Hindus and Muslims on terms of equality or helped bring the two communities nearer to one another.

They were keen on maintaining only orthodox Muslim rule and showed a general disregard for others. Since it was believed that Muhammad bin Tughlaq was not orthodox, Sheikh Nasiruddin Chiragh obtained a promise from Firoz Tughlaq before supporting the latter's claim to the throne, to the effect that he would rule according to the Shariat.

In 1409, when Raja Ganesh (Kans of Muslim chroniclers) obtained the throne of Bengal and sought to establish his authority by keeping the prominent Ulama and Sufis under control, Sheikh Nurul Haqq (Qutbul Alam) wrote to Sultan Ibrahim Sharqi of Jaunpur to come and save the Muslims of Bengal. Sultan Ibrabim responded to the call and Raja Ganesh, finding himself too weak to meet the challenge, came to the Sheikh and begged for his intercession, promising to agree to any conditions.

Sheikh Nurul Haqq said he would intercede for him if he accepted Islam. The Raja retired in favour of his son Jadu, who ascended the throne as Sultan Jalaluddin Shah. Sheikh Nurul Haqq induced Sultan Ibrahim, much against his will, to withdraw his armies. Sheikh Abdul Quddus combined spirituality with dogmatism. His letters to Sultan Sikandar Lodi and Babur (1526-30) show that he was as anxious to maintain Muslim rule as any wordly Muslim, that he had no scruples in using the language of a courtier in asking the rulers to establish the Shariah Akbar's attempt at secularizing the state had exasperated the divines, and Mulla Shah Ahmad and Sheikh Farid Bukhari exhorted court dignitaries to alter the state of things in the very beginning of Jahangir's reign, otherwise it would be difficult to accomplish anything later on. There are many other such instance. It is understandable if disgruntled nobles and courtiers invited foreigners to rescue Islam, but the Sufi Masheikh by such actions compromised their image as Indians first and respecters of all people as equals. They were as opposed to national integration as any orthodox Muslim. Similarly, many modern scholars have shown that some Sufi Masheikh too resorted to aggressive and violent means in fighting infidelity. Even Sheikh Muinuddin Chishti's picture of tolerance is replaced by a portrait of him as a warrior for Islam. Since I have studied this problem in detail elsewhere, I would not like to repeat the cases of aggressive proselytization of Sufi Masheikh mentioned therein.

However, one shocking instance of forcible conversion not mentioned in my book referred to above, may be given here. Saiyyad Jalaluddin Bukhari Makhdum-i-Jahanian of Sind (d.1384) fell very seriously ill. Nawahun, the *darogha* of Uchch, called on him to enquire about his health.

As a matter of courtesy and to raise his sinking spirits, Nahawun said: May God restore your health your holiness is the last of the saints as the Prophet Muhammad was the last of the prophets. Sayyid Jalaluddin Bukhari even on death-bed construed it as an expression of faith in Islam and demanded a formal declaration of conversion from him. Nawahun firmly declined to make any such declaration.

Thereupon he was charged with apostasy. He fled to the court of Firoz Shah Tughlaq in search of asylum and redress. When Sayyid Jalaluddin Bukhari expired, his younger brother Sadruddin Raju Qattal, rushed to Delhi in order to persuade Firoz Shah to execute Nawahun. Though some scholars of the capital did not agree with the viewpoint of Raju Qattal, the latter prevailed upon Firoz Shah in obtaining his permission for Nawahun's execution as a renegade.

Poor or rich, the Sufi Masheikh lived as householders. Except Nizamuddin Auliya and Nasiruddin Chiragh, all Sufi Sheikhs married, and had large families. Since the word saint is associated with celibacy in people's minds of most religions, it would be pertinent to state that marriage is enjoined on every Muslim, and celibacy is frequently condemned by

Muhammad. It is related in the Traditions that Muhammad said: When the servant of God marries, he perfects half his religion Consequently in Islam, even the ascetic orders are rather married than single. Sheikh Muinuddin Chishti took two wives - Ummatullah and Asmatullah, and had three sons and one daughter. He had married in his old age only to realize that his spiritual powers had greatly suffered on that account. Sheikh Qutbuddin Bakhtiyar Kaki Ushi also married twice, late in life.

He divorced one of his wives, soon after marriage, as her presence upset his programme of prayers. He had four sons. Sheikh Farid had a number of wives and a large family. Sheikh Nasiruddin Chiragh is reported to have stated that Sheikh Farid had a number of wives (*harem bisyar bud*). He had at least four wives and eight children. Sheikh Hamiduddin had led a very voluptuous life in his early years, but when he joined the circle of Sheikh Muinuddin Chishti, he adopted the life of a mystic in all sincerity. He had a number of children. Sheikh Qutbuddin Husain Kirmani, uncle of the author of *Siyar-ul-Auliya*, used to put on the garments of the finest Chinese silks and Kamkhawab and always used to have pan in his mouth. Sheikh Nizamuddin Auliya also relished betel.

All this was normal life and all these were normal pleasures. But Sufi Masheikh, known by many names like Wali, Shah, Qalandar, Murshid, Marabout, Sheikh, Faqir and Darwesh, indulged in all kinds of pleasures and luxuries. The case of Sidi Maula was exceptional. He had ready at hand brand new *tankahs* under every coverlet to spend. So many people dined at his *khanqah* that, if Barani is to be believed, two thousand *man* of flour (*maida*), two to three hundred *man* of sugar and a hundred to two hundred man of vegetables used to be consumed in his kitchen every day. But others were equally non-poor and generous. We know that Sheikh Farid was destitute to the end of his days, but we also know that gifts were received and distributed. It could be said generally of every *khanqah* that even in the bad days a person was sure to get some sort of a meal and, with luck, a share of money in every *khanqah* ideals of austerity fought against satisfaction of physical needs, so that there was no dearth of money and parasites because of the well-to-do admirers of the Sheikh.

Sama or devotional music was a common feature of the *khanqah*. During *sama*, the Sheikhs and Qalandars placed strong insistence on the practice of *Nazar-ilal murd* or gazing at good looking boys. One reason why Ghiyasuddin Tughlaq could not see eye to eye with Nizamuddin Auliya was the latter's fondness for *sama* and his ecstatic fits.

The Sultan was free from unnatural lust (*lawatat*) and did not allow handsome beardless boys from coming near him. In the *khanqahs* were also used drugs of the hashish family, and even drinking was common. Love affairs of sufis were of common occurrence.

Ahmad Yadgar mentions the case of a *faqir* who fell for the newly wed bride of the son of Tatar Khan. He relates another story about the love of a *darwesh* and a woman. Love between a Hindu girl and a *darwesh* created flutter and tension. The Sheikhs used to marry in high families and possessed a clout which sometimes became a problem for Sultans. A sixteenth century Suhrawardi writer says that Sheikh Sadruddin Arif had married a divorced wife of Prince Muhammad, the eldest son of Balban. The circumstances of this marriage are given as follows: The prince divorced his wife, whom he passionately loved, in a fit of fury. When he recovered his normal state of mind, he felt deeply pained for what he had done. Legally he could not take her back into his *harem* unless she was married to someone else and then divorced by him. A man of genuine piety was searched to restore the broken relationship.

Sheikh Arif, the most outstanding saint of the town, promised to marry the princess and divorce her the next day. But, after the marriage, he refused to divorce her on the ground that the princess herself was not prepared to be divorced. This incident led to bitterness between the saint and the prince. The latter even thought of taking action against the Sheikh, but a Mongol invasion cut short the thread of his life. Sheikh Salim Chishti had great influence with emperor Akbar, much more than Sadruddin Arif had in the time of Balban. And both Badaoni and Father Monserrate make unflattering comments about Sheikh Salim. The Sufi Masheikh lived a full-fledged life, different from saints of other religions. But among Indian Muslims their memory has always been cherished with utmost reverence. It is said that saint-worship among Muslims is a practice unique to India.

Dargahs of Sufis, real or figurative, are found all over the country and Muslims flock to them in large numbers. It is a legacy of medieval times. One reason for this can be that most Indian Muslims are converted Hindus, who, when their places of worship were converted into (*khanqahs* and later) *dargahs*, did not give up visiting them. For instance, at the most holy *dargah* of Sheikh Muinuddin Chishti, the Sandal Khana mosque is believed to have been built on the site of a Dev temple. The other is that stories of miracles of saints give a hope and a chance to people to obtain fulfilment of their desires. Hence besides Muslims, a few Hindus also resort to such shrines.

REFERENCES

Currie, P.M. *The Shrine and Cult of Muin-ul-din Chishti of Ajmer*, Oxford, Delhi, 1989.

Stein, Burton : *Peasant State and Society in Medieval South India*, Oxford University Press, Delhi, 1980.

Sunder, Prem : *Caste Class and Society : Then and Now*, Educational Pub, Delhi, 2010.

Tillotson, G. H. R.: *Mughal India*, New York, Penguin Books, 1990.

Chapter 5

Hindu Society, Culture and Civilization in Muslim Period

HINDU SOCIETY

The advent of Indo-Turkish rule meant an abrupt end to official patronage for those Brahmans who had served the Sena government as ritual priests, astrologers, ministers, advisors, or financial officers. Doubtless, many of these fled into the eastern hinterland along with the Sena household in 1204, or soon thereafter. In time, however, most Brahmans moved from an initial position of disdain for the new political order to one of uneasy accommodation with it. By the fifteenth and sixteenth centuries, the predominant view was that government employment was perfectly possible as long as one did not engage in marital relations with Mlecchas ("polluted outsiders"). For, ultimately, the Brahmans and the higher Muslim officers of the sultanate needed each other: the former were historically conditioned to look to a ruling class for patronage and livelihood, while the latter required the administrative talents that Brahmans had traditionally monopolized. Hence, while the period before 1415 witnessed few instances of Brahmans serving the sultanate, the picture changed dramatically after the Raja Ganesh revolution. That chieftain's own converted son, Sultan Jalal al-Din Mohammad, signaled the change by honoring Brahman poets. By the reign of Sultan 'Ala al-Din Husain Shah, many Brahmans had taken service in the court.

Serving the sultanate proved far less traumatic for the Kayasthas, who had been the dominant landholding caste prior to the conquest and who continued in this role under Muslim rule. Indeed, after the conquest, the Kayasthas absorbed remnants of Bengal's old ruling dynasties—the Sena, Pala, Chandra, Varman, and so on—and in this way became the region's surrogate Kshatriya or "warrior" class. Judging from the correspondence of Maulana Muzaffar Shams Balkhi, who in 1397 complained bitterly of the power enjoyed by Hindus, it seems that Muslim rulers had from a very early time confirmed the Kayasthas in their ancient role as landholders and political intermediaries.

Looking at Bengal's Hindu society as a whole, it seems likely that the caste system—far from being the ancient and unchanging essence of Indian civilization as supposed by generations of Orientalists—emerged into something resembling its modern form only in the period 1200–1500. Central to this process, as Ronald Inden has argued, was the collapse of Hindu kingship. Before the Turkish conquest, the Sena king had maintained order by distributing wealth and by judging between socially high and low in the context of his court and its rituals. With the dissolution of Hindu kingship that followed the Turkish conquest, however, these functions appear to have been displaced onto society at large. Hindu social order was now maintained by the enforcing of group endogamy, the regulation of marriage by "caste" councils, and the keeping of genealogies by specialists. In the western delta, one sees the result of these processes in the detailed list of Hindu communities mentioned by the poet Mukundaram, who describes a hierarchy of four tiers of occupationally differentiated endogamous groups (*jati*). The first tier included Brahmans, Kayasthas, and Baidyas, or traditional healers. The second included productive classes such as cultivators, herders, iron smiths, potters, weavers, gardeners, barbers, candy makers, spice merchants, brass smiths, gold merchants, and so on. These were followed by a third tier composed of the ritually less pure castes: fishermen, oil pressers, woodcutters, launderers, tailors, molasses makers, carpenters, ferrymen, and beggars. At the very end of the list, compelled to live outside the poet's imaginary city, were the grass cutters, leatherworkers, prostitutes, and Dom tribals, who were scavengers and sweepers.

HINDU RELIGION

As elsewhere in India, there arose in Bengal a need to harmonize Vedic religion, which focused on male deities, with indigenous Indian cults, in which female deities dominated. One way this was accomplished was in the context of the orthodox Shiva cult, which before the Turkish conquest had been presided over by Brahmans and lavishly patronized by Hindu kings such as the early Senas, for whom œiva was the kingdom's cosmic overlord. The cosmic reunion of œiva and Shakti—that is, pure consciousness, corresponding to the male principle; and pure energy, corresponding to the female principle—was typically concretized in aniconic symbols placed in temples, access to which was controlled by Brahman priests. However, this state-supported cult declined when Indo-Turkish conquerors withdrew the royal patronage on which such public cults depended.

Both before and after the conquest, numerous popular cults dedicated to various manifestations of the Goddess also flourished. Celebrated in a literary genre called *mangala-kavya*, these cults thrived among those groups least touched by Indo-Aryan culture and least integrated into the hierarchic scheme of social organization as promoted by Brahmans. They were also among the oldest, the most vibrant, and the most authentically Bengali religious traditions in the delta. In their earliest form, Goddess cults seem to have sprung from ancient female domestic rites not presided over by Brahman priests, as in the cult of the snake goddess Manasa, whose core story was anciently recited by women and for women as a component of their domestic rites. But throughout the period 1200–1600 and doubtless for some time earlier, Brahman ideologues sought to appropriate such cults by identifying female divine power in all its manifestations with the Shakti, or pure energy, which is the counterpart of the Brahmanical god œiva. Thus œiva was understood as son to Dharma; husband to Chandi/Durga, Kali/Ganga, and Sitala; father to Manasa and Neto; guru/father to various Nath saints; master/father to Daksin Ray; and father-in-law to Sasthi. Noting these relationships, W. L. Smith aptly describes œiva as "the hub around which the Bengali divine hierarchy revolves." But these folk deities experienced varying degrees of accommodation with Brahmanical orthodoxy, ranging from a rather complete incorporation into the Hindu pantheon, with full benefits of Brahmanical patronage, to a more marginal place within that pantheon, with only hesitant acceptance by Brahmans.

Extending at least to A.D. 1000, with its core myths and rituals dating from the period 500–1000, if not earlier, the cult of the snake goddess Manasa was well established by the time of the Turkish conquest. Yet this cult, having first emerged among low-ranked tribals of Burdwan, failed to achieve full acceptance in Brahmanic literature, and it was to some extent resisted by orthodox Shivas. Nor did Manasa enjoy a satisfactory connection with œiva.

Like other folk deities, she had a kin tie with the great god—in her case as a daughter—but she could never compete with deities identified as œiva's wife, such as her principal rival, the goddess Chandi. The cult's struggle to gain full acceptance is evident in its central myth. Having already gained a following among ritually low-ranking communities like fishermen and cowherds, Manasa was convinced that she could win universal human devotion only through gaining the submission of Chando, an upper-caste merchant and fervent devotee of œiva. Although Chando initially despised Manasa and viewed her as one of inferior status, he ultimately (though reluctantly) recognized Manasa's popularity and submitted to her cult. The story thus suggests a steadily widening circle of the cult's social basis: from cowherds to fishermen, to farmers, to upper-class women, to upper-class men, and finally to Brahman priests.

If the Manasa cult enjoyed only a limited or reluctant acceptance among Bengal's upper castes in our period, it fared much better among the masses, especially in the delta's less-Aryanized east. In 1540 the poet Vrindavan Das, though himself not devoted to any of the Goddess cults, affirmed their popularity when he wrote:

All "religious" people know this only:

They sing the song of Mangal Candi at the jagaran *[the last night of the festival for the goddess Chandi],*

With pomp some give puja *to Visahari [Manasa],*

And another puts on a puppet show at great expense.

Relief images of stone preserved in the Chittagong University Museum can be confidently identified with the goddess Manasa. Two of these stand several feet in height and depict the deity with a hood of seven snakes over her head, her left hand holding another snake, and her principal iconographic symbol, a sacred pot, at her feet. The appearance of such votive images, evidently intended for installation in simple, thatched shrines dedicated to her worship, marked an important step in the progression of the Manasa cult from a domestic rite to an established cult, complete with officiating priests, even though these may not have been Brahmans.

Enjoying far more support among Brahmans, and at the mass level perhaps the widest support of any cult in the premodern Bengali pantheon, was the cult of the goddess Chandi. Like her rival Manasa, Chandi was a forest goddess whose cult had sprung up from the delta's aboriginal society. But Chandi's identification as the wife of the great god œiva rendered her more mild and generous than the nasty, manipulative Manasa. Moreover, though Chandi's cultic literature is also very ancient, it appeared in written form only in the late sultanate period, the best-known text being Mukundaram's *Candi-Mangala* (ca. 1590). Perhaps because the written versions of the myth appeared so late in the cult's evolution, Chandi emerges in Mukundaram's work as rather well integrated into the Indo-Aryan pantheon and with Brahmanic values. She is portrayed, for example, as having put an end to the primordial chaos prevailing at a time before gods and Brahmans imposed order on earth. Furthermore, she not only protects all the animals of the woods, but presides over their hierarchic ranking in a scheme exactly mirroring the ideal human society as seen from the Brahmanical perspective. And finally, her protection of the animals is conditioned on their renunciation of mutual violence, for society is to accord with the norms of *dharma*, or righteous law.

The myth's story line also illustrates the post-eighth-century Hindu conception of the interrelationship of religion and politics. In a world where both deities and kings seek to enlarge their circles of authority, a deity "entrusts" earthly sovereignty to an appointed king on condition that he propagate and promote that deity's cult in human society. Craving human devotion like most Indian deities, Chandi embarks on a project designed to establish a royal kingdom on earth. Here the narrative focuses on a low-caste hunter named Kalaketu, to whom the goddess assigns the sovereignty of her forest kingdom.

In return for this, the hunter must renounce the hunt, build and populate a city in the forest, and construct a glorious temple dedicated to her, in this way propagating Chandi's cult among humans. All this underscores the goddess's fundamentally political role, seen in the dual sovereignty that she and her human protege exercise over the forest kingdom. As Chandi's earthly representative, Kalaketu rules on behalf of that goddess, behind whom stands the kingdom's cosmic overlord—her spouse, œiva. Yet, for all her dharmic trappings and her trucking with the highest gods of the Indo-Aryan pantheon, Chandi remains of the forest—that dark domain of jungle beasts and non-Aryan tribes—and not of the city, the proper domain of Brahmans and their ritual performances. Moreover, Chandi's protege Kalaketu is a hunter who pursues a violent and unclean livelihood typical of Bengal's indigenous tribes, amongst whom the myth had originally evolved. No amount of Brahmanical revision could disguise the underlying association of both goddess and king with non-Aryan, indigenous Bengali culture.

It is worth recalling that the only known nativist rebellion mounted against the sultanate was waged in the name of Chandi, this thoroughly Bengali goddess and protectress of the forest. Dated A.D. 1417—18 and minted in Chittagong, Sonargaon, and Chhota Pandua—that is, the delta's forested southern and eastern hinterland—the coins of Danuja Marddana Deva and his son Mahendra Deva bore the Sanskrit legend *uri Candi Carana Parayana*, "devoted to the feet of Goddess Chandi." Inasmuch as armed insurrection against established political authority is always serious business, we may be sure that rebel leaders would have invoked only such supernatural assistance as was judged most powerful and most likely to respond to human entreaties. Chandi's appearance on the Deva kings' coins during this rebellion clearly attests to her widespread popularity, and to belief in her protective power.

DEVELOPMENT OF HINDU RELIGION AND CULTURE

From epigraphic, artistic, and literary evidence—notably the Sanskrit poem *Gita Govinda*, composed by the thirteenth-century poet Jayadeva—we know that the Vishnu cult had been gaining royal favour immediately prior to the Turkish conquest. During the first several centuries of Turkish rule, however, this public cult, like that of œiva, suffered from the withdrawal of state patronage. It next appeared in deltaic Bengal as a popular devotional movement unmediated by priestly rituals or court patronage, and marked by the appearance of vernacular literature glorifying the various incarnations of Vishnu. Sometime in the fifteenth century, Kirtivas Pundit made a Bengali translation of the *Ramayana*, the famous epic of Rama. Yet what ultimately won over the mainstream of Bengali Vaishnavas was Vishnu's incarnation, not as Rama, but as Krishna—the naughty child-god, the slayer of the snake king Kaliya, the seducer of the pastoral Gopi women, and especially, the lover of Radha. The popularization of a new Krishna literature can be attributed, in part, to patronage by the Muslim court at Gaur. Between 1473 and 1480, the Kayastha poet Maladhara Basu composed his *uri Krishna-Vijaya*, "The Triumph of Lord Krishna," under the patronage of Sultan Rukn al-Din Barbak (r. 1459–74). Somewhat later, Sultan 'Ala al-Din Husain Shah (r. 1493–1519) patronized composition by Yasoraj Khan of the *Krishna-Mangala*, now lost. The most famous early poem of the Krishna story was the *uri Krishna-Kirtan*. Composed by Chandi Das, probably in the fifteenth century, this work explores the devious tactics deployed by the lusty young Krishna in winning the love of the cowherdess Radha. Once won, Radha's passionate love for the divine Krishna became the central motif of Bengali devotionalism, or *bhakti*.

The movement crystallized around a single, charismatic personality who appeared in West Bengal early in the sixteenth century—the saint and mystic Chaitanya (d. 1533). Born a Brahman in 1486, Chaitanya began his career studying and teaching at Nadia, then a bastion of Brahmanical learning, but in 1508 he met a devotee of Krishna while on a trip in Bihar, and his life took a decisive turn. Once initiated into the cult, Chaitanya renounced his former life for that of an ecstatic worshiper of Vishnu manifested as Krishna. Upon returning to Bengal he became the center of a group of devotees who established a tradition of devotional worship through enraptured dance and songs (*Kirtan*) praising Krishna. The practice soon became a public one, as Chaitanya and his followers took to parading through the streets of Nadia shouting the name of God in moods of raptured devotion. Although officers of the sultanate placed curbs on the cult's ecstatic excesses when they disturbed the public peace, the true adversaries of the growing neo-Vaishnava movement were neither local Muslims nor the court at Gaur—which actually patronized Vaishnava literature—but Brahman supporters of the cults of Chandi and Manasa. First, in their view, the Vaishnava custom of communal song, the *Kirtan*, not only disturbed the peace but lacked scriptural authority. Second, Chaitanya had identified himself with God ("Gaurhari"). Third, he had usurped from Brahmans their monopoly over the use of mantras, or sacred oral formulae. And finally, his cult was charged with having attracted followers from amongst the lower classes, a point hinting at the social basis of the leading Hindu sects in this period. Since Goddess cults enjoyed broad popular support, the uakta

Brahmans, as patrons of those cults, viewed the lower classes as their own natural constituency, even though they were sometimes ambivalent about extending their support to such cults. Chaitanya's movement thus threatened to cut into their pool of religious clients.

Despite initial Brahman attempts to resist the movement, and later to control it by incorporating it into a broader Brahmanical framework, Vaishnavism managed to carve out and maintain for itself an autonomous identity in the delta's religious landscape. By emphasizing non-Brahman inclusiveness as opposed to high-caste exclusiveness, the practice of devotion rather than ritual, and the use of Bengali rather than Sanskrit, the movement posed a real alternative to the Brahman-supported Shiva movement, with its ties to various Goddess cults. Devotional and hagiographical literature composed in the sixteenth century dramatized the assurance of salvation through love of Krishna and fixed the historical Chaitanya as one who was at least divinely inspired, if not identified with both Krishna and his lover Radha. Even during his lifetime, Chaitanya had been deified by enthusiastic devotees, and by the end of the century, when his name was included among those of the gods praised in the introductory lines of contemporary poems, his divinity seems to have been widely accepted.

Vaishnava piety spread dramatically across Bengali Hindu society. In his idealized image of a Bengali kingdom the poet Mukundaram included Vaishnavas among the city's Brahmans, referring to them as homesteaders who engaged in devotional singing, or as prosperous city-dwellers living amidst beautiful Vishnu temples adorned with golden spires and fluttering flags. This suggests that by the late sixteenth century, while the ecstatic spirit of Chaitanya's devotional movement was still vibrant, the upper castes had already begun to ally themselves with the movement, in the process redefining it along orthodox lines. In subsequent centuries, Vaishnava piety, though originating in cities, would make deep inroads among Bengal's Hindu artisan and cultivating castes. By 1893 James Wise could write, "It may be said with perfect truth that Vaishnavism, in one or another of its diverse forms, to the exclusion of Saivism and all other [Hindu] creeds, is the faith professed by the agricultural, artizan, and fisher tribes of Bengal."

In sum, Hindu society in the sultanate period was dominated by two principal religious orientations—the various Goddess cults and Vaishnava devotionalism—with Brahmans endeavoring to appropriate both. In terms of geographical reach, the Vaishnava movement appears to have been centered in western Bengal, whereas the cults dedicated to the Goddess prevailed throughout the delta, especially in the south and the east, where rebellious Hindu political movements rose up in the name of Chandi. Although the public Uiva cult never recovered from the withdrawal of court patronage that followed the Turkish conquest, its uakta Brahman patrons eventually succeeded in grafting the high god to indigenous cults, and especially to that focusing on the goddess Chandi. Similarly, Vaishnava Brahmans in time managed to check the unrestrained emotionalism of Chaitanya's movement.

It was in the context of these religious currents that Islamic devotionalism became a force in its own right in the Bengal delta. Thus far we have seen Muslims as rulers, soldiers, Sufis, merchants, administrators, or judges. But we have not yet seen them in the role of the ordinary cultivators who came to pervade the modern Bengali countryside. Indeed, Bengali Muslim cultivators would eventually form the basis of one of the largest Muslim communities on earth. This raises the question of Islamization, and the contested issue of conversion to Islam.

FOUR CONVENTIONAL THEORIES OF ISLAMIZATION IN INDIA

Theories purporting to explain the growth of Islam in India may be reduced to four basic modes of reasoning. Each is inadequate. The first of these, which I shall call the Immigration theory, is not really a theory of conversion at all since it views Islamization in terms of the diffusion not of belief but of peoples. In this view, the bulk of India's Muslims are descended from other Muslims who had either migrated overland from the Iranian plateau or sailed across the Arabian Sea. Although some such process no doubt contributed to the Islamization of those areas of South Asia that are geographically contiguous with the Iranian plateau or the Arabian Sea, this argument cannot, for reasons to be discussed below, be used to explain mass Islamization in Bengal.

The oldest theory of Islamization in India, which I shall call the Religion of the Sword thesis, stresses the role of military force in the diffusion of Islam in India and elsewhere. Dating at least from the time of the Crusades, this idea received big boosts during the nineteenth century, the high tide of European imperial domination over Muslim peoples, and subsequently in the context of the worldwide Islamic reform movements of the late twentieth century. Its general tone is captured in the way many nineteenth- and twentieth-century Orientalists explained the rise of Islam in seventh-century Arabia, as illustrated in these lurid lines penned in 1898 by Sir William Muir:

> It was the scent of war that now turned the sullen temper of the Arab tribes into eager loyalty....Warrior after warrior, column after column, whole tribes in endless succession with their women and children, issued forth to fight. And ever, at the marvelous tale of cities conquered; of rapine rich beyond compute; of maidens parted on the very field of battle "to every man a damsel or two"...fresh tribes arose and went. Onward and still onward, like swarms from the hive, or flights of locusts darkening the land,

tribe after tribe issued forth and hastening northward, spread in great masses to the East and to the West.

In the end, though, after the thundering hooves have passed and the dust has settled, in attempting to explain the Arab conquests, Muir leaves us with little of substance. Rather, he simply asserts the Arabs' fondness for the "scent of war," their love of "rapine," and the promise of "a damsel or two." Muir's vision of a militant, resurgent Islam gone berserk reflected, in addition to old European associations of Islam with war and sex, colonial fears that Europe's own Muslim subjects might, in just such a locustlike manner, rise up in revolt and drive the Europeans back to Europe. Sir William, after all, was himself a senior British official in colonial India, as well as an aggressive activist for the Christian missionary movement there.

If colonial officials could imagine that the reason for the rise of Islam was its inherently militant nature, they had little difficulty explaining its extension in India in similar terms. Yet as Peter Hardy has observed, those who argued that Indian Muslims were forcibly converted have generally failed to define either *force* or *conversion,* leaving one to presume that a society can and will alter its religious identity simply because it has a sword at its neck. Precisely how this mechanism worked, either in theoretical or in practical terms, has never, however, been satisfactorily explained. Moreover, proponents of this theory seem to have confused conversion to the Islamic religion with the extension of Turko-Iranian rule in North India between 1200 and 1760, a confusion probably originating in too literal a translation of primary Persian accounts narrating the "Islamic" conquest of India. As Yohanan Friedmann has observed, in these accounts one frequently meets with such ambiguous phrases as "they submitted to Islam", or "they came under submission to Islam", in which "Islam" might mean either the religion, the Muslim state, or the "army of Islam." But a contextual reading of such passages usually favours one of the latter two interpretations, especially as these same sources often refer to Indo-Turkish armies as the *lashkar-i Islam*, or "army of Islam," and not the *lashkar-i Turkan*, or "army of Turks." In other words, it was the Indo-Muslim state, and, more explicitly, its military arm, to which people were said to have submitted, and not the Islamic faith. Nor does the theory fit the religious geography of South Asia. If Islamization had ever been a function of military or political force, one would expect that those areas exposed most intensively and over the longest period to rule by Muslim dynasties—that is, those that were most fully exposed to the "sword"—would today contain the greatest number of Muslims. Yet the opposite is the case, as those regions where the most dramatic Islamization occurred, such as eastern Bengal or western Punjab, lay on the fringes of Indo-Muslim rule, where the "sword" was weakest, and where brute force could have exerted the least influence. In such regions the first accurate census reports put the Muslim population at between 70 and 90 percent of the total, whereas in the heartland of Muslim rule in the upper Gangetic Plain—the domain of the Delhi Fort and the Taj Mahal, where Muslim regimes had ruled the most intensively and for the longest period of time—the Muslim population ranged from only 10 to 15 percent. In other words, in the subcontinent as a whole there is an *inverse* relationship between the degree of Muslim political penetration and the degree of Islamization. Even within Bengal this principle holds true. As the 1901 *Census of India* put it:

> *None of these [eastern] districts contains any of the places famous as the head-quarters of Mohammedan rulers. Dacca was the residence of the Nawab for about a hundred years, but it contains a smaller proportion of Muslims than any of the surrounding districts, except Faridpur. Malda and Murshidabad contain the old capitals, which were the center of Musalman rule for nearly four and a half centuries, and yet the Muslims form a smaller proportion of the population than they do in the adjacent districts of Dinajpur, Rajshahi, and Nadia.*

Indeed, it has even been proposed that, far from promoting the cause of Islamization, the proximity of Muslim political power in some cases actually hindered it. According to S. L. Sharma and R. N. Srivastava, Mughal persecution of the nominally converted Meo community of Rajasthan had the effect, not of strengthening the Meos' Islamic identity, but of reinforcing their resistance to Islam.

A third theory commonly advanced to explain Islamization in India is what I call the Religion of Patronage theory. This is the view that Indians of the premodern period converted to Islam in order to receive some non-religious favour from the ruling class—relief from taxes, promotion in the bureaucracy, and so forth. This theory has always found favour with Western-trained secular social scientists who see any religion as a dependent variable of some non-religious agency, in particular an assumed desire for social improvement or prestige. Many instances in Indian history would appear to support this theory. In the early fourteenth century, Ibn Battuta reported that Indians presented themselves as new converts to the Khalaji sultans, who in turn rewarded them with robes of honour according to their rank. According to nineteenth-century censuses, many landholding families of Upper India had declared themselves Muslims in order to escape imprisonment for nonpayment of revenue, or to keep ancestral lands in the family. The theory might even be stretched to include groups employed by Muslim rulers that assimilated much Islamic culture even if they did not formally convert. The Kayasthas and Khatris of the Gangetic Plain, the Parasnis of Maharashtra, and the Amils of Sind all cultivated Islamic culture while meeting the government's need for clerks and administrative servants, a process that Aziz Ahmad once compared with nineteenth-and twentieth-century "Westernization." The acculturation of captured soldiers or slaves perhaps formed another dimension of this process. Severed from their families, and with no permanent sociocultural ties to their native homes, these men not surprisingly fell into the cultural orbit of their patrons.

Although this thesis might help explain the relatively low incidence of Islamization in India's political heartland, it cannot explain the massive conversions that took place along the political fringe—as in Punjab or Bengal. Political patronage, like the influence of the sword, would have decreased rather than increased as one moved away from the centers of that patronage. What we need is some theory that can explain the phenomenon of mass Islamization on the periphery of Muslim power and not just in the heartland, and among millions of peasant cultivators and not just among urban elites.

To this end a fourth theory, which I call the Religion of Social Liberation thesis, is generally pressed into service. Created by British ethnographers and historians, elaborated by many Pakistani and Bangladeshi nationals, and subscribed to by countless journalists and historians of South Asia, especially Muslims, this theory has for long been the most widely accepted explanation of Islamization in the subcontinent. The theory postulates a Hindu caste system that is unchanging through time and rigidly discriminatory against its own lower orders. For centuries, it is said, the latter suffered under the crushing burden of oppressive and tyrannical high-caste Hindus, especially Brahmans. Then, when Islam "arrived" in the Indian subcontinent, carrying its liberating message of social equality as preached (in most versions of the theory) by Sufi Shaikhs, these same oppressed castes, seeking to escape the yoke of Brahmanic oppression and aware of a social equality hitherto denied them, "converted" to Islam en masse.

It can be seen that by juxtaposing what it perceives as the inherent justice of Islam and the inherent wickedness of Hindu society, the Religion of Social Liberation theory identifies motives for conversion that are, from a Muslim perspective, eminently praiseworthy. The problem, however, is that no evidence can be found in support of the theory. Moreover, it is profoundly illogical. First, by attributing present-day values to peoples of the past, it reads history backward. Before their contact with Muslims, India's lower castes are thought to have possessed, almost as though familiar with the writings of Jean-Jacques Rousseau or Thomas Jefferson, some innate notion of the fundamental equality of all humankind denied them by an oppressive Brahmanic tyranny. In fact, however, in thinking about Islam in relation to Indian religions, premodern Muslim intellectuals did not stress their religion's ideal of social equality as opposed to Hindu inequality, but rather Islamic monotheism as opposed to Hindu polytheism. That is, their frame of reference for comparing these two civilizations was theological, not social. In fact, the idea that Islam fosters social equality (as opposed to religious equality) seems to be a recent notion, dating only from the period of the Enlightenment, and more particularly from the legacy of the French Revolution among nineteenth-century Muslim reformers.

Second, even if Indians *did* believe in the fundamental equality of mankind, and even if Islam *had* been presented to them as an ideology of social equality—though both propositions appear to be false—there is abundant evidence that Indian communities failed, upon Islamization, to improve their status in the social hierarchy. On the contrary, most simply carried into Muslim society the same birth-ascribed rank that they had formerly known in Hindu society. This is especially true of Bengal. As James Wise observed in 1883: "In other parts of India menial work is performed by outcast Hindus; but in Bengal any repulsive or offensive occupation devolves on the Mohammedan. The Beldar [scavenger, and remover of carcasses] is to the Mohammedan village what the Bhuinmali is to the Hindu, and it is not improbable that his ancestors belonged to this vile caste."

Finally, as with the Sword and Patronage theories, the Religion of Social Liberation theory is refuted by the facts of geography. In 1872, when the earliest reliable census was taken, the highest concentrations of Muslims were found in eastern Bengal, western Punjab, the Northwest Frontier region, and Baluchistan. What is striking about those areas is not only that they lay far from the center of Muslim political power but that their indigenous populations had not yet, at the time of their contact with Islam, been fully integrated into either the Hindu or the Buddhist social system. In Bengal, Muslim converts were drawn mainly from Rajbansi, Pod, Chandal, Kuch, and other indigenous groups that had been only lightly exposed to Brahmanic culture, and in Punjab the same was true of the various Jat clans that eventually formed the bulk of the Muslim community.

But this is hardly surprising. The *Baudhayana-Dharmasutra*, a late Vedic text (fifth-sixth centuries B.C.) reflecting the values of self-styled "clean" castes, divided the subcontinent into three concentric circles, each one containing distinct sociocultural communities. The first of these, Aryavarta, or the Aryan homeland, corresponded to the Upper Ganges-Jumna region of north-central India; there lived the "purest" heirs to Brahmanic tradition, people styling themselves highborn and ritually clean. The second circle contained an outer belt (Avanti, Anga-Magadha, Saurastra, Daksinapatha, Upavrt, and Sindhu-Sauvira) corresponding to Malwa, East and Central Bihar, Gujarat, the Deccan, and Sind. These regions lay within the pale of Indo-Aryan settlement, but they were inhabited by people "of mixed origin" who did not enjoy the same degree of ritual purity as those of the first region. And the third concentric circle contained those outer regions inhabited by "unclean" tribes considered so far beyond the pale that penances were prescribed for those who visited such places. Peoples living in this third circle included the Arattas of Punjab, the Sauviras of southern Punjab and Sind, the Pundras of North Bengal, and the Vangas of central and East Bengal.

Now, the theory of Social Liberation assumes the prior existence of a highly stratified Hindu social order presided over by an entrenched and oppressive Brahman community. If the theory were valid, then, the greatest incidence of conversion to Islam should logically have occurred in those areas where Brahmanic social order was most deeply entrenched—namely, in the core region of Aryavarta. Conversely, Islam should have foundits fewest adherents in those areas having the least exposure to Brahmanic civilization, that is, along the periphery or beyond the pale of that civilization, in the outermost of the three concentric circles cited in the *Baudhayana-Dharmasutra*. But it is precisely in that outer circle—the area roughly coinciding with the areas included in the original (1947) state of Pakistan, with its eastern and western wings—that the vast majority of South Asian Muslims reside. The modern, pre-Partition distribution of South Asian Muslims thus indicates an outcome precisely opposite to the one predicted by the theory—namely, the less the prior exposure to Brahmanic civilization, the greater the incidence of subsequent Islamization. If the aboriginal peoples inhabiting India's "periphery" had never been fully absorbed in a Brahman-ordered society in the first place, the matter of their escaping an oppressive Hindu social order cannot arise logically, just as it did not arise empirically.

THE INTERACTION OF ISLAM AND HINDUISM

AN Aspect of the cultural life of Islamic India that demands special consideration is the nature of the interaction of faith and practice that took place between Islam and Hinduism. There are, however, a variety of factors involved that make the study of this interaction exceedingly complex and prevent any very assured conclusions being attained. One is simply the lack of evidence, for the religious movements of medieval India have left few records. Then there is the uncertainty at times whether a pattern of behavior and belief in both religions has a common origin in one, or if it grew up independently in both cultures. The intricate question of the relation of Hindu and Islamic mystical movements is an example of this difficulty. Finally, since one is confronted not just with the problem of identifying Islamic influence on Hinduism but also Hindu influences on

Islam, it is clear that the process of interaction may be complicated by a double movement. Original Hindu influences, for example, may have passed over into Islam; the movement or process that resulted from this may then in turn influence Hinduism, causing a rather different phenomenon. Mysticism again provides a possible illustration.

The most obvious result of the religious impact of Islam on Hinduism is, of course, the existence of a large Muslim population in India. The view that Islam propagated itself in India through the sword cannot be maintained; aside from other evidence, the very distribution of the Muslim population does not support it. If the spread of Islam had been due to the might of the Muslim kings, one would expect the largest proportion of Muslims in those areas which were the centers of Muslim political power. This, however, is not the case.

The percentage of Muslims is low around Delhi, Lucknow, Ahmadabad, Ahmadnagar, and Bijapur, the principal seats of Muslim political power. Even in the case of Mysore, where Sultan Tipu is said to have forced conversion to Islam, the ineffectiveness of royal proselytism may be measured by the fact that Muslims are scarcely 5 percent of the total population of the state. On the other hand, Islam was never a political power in Malabar, yet today Muslims form nearly 30 percent of its total population. In the two areas in which the concentration of Muslims is heaviest—modern East and West Pakistan—there is fairly clear evidence that conversion was the work of Sufis, mystics who migrated to India throughout the period of the sultanate.

In the western area the process was facilitated in the thirteenth century by the thousands of Muslim theologians, saints, and missionaries who fled to India to escape the Mongol terror. The names and careers of some of these are well known. Thus Pir Shams Tabriz came to Multan; Khwaja Qutb-ud-din Bakhtiyar went to Delhi; and Syed Jalal settled in Uch, the great fortress south of Multan. The influence of such men, and of many others, can be traced through the families of their spiritual descendants.

In Bengal, the Muslim missionaries found the greatest response to their message among the outcastes and the depressed classes, of which there were large numbers in Bengal. To them, the creed of Islam, with its emphasis on equality, must have come as a liberating force. Then too, the acceptance of the religion of the conquerors would have been a powerful attraction, since it would undoubtedly carry with it possibilities of advancement they had never known before. Another factor in the large number of conversions is the somewhat peculiar religious history of Bengal. From the eighth to the twelfth century the Pala dynasty had supported Buddhism. Then in the twelfth century the Sena dynasty, which had its roots in South India, began to encourage Hindu orthodoxy. The result was probably a good deal of religious unrest and uncertainty, which made it possible for Islam to find an opening for its work of proselytization. When the Islamic missionaries arrived they found in several instances that the conquering armies had destroyed both the temples of revived Hinduism and the monasteries of the older Buddhism; in their place—often on the same sites—they built new shrines. Moreover, they very frequently transferred ancient Hindu and Buddhist stories of miracles to Muslim saints, fusing the old religion into the new on a level that could be accepted by the masses.

By the end of the fourteenth century Islam had permeated all parts of India, and the process was fully under way which led to the conversion of a large section of the Indian population to Islam, and resulted in far-reaching cultural and spiritual changes outside the Muslim society. The developments in the cultural sphere—development of regional languages, the rise of Hindustani, and the evolution of Indo-Muslim music and architecture—have been outlined in the preceding chapter; here an attempt will be made to examine those religious movements which seem to owe something to the interaction of Hinduism and Islam.

The process of interaction is undeniably obscure, and knowledge of many vital links is lacking, but what is certain is that the period was of great importance for the development of the religious and cultural traditions of modern India. The fifteenth century, it has been observed, "was marked by an extraordinary outburst of devotional poetry inspired by these religious movements, and this stands out as one of the great formative periods in the history of northern India, a period in which on the one hand the modern languages were firmly established as vehicles of literary expression, and on the other the faith of the people was permeated by new ideas."

The religious schools and movements which arose in the fifteenth and sixteenth centuries are generally characterized as variants of bhakti, or devotional religion, and the influence of Islam has been seen as a determining factor. This understanding of the movements is, however, an oversimplification of a very complex phenomenon. It is important to remember, first of all, that many of the elements associated with the religious movements at the end of the sultanate had already been dominant in Hinduism itself for many centuries. This is especially true of those areas of South India where Muslim influence had not been strong. It is also quite possible that the Islamic mystics, the Sufis, had been directly or indirectly influenced by Hindu thought and institutions before the conquest of India. Hinduism in the fifteenth century, then, was receiving in an elaborated form what it had already given to Islam. But of even greater importance in examining the religious movements of the fourteenth and fifteenth centuries is an awareness of two very different attitudes which Hindu religious leaders had toward Islam. One group accepted what was congenial to it in the new spiritual system; the other group adopted a few elements from the spiritual structure of the dominant race in order to strengthen Hinduism and make it better able to withstand Islam. Both reacted to Islam, but one was sympathetic while the other was hostile. The two trends are similar to the growth of the tolerant, cosmopolitan Brahmo Samaj and the militant Arya Samaj, when Hinduism was confronted with Christianity in the nineteenth century. Kabir, Guru Nanak, Dadu, and other founders of syncretic sects are included in the first group, while the movement in Bengal, associated with Chaitanya, mirrors the latter tendency.

RELIGIOUS LEADERS

One of the earliest of the religious leaders, and probably the most influential, was Kabir. His dates are uncertain, some scholars giving his birth date as 1398, and some as late as 1440, but it is generally agreed that he flourished in the middle of the fifteenth century. There has also been much controversy concerning his religious origins, but it is quite certain that he was born into a Muslim family. The names of Kabir and Kamal, his son, are both Islamic. According to the popular *Tazkirah-i-Auliya-i-Hind* (Lives of Muslim Saints), he was a disciple of the Muslim Sufi, Shaikh Taqi. A further indication of his Muslim origin is that his grave at Maghar has always been in the keeping of Muslims. But Kabir was above all a religious radical who denounced with equal zest the narrowness of Islamic and Hindu sectarianism. According to one tradition he was a disciple of Ramananda, the great mystic who is credited with the spread of bhakti doctrines in North India. That Ramananda himself was influenced by Islam is not certain, but his willingness to admit men of all castes, including Islam, as his disciples, suggests the possibility of this. The right conclusion seems to be that Kabir was a Muslim Sufi who, having come under Ramananda's influence, accepted some Hindu ideas and tried to reconcile Hinduism and Islam. However it was the Hindus, and particularly those of the lower classes, to whom his message appealed.

With many of his works not available for study, and serious doubts existing about the genuineness of others, it is difficult to assess Kabir properly, but there is no difference of opinion about the general tenor of his writings. He often uses Hindu religious nomenclature, and is equally at home in Hindu and Muslim religious thought, but there is no doubt that one of the most salient features of his teachings is denunciation of polytheism, idolatry, and caste. But he is equally unsparing in his condemnation of Muslim formalism, and he made no distinction between what was sane and holy in the teachings of Hinduism and Islam. He was a true seeker after God, and did his best to break the barriers that separated Hindus from Muslims. What has appealed to the millions of his followers through the ages, however, is his passionate conviction that he had found the pathway to God, a pathway accessible to the lowest as well as the highest. That he has in the course of time become a saint of the Hindus rather than of the Muslims is a reflection of the temper of Hinduism, which finds it easier than Islam to bring new sects and doctrines within its spiritual hegemony.

The second great religious leader whose work shows undoubted Islamic influence is Guru Nanak (1469–1539). The Sikh religion, of which Nanak was the founder, is noted for its militant opposition to Islam, but this is largely a product of historical circumstances in the seventeenth century. Nanak's own aim was to unite both Hindu and Muslim through an appeal to what he considered the great central truths of both. He acknowledged Kabir as his spiritual teacher, and their teachings are very similar. His debt to Islam is shown in his rigorous insistence on the will and majesty of God, while the underlying structure of his thought, with its tendency to postulate a unity that comprehends all things, suggests his Hindu inheritance. Accompanied by two companions, one a Muslim and the other a Hindu, he wandered throughout North India and, according to some accounts, to Arabia, preaching his simple gospel. The followers he gained became, in the course of a century, a separate religious community, but the Sikh scriptures, of which Nanak's sayings provide the core, are a reminder of the attempt to bridge the gap between Hinduism and Islam.

Dadu (1544–1603) was the third of the religious leaders through whose teachings Islamic ideas found wide currency among non-Muslims. While he does not belong chronologically in a survey of the early interaction of Hinduism and Islam, since he lived into the seventeenth century, his membership in a Kabir sect makes a brief consideration of his career useful. Furthermore, his biography shows the same process at work that is seen in the accounts of the life of Kabir. Dadu is stated by his later followers to have been the son of a Nagar Brahman, but recent researches have shown that he was born in a family of Muslim cotton-carders. This is borne out by his own works and the fact that all the members of his family have Muslim names: his father's name was Lodi, his mother's, Basiran; his sons were Garib and Miskin and his grandson, Faqir. His teacher was Shaikh Budhan, a Muslim saint of the Qadri order. The early Hindu followers of Dadu were not disturbed by the knowledge that he was a Muslim by birth, but later ones were. The legend of his Brahmanical origin made its first appearance in a commentary on the *Bhaktamala*, written as late as 1800. It is said that until recent times documents existed at the monasteries of the followers of Dadu which suggested that he had been a Muslim, but that these were destroyed by the keepers who were unwilling to admit that his origins were not Hindu.

The metamorphosis which the life story and teachings of Kabir and Dadu have undergone is not merely the work of those who were anxious to secure for their heroes high lineage and a link with Hinduism; it is symptomatic of the general movement of separation that became common in both Islam and Hinduism in later centuies. As the Muslims grew more orthodox, they turned away from men such as Kabir and Dadu, while the Hindus accepted them as saints, but forgot their Islamic origins. In order to conform to the requirements of the Hindu bhakti tradition, they have undergone a transformation that at times necessitates a falsification of history. Two poet-saints who are clearly in the Hindu Bhakti tradition but show traces of Islamic influence are Namadeva and Tukaram, the great religious figures of the Maratha country. Namadeva, who lived in the late fourteenth or early fifteenth century, used a number of Persian and Arabic words, suggesting that even at this early time the influence of Islam was felt by a man, in a remote area of the country, whose only concern seems to have been with religion. The writings of Tukaram (1598–1649), the greatest of the Marathi poets, contain many obvious references to Islam, such as the following:

First among the great names is Allah, never forget to respect it.

Allah is verily one, the prophet is verily one.

There Thou art one, there Thou art one, There Thou art one, O friend.

There is neither I nor thou.

In general the attitude of the Marathas to Muslim saints was one of respect, the most vivid example of this being the great faith Shivaji's grandfather had in Shah Sharif of Ahmadnagar. In honour of the saint he gave his sons the names of Shahji and Sharifji. While a full study of the religious and social ferment of Maharashtra in the fifteenth and sixteenth centuries has yet to be made; it seems certain that the new religious life did not take the form of a Hindu revivalism that emphasized the separation of the Hindus from Islam. Antagonism toward Muslims came later, and, as was the case with the Sikhs, had definite antecedents in particular historical events.

The creative spiritual and literary movement provided the basis on which the Maratha nation could be built, and its emergence as the great antagonist of Muslim power in India was based on political, not religious, factors. The evidence from the songs of Namadeva and Tukaram strongly suggests that they were not reacting in any hostile fashion to Islam. For this reaction one must look to Chaitanya and the Vaishnavite movement in Bengal.

Chaitanya (1485–1533) of Bengal represents an aspect of the Bhakti movement that is very different from that seen in the lives and teachings of Kabir and his successors. Chaitanya's concern, unlike that of Kabir, was not with bringing people to an understanding of a God beyond all creeds and formulations; it was to exalt the superiority of Krishna over all other deities. It was, in other words, a revivalist, not a syncretic, movement, a return to a worship of Vishnu under one of his most appealing forms, the loving ecstatic Krishna. The attitude of Bengal Vaishnavites toward Islam was the antithesis of the attitude advocated by Kabir and Nanak. Conscious of the appeal being made by Islam, they did not try to reform Hinduism by adopting any of the attractive features of the rival faith. Instead, they emphasized precisely those features, such as devotion to Krishna, which were most antipathetic to the Islamic spirit. Another difference between Chaitanya's movement and that of Kabir is the attitude toward caste. While it is true that Chaitanya made disciples from all classes, one does not find the same note of condemnation of caste as one does in Kabir. According to some students of the period, this indicates the essential difference between the two aspects of Bhakti in the fifteenth and sixteenth centuries: only where Hinduism was directly influenced by Islam was there evidence of concern for social inequities.

Because of the interest that is attached to such great names as that of Kabir, there is a tendency to think of the movement of interaction between the two faiths as mainly from Islam to Hinduism. This was not true, however, for Muslim society was deeply influenced by its contacts with Hinduism. Some contacts had been made even before Islamic rule was established in India; for example the probable Hindu element in certain forms of Islamic mysticism, and the intellectual interchanges that had taken place after the conquest of Sind in the seventh and eighth centuries. During the sultanate, changes of a quite different order were apparent.

One of these concerns the lives of converts to Islam. Here the important point to keep in mind is that when one sees Hindu practices followed by Indian Muslims, it is not a case of Hindu influence, but simply of incomplete change from the old way of life. Indian Muslims did not start with orthodox Islam, but began by accepting a few basic features, and only in the course of time, particularly during the last two centuries, have they become more orthodox. The process is less complete in the lower classes, or those groups which, like the Khojas, adopted a somewhat composite form of religion. More than religious beliefs, Indian Islam retained certain characteristic features of Hindu society which, if not religious in themselves, certainly had been given religious sanction. One of these was the place given to caste, with converts clinging to some memory of their former status in a hierarchical society, while what may be called Muslim castes developed as Indian Muslims classified themselves as Sayyid, Shaikh, Mughal, or Pathan. This structure was never very rigid; as Bernier commented, anyone who put on a white turban called himself a Mughal. An old saying makes the same point: "Last year I was a Julaha (weaver); this year a Shaikh; and next year if the harvest be good, I shall be a Sayyid." And in the mosque the Islamic ideals of brotherhood and equality remained triumphant.

HINDU PRACTICE AND MARRIAGE

Muslims in India also adopted the Hindu practices of early marriages and of objection to widow remarriage. Some social ceremonies connected with births, deaths, and marriages may also be traced to Hindu origin. Some writers think that reverence for pirs, or saints, and their graves, a marked feature of popular Indian Islam, is a carry-over of Hindu practices. This interpretation overlooks the fact, however, that even outside India pirs and their tombs are objects of great attention and veneration.

The main influence of Hinduism on Islam, however, is probably seen not so much in these specific instances as in a general softening of the original attitude of the conquerors, particularly the Turks, in religious matters. This softening is to be seen partly as a movement of Hindu attitudes toward the universe into Islamic thought; it is also partly a recognition of the position of Islam in India. More striking than the amount of interaction that took place in the first three centuries of Muslim rule was the fact that there was not more. The impression one gains is that there was never a very conscious attempt to create understanding, except on the part of Kabir and Nanak, and that the contacts between the two great religions were, on the whole, remarkably superficial as far as the total life of the country was concerned. Writing in 1030, before the full tide of conquest had begun, Al-Biruni spoke of how the Hindus differed from the Muslims in every respect, and, because of the raids by Mahmud of Ghazni, "cherish the most inveterate aversion toward all Muslims." Nearly three centuries later another traveller, Ibn Battuta, remarked that Hindus and Muslims lived in entirely separate communities. For Hindus, there could be no intermarriage with Muslims nor even interdining. "It is the custom among the heathen of the Malabar country," he remarked, "that no Muslim should enter their houses or use their vessels for eating purposes. If a Muslim is fed out of their vessels, they either break the vessels or give them away to the Muslims."

THE RISE OF EARLY MEDIEVAL HINDU CULTURE

Even while Indo-Buddhist civilization expanded and flourished overseas, however, Buddhist institutions were steadily declining in eastern India. Since Buddhists there had left life-cycle rites in the hands of Brahman priests, Buddhist monastic establishments, so central for the religion's institutional survival, became disconnected from the laity and fatally dependent on court patronage for their support. To be sure, some Bengali dynasties continued to patronize Buddhist institutions almost to the time of the Muslim conquest. But from as early as the seventh century,

Brahmanism, already the more vital tradition at the popular level, enjoyed increasing court patronage at the expense of Buddhist institutions. By the eleventh century even the Palas, earlier such enthusiastic patrons of Buddhism, had begun favoring the cults of two gods that had emerged as the most important in the newly reformed Brahmanical religion—Œiva and Vishnu. These trends are seen most clearly in the later Bengali dynasties—the Varmans (ca. 1075–1150) and especially the Senas (ca. 1097–1223), who dominated all of Bengal at the time of the Muslim conquest. The kings of the Sena dynasty were descended from a warrior caste that had migrated in the eleventh century from South India (Karnataka) to the Bhagirathi-Hooghly region, where they took up service under the Palas. As Pala power declined, eventually evaporating early in the twelfth century, the Senas first declared their independence from their former overlords, then consolidated their base in the Bhagirathi-Hooghly area, and finally moved into the eastern hinterland, where they dislodged the Varmans from their capital at Vikrampur. Moreover, since the Senas had brought from the south a fierce devotion to Hindu culture (especially Œaivism), their victorious arms were accompanied everywhere in Bengal by the establishment of royally sponsored Hindu cults. As a result, by the end of the eleventh century, the epicenter of civilization and power in eastern India had shifted from Bihar to Bengal, while royal patronage had shifted from a primarily Buddhist to a primarily Hindu orientation. These shifts are especially evident in the artistic record of the period.

Behind these political developments worked deeper religious changes, occurring throughout India, that served to structure the Hindu religion as it evolved in medieval times and to distinguish it from its Vedic and Brahmanical antecedents. As Ronald Inden has argued, the ancient Vedic sacrificial cult (ca. 1000–ca. 300 B.C.) experienced two major historical transformations. The first occurred in the third century B.C., when the Mauryan emperor Ashoka established Buddhism as his imperial religion. At that time the Vedic sacrifice, which was perceived by Buddhists as violent and selfish, was replaced by gift-giving (*dana*) in the form either of offerings to Buddhist monks by the laity or of gifts of land bestowed on Buddhist institutions by Buddhist rulers. In response to these developments, Brahman priests began reorienting their own professional activities from performing bloody animal sacrifices to conducting domestic life-cycle rites for non-Brahman householders. At the same time, they too became recipients of gifts in the form of land donated by householders or local elites, as began occurring in Bengal from the fifth century A.D. This first transformation of the Vedic sacrifice did not, however, cause a rupture between Buddhism and Brahmanism. In fact, the two religions coexisted quite comfortably, the former operating at the imperial center, the latter at the regional periphery.

The second transformation of the Vedic sacrifice occurred in the seventh and eighth centuries, when chieftains and rulers began building separate shrines for the images of deities. The regenerative cosmic sacrifice of Vedic religion, which Buddhists had already transformed into rites of gift-giving to monks, was now transformed into a new ceremony, that of the "Great Gift" (*mahadana*), which consisted of a king's honoring a patron god by installing an image of him in a monumental temple. These ideas crystallized toward the end of the eighth century, when, except for the Buddhist Palas, the major dynasties vying for supremacy over all of India—the Pratiharas of the north, the Rashtrakutas of the Deccan, and the Pandyas and Pallavas of the south—all established centralized state cults focusing on Hindu image worship. Instead of worshiping Vedic gods in a general or collective sense, each dynasty now patronized a single deity (usually Vishnu or œiva), understood as that dynasty's cosmic overlord, whose earthly representative was the gift-giving king. These conceptions were physically expressed in monumental and elaborately carved temples that, like Buddhist stupas, were conceptually descended from the Vedic sacrificial fire altar. Brahmans, meanwhile, evolved into something much grander than domestic priests who merely tended to the life-cycle rituals of their non-Brahman patrons. Now, in addition to performing such services, they became integrated into the ritual life of Hindu courts, where they officiated at the kings' "Great Gift" and other state rituals.

Copper-plate inscriptions issued from the tenth through the twelfth centuries show how these ideas penetrated the courts of Bengal. Detailed lists of state officers found in inscriptions of the major dynasties of the post-tenth-century period—Pala, Chandra, Varman, and Sena—all show an elaboration of centralized state systems, increasing social stratification, and bureaucratic specialization. Moreover, donations in land became at this time a purely royal prerogative, while the donations themselves (at least those in the northern and western delta) consisted of plots of agricultural land whose monetary yields were known and specified, indicating a rather thorough peasantization of society. And, except in the case of Samatata, recipients of these grants were Brahmans who received land not only for performing domestic rituals, as had been the case in earlier periods, but for performing courtly rituals. Indeed, the granting of land to Brahmans who officiated at court rituals had become a kingly duty, a necessary component of the state's ideological legitimacy.

In these centuries, then, the ideology of medieval Hindu kingship became fully elaborated in the delta. The earliest Sena kings, it is true, had justified their establishment of power in terms of their victorious conquests, and in this respect they differed little from their own conquerors, the Turks of the early Delhi sultanate. Yet the Senas' political theory was based on a religious cosmology fundamentally different from that of their Muslim conquerors. In the Islamic conception, the line separating the human and superhuman domains was stark and unbridgeable; neither humans nor superhumans freely moved or could move from one domain to the other. In the Sena conception, however, as in medieval Hindu thought generally, the line between human and superhuman was indistinct. Since it was the king's performance of royally sponsored rituals that served to uphold *dharma*—that is, cosmic, natural, and human order as understood in classical Indian thought—movement between the two domains could be actuated by the intervention of the king's ritual behavior. "He was never tired of offering sacrifices," one inscription boasts of Vijaya Sena (ca. 1095–1158), and through his power Dharma [*dharma*], though she had become one-legged in the course of time, could move about on the earth, quickly taking the help of the rows of sacrificial pillars. That sacrificer [the king] calling down the immortals from the slopes of [the cosmic mountain] Meru full of the enemies killed by himself, brought about an interchange of the inhabitants of heaven and earth. (For) by (the construction of) lofty "houses of gods" (i.e. temples) and by (the excavation of) extensive lakes the areas of both heaven and earth were reduced and thus they were made similar to one another.

By ritually bringing about "an interchange of the inhabitants of heaven and earth," the king symbolically erased the distinction between the human and superhuman domains. Like Hindu kings elsewhere in eleventh-and twelfth-century India, the Senas projected their vision of the cosmos and their own proper place in it through the medium of architecture, specifically the monumental royal temple. By replicating cosmic order in the medium of stone monuments, in which they placed an image of their patron overlord, and by placing themselves and their temples at the center of the earthly stage, these kings mimicked the manner in which their patron overlord presided over cosmic order. Thus Vijaya Sena proclaimed:

[The king] built a lofty edifice of Pradyumnevara, the wings, and plinth and the main structure of which occupied the several quarters, and the middle and the uppermost parts stretched over the great oceanlike space—(it is) the midday mountain of the rising and setting Sun who touches the Eastern and Western mountains, the supporting pillar of the house which is the three worlds and the one that remains of the mountains.... If the creator would make a jar, turning on the wheel of the earth Sumeru like a lump of clay, then that would be an object with which could be compared the golden jar placed by him (i.e., the king) on (the top of) this (temple).

The Sena kings also expressed their kingly authority by performing the "Great Gift" ceremony in honour of their patron overlord, who under the last pre-conquest king, Lakshmana Sena, was Vishnu. Although this great god was the ritualized recipient of the "Great Gift," its effective recipients were officiating Brahman priests.

THE DIFFUSION OF BENGALI HINDU CIVILIZATION

By the time of the Muslim conquest, then, the official cult of a cosmic overlord, monumental state temples, and royally patronized Brahman priests had all emerged as central components of the Senas' religious and political ideology. It was not the case, however, that by that time early Indo-Aryan civilization and its later Hindu offshoot had penetrated all quarters of the Bengal delta evenly. Rather, the evidence indicates that Bengal's northwestern and western subregions were far more deeply influenced by Indo-Aryan and Hindu civilization than was the eastern delta, which remained relatively less peasantized and less Hinduized. This is seen, for example, in pre-thirteenth-century land use and settlement patterns. A seventh-century grant of land on the far eastern edge of the delta, in modern Sylhet, describes the donated territory as lying "outside the pale of human habitation, where there is no distinction between natural and artificial; infested by wild animals and poisonous reptiles, and covered with forest out-growths." In such regions, grants of uncultivated land were typically made in favour of groups of Brahmans or to Buddhist monasteries with a view to colonizing the land and bringing it into cultivation. One plate issued by a tenth-century Chandra king granted an enormous area of some one thousand square miles in Sylhet to the residents of eight monasteries; it also settled about six thousand Brahmans on the land.

But in the west the situation was different. In the Bhagirathi-Hooghly region, most land grants were made to individual Brahmans and were typically small in size. After the ninth century, royal donations in this area aimed not at pioneering new settlements but at supporting Brahmans on lands already brought under the plow. These grants typically gave detailed measurements of arable fields, specified their revenue yields, and instructed villagers to pay their taxes in cash and kind to the donees. Such terms and conditions point to a far greater intensity of rice cultivation, a higher degree of peasantization, and a greater population density in the Bhagirathi-Hooghly region than was the case in the relatively remote and more forested eastern delta.

There are several reasons for the greater penetration of Indo-Aryan culture in the western delta than in the east. One has to do with persistent facts of climate. Moving down the Gangetic Plain, the monsoon rainfall increases as the delta is approached, and within the delta it continues to increase as one crosses to its eastern side. The Bhagirathi-Hooghly region, comprising most of today's West Bengal, gets about fifty-five inches of rain annually, whereas central and eastern Bengal get between sixty and ninety-five inches, with the mouth of the Meghna receiving from one hundred to one hundred and twenty and eastern Sylhet about one hundred and fifty inches. If this climatic pattern held in ancient times, the density of vegetation in the deltaic hinterland, formerly covered with thick forests, mainly of *ual* (*Shorea robusta*), would have increased as one moved eastward. Cutting it would have required much more labour and organization, even with the aid of iron implements, than in the less densely forested westerly regions.

Also at work here were patterns of Brahman immigration to and within Bengal. West Bengal was geographically contiguous to the upper and middle Gangetic zone, long established as the heartland of Indo-Aryan civilization. Hence, when from the ninth century an increasing number of scholarly and ritually pure Brahmans migrated from this area into Bengal, most received fertile lands in the western delta. On the other hand recipients of lands further to the east, in the modern Comilla and Chittagong area, tended to be local Brahmans or migrants from neighboring parts of the delta. This suggests an eastward-sloping gradient of ritual status, with higher rank associated with the north and west, and lower rank with the less-settled east.

Finally, the different degree of Aryanization in the eastern and western delta was related to ancient Bengal's sacred geography, and in particular to the association of the Ganges River with Brahmanically defined ritual purity. This river was already endowed with great sanctity when Indo-Aryans entered the delta, and for centuries thereafter Hindus made pilgrimage sites of towns along its banks in western Bengal—for example, Navadwip, Katwa, Tribeni, Kalighat, and Ganga Sagar. With reference to the eastern delta, on the other hand, the geographer S. C. Majumdar notes that "no such sanctity attaches to the Padma below the Bhagirathi offtake nor is there any place of pilgrimage on her banks." This was because from prehistoric times through the main period of Brahman settlement in the delta, the principal channel of the Ganges flowed down the delta's westernmost corridor through what is now the Bhagirathi-Hooghly channel. It did not divert eastward into the Padma until the sixteenth century, long after the Turkish conquest. As a result, the river's sanctity lingered on in West Bengal—even today the Bhagirathi-Hooghly River is sometimes called the Adi-Ganga, or "original Ganges"—while the eastern two-thirds of the delta, cut off from the Ganges during the formative period of Bengal's encounter with Indo-Aryan civilization, remained symbolically disconnected from Upper India, the heartland of Indo-Aryan sanctity and mythology.

By the thirteenth century, then, most of Bengal west of the Karatoya and along the Bhagirathi-Hooghly plain had become settled by an agrarian population well integrated with the Hindu social and political values espoused by the Sena royal house. There, too, indigenous tribes had become rather well assimilated into a Brahman-ordered social hierarchy. But in the vast stretches of the central, eastern, and northeastern delta, the diffusion of Indo-Aryan civilization was far less advanced. In the Dhaka area, the city of Vikrampur, though an important administrative center, from which nearly all of Bengal's copper-plate inscriptions were issued in the tenth through twelfth centuries, shrank before its neighbors to the west in both size and sacredness. And in the extreme southeast, the impressive urban complex at Lalmai-Mainamati, with its distinctive artistic tradition, its extensive history of Buddhist patronage, and its cash-nexus economy, appears somewhat disconnected from the Gangetic culture to the west, looking outward to wider Indian Ocean commercial networks.

In sum, although the eastern delta had certainly begun to be peasantized, especially along the valleys of the larger river systems, such as at Vikrampur and Lalmai, the process had not advanced there to the extent that it had in the west and northwest of Bengal. East of the Karatoya and south of the Padma lay a forested and marshy hinterland, inhabited mainly by non-Aryan tribes not yet integrated into the agrarian system that had already revolutionized Magadha and most of western Bengal. As a result, in 1204, when Mohammad Bakhtiyar's Turkish cavalry captured the western Sena city of Nudiya, it was to this eastern hinterland that King Lakshmana Sena and his retainers fled. It was also in this region that subsequent generations of pioneers would concentrate their energies as Bengal's economic and cultural frontiers continued to migrate eastward.

THE ARTICULATION OF POLITICAL AUTHORITY

The world is a garden, whose gardener is the state. We arrived before the Sultan. He was seated on a large gilt sofa covered with different-sized cushions, all of which were embedded with a smattering of precious stones and small pearls. We greeted him according to the custom of the country—hands crossed on our chests and heads as low as possible.

It is more challenging, however, to reconstruct the changing meaning of that authority, both to the rulers and to the subject population. All political behavior derives its meaning through the prism of culture. Equally, invocations of political symbols most effectively confer authority on rulers when they and their subjects share a common political culture. But what happened in the cases of "conquest dynasties," as in Bengal, where the conquering class was of a culture fundamentally different from that of the subject population? How did rulers in such circumstances remain in effective control without resorting to the indefinite and prohibitively costly use of coercive force? To raise these questions is to suggest that the political frontier in Bengal may be understood not only as a moving line of garrisons, mint towns, and architectural monuments. Also involved was the more subtle matter of accommodation, or the lack of it, between a ruling class and a subject population that, as of 1204, adhered to fundamentally different notions of legitimate political authority. The transformation of these concepts of legitimacy over time—their divergence from or convergence with one another—constitutes a political frontier far less tangible than a military picket line, but one ultimately more vital to understanding the dynamics of Bengal's premodern history.

REFERENCES

Bernard, Jessie: *Social Problems at Midcentury: Role, Status and Stress in a Context of Abundance,* New York: Holt, Rinehart and Winston, 1957.

Stein, Burton : *Peasant State and Society in Medieval South India*, Oxford University Press, Delhi, 1980.

Duboi, Abbe: *Hindu Manners, Customs and Ceremonies*, Fifth Indian Impression, CUP, 1985.

Sunder, Prem : *Caste Class and Society : Then and Now*, Educational Pub, Delhi, 2010.

Chapter **6**

Economic and Social Developments under the Mughals

It was the normal policy of the Timurid rulers, both in their original Central Asian homelands and in India, to encourage trade. As in much else, Sher Shah Suri during his brief reign (1538–1545) set a pattern that was followed by the later Mughals, especially Akbar, when he encouraged trade by linking together various parts of the country through an efficient system of roads and abolishing many inland tolls and duties. The Mughals maintained this general policy, but their rule was distinguished by the importance which foreign trade attained by the end of the sixteenth century. This was partly the result of the discovery of the new sea-route to India; but even so, progress would have been limited if conditions within the country had not been favourable.

TRADE, INDUSTRY AND MANUFACTURE UNDER MUGHALS

Both Akbar and Jahangir interested themselves in the foreign seaborne trade, and Akbar himself took part in commercial activities for a time. The Mughals welcomed the foreign trader, provided ample protection and security for his transactions, and levied a very low custom duty (usually no more than 2½ percent ad valorem). Furthermore, the expansion of local handicrafts and industry resulted in a reservoir of exportable goods. Indian exports consisted mainly of manufactured articles, with cotton cloth in great demand in Europe and elsewhere. Indigo, saltpeter, spices, opium, sugar, woolen and silk cloth of various kinds, yarn, asafoetida, salt, beads, borax, turmeric, lac, sealing wax, and drugs of various kinds, were also exported. The principal imports were bullion, horses, and a certain quantity of luxury goods for the upper classes, like raw silk, coral, amber, precious stones, superior textiles (silk, velvet, brocade, broadcloth), perfumes, drugs, china goods, and European wines. By and large, however, in return for their goods Indian merchants insisted on payment in gold or silver. Naturally this was not popular in England and the rest of Europe, and writers on economic affairs in the seventeenth century frequently complained, as did Sir Thomas Roe, that "Europe bleedeth to enrich Asia." The demand for articles supplied by India was so great, however, and her requirements of European goods so limited, that Europe was obliged to trade on India's own terms until the eighteenth century, when special measures were taken in England and elsewhere to discourage the demand for Indian goods.

The manufacture of cotton goods had assumed such extensive proportions that in addition to satisfying her own needs, India sent cloth to almost half the world: the east coast of Africa, Arabia, Egypt, Southeast Asia, as well as Europe. The textile industry, well established in Akbar's day, continued to flourish under his successors, and soon the operations of Dutch and English traders brought India into direct touch with Western markets. This resulted in great demand for Indian cotton goods from Europe, which naturally increased production at home. Even the silk industry—especially in Bengal—was in flourishing condition. Bernier wrote: "There is in Bengal such a quantity of cotton and silk, that the kingdom may be called the common storehouse for these two kinds of merchandise, not of Hindoustan or the Empire of the Great Mogul only, but of all the neighbouring kingdoms, and even of Europe."

Apart from silk and cotton textiles, other industries were shawl and carpet weaving, woollen goods, pottery, leather goods, and articles made of wood. Owing to its proximity to sources of suitable timbers, Chittagong specialized in shipbuilding, and at one time supplied ships to distant Istanbul. The commercial side of the industry was in the hands of middlemen, but the Mughal government, like the earlier sultans, made its own contribution. The emperor controlled a large number of royal workshops, busily turning out articles for his own use, for his household, for the court, and for the imperial army. Akbar took a special interest in the development of indigenous industry. He was directly responsible for the expansion of silk weaving at Lahore, Agra, Fathpur-Sikri, and in Gujarat. He opened a large number of factories at important centers, importing master weavers from Persia, Kashmir, and Turkistan. Akbar frequently visited the workshops near the palace to watch the artisans at work, which encouraged the craftsmen and raised their status. It is said that he took such an interest in the industry that to foster demand he "ordered people of certain ranks to wear particular kinds of locally woven coverings ... an order which resulted in the establishment of a large number of shawl manufactories in Lahore; and inducements were offered to foreign carpet-weavers to settle in Agra, Fathepur Sikri, and Lahore, and manufacture carpets to compete with those imported from Persia." In the course of time, the foreign traders established close contracts with important markets in India, and new articles which were more in demand in Western Europe began to be produced in increasing quantities. Among the foreign inventions that excited Akbar's interest was an organ, "one of the wonders of creation," that had been brought from Europe.

Urban Life

All foreign travellers speak of the wealth and prosperity of Mughal cities and large towns. Monserrate stated that Lahore in 1581 was "not second to any city in Europe or Asia." Finch, who travelled in the early days of Jahangir, found both Agra and Lahore to be much larger than London, and his testimony is supported by others. Other cities like Surat ("A city of good quantity, with many fair merchants and houses therein"), Ahmadabad, Allahabad, Benares, and Patna similarly excited the admiration of visitors. The new port towns of Bombay, Calcutta, Madras, and Karachi developed under British rule, but they had their predecessors in Satgaon, Surat, Cambay, Lari Bunder, and other ports.

The efficient system of city government under the Mughals encouraged trade. The pivot of urban administration was the kotwal, the city governor. In addition to his executive and judicial powers, it was his duty to prevent and detect crime, to perform many of the functions now assigned to the municipal boards, to regulate prices, and in general, to be responsible for the peace and prosperity of the city. The efficient discharge of these duties depended on the personality of the individual city governor, but the Mughals tried to ensure high standards by making the kotwal personally responsible for the property and the security of the citizens. Akbar had decreed (probably following Sher Shah Suri's example of fixing the responsibility on village chiefs for highway robberies in their territory) that the kotwal was to either recover stolen goods or be held responsible for their loss. That this was not only a pious hope is borne out by the testimony of several foreign travellers who state that the kotwal was personally liable to make good the value of any stolen property which he was unable to recover. The kotwals often found pretexts to evade the ultimate responsibility, but in general they took elaborate measures to prevent thefts.

Most of this flourishing commerce was in the hands of the traditional Hindu merchant classes, whose business acumen was proverbial. Their caste guilds added to the skills in trade and commerce that they had learned through the centuries. Not only were their disputes settled by their panchayats, but they would frequently impose pressure on the government by organized action. Foreign visitors record that the governors and kotwals were very sensitive to this, and in spite of hardships inseparable from a despotic system of administration, the business communities had their own means of obtaining redress.

Bernier, writing during Aurangzeb's time, declared that the Hindus possessed "almost exclusively the trade and wealth of the country." If Muslims enjoyed advantages in higher administrative posts and in the army, Hindu merchants maintained the monopoly in trade and finance that they had during the sultanate. A Dutch traveller in the early seventeenth century was struck by the fact that few Muslims engaged in handicraft industries, and that even when a Muslim merchant did have a large business, he employed Hindu bookkeepers and agents. Banking was almost exclusively in Hindu hands.

In the years of the decline of the Mughals, a rich Hindu banker would finance his favourite rival claimant for the throne. The role of Jagat Seth of Murshidabad in the history of Bengal is well known.

Even the "war of succession" out of which Aurangzeb emerged victorious was financed by a loan of five and a half lakhs of rupees from the Jain bankers of Ahmadabad. Here one sees a contrast with British rule, when the British not only monopolized the higher civil service posts but also controlled most of the major industries as well as the great banks and trading agencies.

Rural Conditions

Conditions in the rural areas during the Mughal period were much the same as at present, with one important difference—the Muslim rulers had scarcely disturbed the old organization of the villages.

The panchayats continued to settle most disputes, with the state impinging very little on village life, except for the collection of land revenue, and even this was very often done on a village basis rather than through individuals, with the age-old arrangements being preserved. The incidence of land revenue was substantially higher under the Mughals and in Hindu states like Vijayanagar than in British India, but the administration was more flexible, both in theory and in practice, in its assessment and collection. Apart from the remission of land revenue when crops failed, there was reduction in government demand even when bumper crops caused prices to fall. For example, between 1585 and 1590 very large sums had to be written off because a series of exceptionally good harvests had resulted in a surplus, and peasants could not sell their crops. The state also advanced loans to the cultivators, and occasionally provided seed as well as implements for digging wells. Loans advanced to the cultivators for seeds, implements, bullocks, or digging of wells were called *taqavi*—an expression which has continued in modern land revenue administration.

Health and Medical Facilities

A feature noticed by many foreign travellers was the good health of the local inhabitants. Fryer, writing of the mortality among the English at Bombay and the adjacent parts, says that "the country people lived to a good old age, supposed to be the reward of their temperance." Bernier also speaks of "general habits of sobriety among the people," though this did not apply to a few cases among the upper classes or the royal family. The European travellers found "less vigour among the people than in the colder climates, but greater enjoyment of health." From their accounts, even the climate would appear to have been healthy. "Gout, stone complaints in the kidneys, catarrh ... are nearly unknown; and persons who arrive in the country afflicted with any of these disorders soon experience a complete cure." The Mughal emphasis on physical fitness and encouragement of out-of-door manly games also raised the general standard of health. The ideal was that everyone was to be trained to be a soldier, a good rider, a keen shikari, and able to distinguish himself in games. Ovington found that the English at Surat were "much less vigorous and athletic in their bodies than Indians." It is possible that the drinking habits of the Europeans made them an easy prey to ill-health in the tropics.

Public hospitals had been provided in Muslim India, at least since the days of Firuz Tughluq (1351–1388), and though it would be ridiculous to compare them with the arrangements introduced by the British, the system seems to have been extended during the Mughal period. Jahangir states in his autobiography that on his accession to the throne he ordered the establishment, at government expense, of hospitals in large cities. That this order was actually made effective is shown by the records of salaries paid by the government and of grants for the distribution of medicine.

The supply of local physicians was not plentiful; and judged by the demand for European doctors, particularly surgeons, they were apparently not equal to all demands. The general health of the inhabitants suggests, however, that the medical services were not completely inadequate, and the local physicians were able to deal with normal problems. As early as 1616 they knew the important characteristics of the bubonic plague and suggested suitable preventive measures. According to an account in *Iqbal Nama*, which was written in Jahangir's reign: "When the disease was about to break out, a mouse would rush out of its hole, as if mad, and striking itself against the door and the walls of the house, would expire. If immediately after this signal the occupants left the house and went away to the jungle, their lives were safe. If otherwise, the inhabitants of the village would be spirited away by the hands of death." As modern scholars have pointed out, this observation includes two facts about the plague whose significance has been corroborated by modern science: the association of the death of rodents with the disease, and the necessity of evacuating the infected quarter.

A crude form of vaccination against smallpox seems to have been employed by Eastern doctors, for it was vaguely realized that the introduction of a mild form of cowpox prevented the virulent form of smallpox. An article in the Asiatic Register of London for 1804 contained a translation of a memorandum by Nawab Mirza Mehdi Ali Khan describing from personal observations the method adopted by a Hindu medical practitioner of Benares. A thread drenched in "the matter of a pustule on the cow" was placed on the arms of a child to cause an easy irruption, thus avoiding a virulent attack of smallpox.

In ancient times, the use of medicines had been well developed among the Hindus, but dissection was considered to be irreligious. The Muslims, who did not have this restriction, performed a number of operations. As Elphinstone pointed out: "Their surgery is as remarkable as their medicine especially when we recollect their ignorance of anatomy. They cut for the stone, couched for the cataract, and extracted the feotus from the womb, and in their early works enunciate no less than one hundred and twenty-seven surgical works." According to Manucci, Muslim surgeons could provide artificial limbs.

Social Customs

The marriage customs of Hindus and Muslims had many similarities. Early marriages were much in vogue amongst the Hindus, with seven considered the proper age for a girl to be married. To leave a daughter unmarried beyond twelve years of age was to risk the displeasure of one's caste. The Muslims also betrothed their children between the ages of six and eight, but the marriage was generally not solemnized before they had attained the age of puberty.

Among the wealthier classes polygamy and divorce are said to have been very common. The custom of secluding women, known as purdah, was very strictly observed. Marriage negotiations were undertaken by the professional broker or the friends of either party. The marriage ceremonies were more or less the same as they are at present, and the character of the average Indian or Pakistani home and the socio-ethical ideas which influence it have not undergone any fundamental change. The son's duty to his parents and the wife's duty to her husband were viewed almost as religious obligations. "Superstitions played a prominent part in the daily life of the people. Charms were used not merely to ensnare a restive husband but also to secure such other ends as the birth of a son or cure of a disease. The fear of the evil eye was ever present … and the young child was considered particularly susceptible. … People believed in all sorts of omens." Astrologers were very much in demand, even at the Mughal court.

The Muslim aristocrats lived in great houses decorated with rich hangings and carpets. Their clothing was made of finest cotton or silk, decorated with gold; and they carried beautiful scimitars. There was a considerable element of ostentatious display involved in this, however, for their domestic arrangements did not match the outward splendour of their dress and equipment. Manucci, a keen observer, refers to Pathans who came to court "well-clad and well-armed, caracolling on fine horses richly caparisoned and followed by several servants," but when they reached home, divested themselves of "all this finery, and tying a scanty cloth around their loins and wrapping a rag around their head, they take their seat on a mat, and live on ... rice and lentils or badly cooked cow's flesh of low quality, which is very abundant in the Mogul country and very cheap."

The courtly manners and the elaborate etiquette of the Muslim upper classes impressed foreign visitors. In social gatherings they spoke "in a very low voice with much order, moderation, gravity, and sweetness. ... Betel and betelnut were presented to the visitors and they were escorted with much civility at the time of departure. Rigid forms were observed at meals. ... Dice was their favourite indoor game. Polo or chaugan—for which there was a special playground at Dacca—elephant-fights, hunting, excursions and picnics, were also very popular." The grandees rode in palkis, preceded by uniformed mounted servants. Many "drove in fine two-wheeled carts, carved with gilt and gold, covered in silk, and drawn by two little bulls which could race with the fastest horses."

The Position of the Hindus

The Hindu upper classes undoubtedly shared in the material culture of the Mughals, for, as already noted, they had a virtual monopoly of trade and finance. Furthermore, they had long held many high posts in the government. The contrast between the position of Hindus under the Mughals and of Indians in general under the British was often made by Indian historians during the period of the nationalist movement. Thus a Hindu historian writing in 1940 could argue that "under Shah Jahan Hindus occupied a higher status in the government than that occupied by the Indians today."

The vitality of the Hindus was shown in more than their ability to maintain footholds within administrative and commercial life. Widespread religious movements, having, as we have seen, their roots partly in the vivifying contacts of Hinduism with Islam, had produced a religious enthusiasm among the masses that was transforming the older Brahmanical religion.

Although Muslim historians ignore this religious revival among the Hindus, there is enough evidence to indicate its importance during Mughal rule. The new regional literature of Bengal and Maharashtra, which owed much to the new movement, is a clear mirror of what was taking place in Hindu society. In Bengal, there was not only the rise of a new literature, but numerous temples were built during the late seventeenth century. The significance of this phenomenon becomes clear if it is remembered that practically throughout the second half of the seventeenth century, Aurangzeb was on the throne. His alleged ceaseless campaign of temple destruction obviously could have been neither thoroughgoing nor universal.

The developments in intellectual life were even more marked. The rise of Navadipa as a great center of Sanskritic learning, and the vogue of navyanyaya (new logic) belong to this period.

In relation to Islam, Hinduism exhibited a new vigor, greater self-confidence, and even a spirit of defiance. Hinduism is not generally thought of as a missionary religion, and it is often assumed that during Muslim rule conversions were only from Hinduism to Islam. This is, however, not true. Hinduism by now was very much on the offensive and was absorbing a number of Muslims. When Shah Jahan returned from Kashmir, in the sixth year of his reign, he discovered that Hindus of Bhadauri and Bhimbar were forcibly marrying Muslim girls and converting them to the Hindu faith. At death these women were cremated according to the Hindu rites. Jahangir had tried to stop this practice but with no success, and Shah Jahan also issued orders declaring such marriages unlawful. Four thousand such conversions are said to have been discovered. Many cases were also found in Gujarat and in parts of the Punjab. Partly to deal with such cases, and partly to conform to his early notions of an orthodox Muslim king, Shah Jahan established a special department to deal with conversions. After the tenth year of his reign, he seems to have ceased trying to prevent the proselytizing activities of the Hindus. There are several later cases of the conversion of Muslims, not recorded by the court historians. A number of Muslims—including at least two Muslim nobles, Mirza Salih and Mirza Haider—were converted to Hinduism by the vairagis, the wandering ascetics of the Chaitanya movement, which had become a powerful religious force in Bengal. There were also cases of conversions from Islam to Sikhism. When Guru Hargovind took up his residence at Kiratpur in the Punjab some time before 1645, he is said to have succeeded in converting a large number of Muslims. It was reported that not a Muslim was left between the hills near Kiratpur and the frontiers of Tibet and Khotan. His predecessor, Guru Arjan, had proselytized so actively that he incurred Jahangir's anger, and, as Jahangir mentions in his autobiography, the Hindu shrines of Kangra and Mathura attracted a number of Muslim pilgrims.

The Hindu position was so strong that in some places Aurangzeb's order for the collection of jizya was defied. On January 29, 1693, the officials in Malwa sent a soldier to collect jizya from a zamindar called Devi Singh. When he reached the place, Devi Singh's men fell upon him, pulled his beard and hair, and sent him back empty-handed. The emperor thereupon ordered a reduction in the jagir of Devi Singh. Earlier, another official had fared much worse. He himself proceeded to the jagir to collect the tax, but was killed by the Hindu mansabdar. Orders to destroy newly built temples met with similar opposition. A Muslim officer who was sent in 1671 to destroy temples at the ancient pilgrimage city of Ujjain was killed in a riot that broke out as he tried to carry out his orders.

Muslim historians, in order to show the extreme orthodoxy of Aurangzeb, have recorded many reports of temple destruction. On a closer scrutiny, however, there seem to be good grounds for believing that all the reports were not correct, and that quite often no action was taken on imperial orders. We read, for example, about the destruction of a certain temple at Somnath during the reign of Shah Jahan and again under Aurangzeb. It is likely that in this and in many similar cases, the temple was not destroyed on the first order. According to accounts by English merchants, Aurangzeb's officers would leave the temples standing on payment of large sums of money by the priests. However, new temples whose construction had not been authorized were often closed.

If the situation is closely examined, it appears that the complaint of Shaikh Ahmad that under Muslim rule as it existed in India, Islam was in need of greater protection than other religions does not appear to have been completely unfounded. Aurangzeb tried, of course, to reverse this trend, and some other rulers also had occasional spells of Islamic zeal, either from political or religious causes. But by and large, it is perhaps fair to say that during Muslim rule, Islam suffered from handicaps which almost outweighed the advantages it enjoyed as the religion of the ruling dynasty. This paradox becomes understandable if the basic Muslim political theory is kept in mind, under which the non-Muslim communities, so long as they paid certain taxes, were left to manage their own affairs. This local and communal autonomy severely circumscribed the sovereignty of the Muslim state, and in most matters the caste guilds and the village panchayats exercised real sovereignty, which they naturally utilized to safeguard their creed and way of life. It was this power which enabled them to evade, or even defy, unwelcome orders from the capital. A curious light on the situation is thrown by the penalties and economic losses which a Hindu had to suffer on the adoption of Islam. Practically until the end of Muslim rule, a Hindu who became a Muslim automatically lost all claim to ancestral property.

This extraordinary position was a natural result of the application of Hindu law, which, according to the Muslim legal system, governed Hindu society even under Muslim government, and under which apostacy resulted in disinheritance. Shah Jahan, who began as an orthodox Muslim, tried to redress the balance by issuing orders that "family pressure should not prevent a Hindu from being admitted to Islam," and laid down that a convert should not be disinherited. Whether these orders could overcome the subtle but solid pressure of the joint family system and the power of the caste panchayats must remain a matter of speculation.

The question, however, of handicaps or advantages of one community against another is not of fundamental significance. The important fact is that during normal times conditions of tolerance prevailed. This was of special interest to European visitors, almost all of whom commented on the concessions enjoyed by non-Muslims under Muslim rule. The Jesuits were critical of this policy of tolerance, declaring the destruction of Hindu temples by Muslims "a praiseworthy action," but noting their "carelessness" in allowing public performance of Hindu sacrifices and religious practices. When Akbar granted the followers of the Raushaniya sect the freedom to follow their religion, Monserrate sadly commented that "He cared little that in allowing everyone to follow his own religion he was in reality violating all religions."

Even in Aurangzeb's reign a cow could not be slaughtered in important places like Surat, and attempts made by some English merchants to obtain beef led to riots. According to one account: "In Surat the Hindus paid a fixed sum to the Mohammadans in return for sparing the cows. In 1608 a riot was caused at Surat by a drunken sailor Tom Tucker who killed a calf. Similar occurrences at Karwar and Honavar led to outbreaks, in one of which the whole factory was murdered." But nothing brings out the Mughal administration's respect for the susceptibilities of the Hindus as well as the experience of the Portuguese missionary traveller, Manrique. "In a village where he stopped for the night, one of his followers, a Musalman, killed two peacocks, birds sacred in the eyes of Hindus, and did his best to conceal the traces of his deed by burying their feathers. The sacrilege was, however, detected, the whole party arrested, and the offender sentenced to have a hand amputated, though this punishment was eventually commuted to a whipping by the local official, who explained that the emperor had taken an oath that he and his successors would let the Hindus live under their own laws and customs and tolerate no breach of them."

Although the Mughals interfered little with Hindu customs, there was one ancient practice which they sought to stop. This was sati, or the custom of widows, particularly those of the higher classes, burning themselves on their husbands' funeral pyres. Akbar had issued general orders prohibiting sati, and in one noteworthy case, personally intervened to save a Rajput princess from immolating herself on the bier of her husband. Similar efforts continued to be made in the succeeding reigns. According to the European traveller Pelsaert, governors did their best to dissuade widows from immolating themselves, but by Jahangir's orders were not allowed to withhold their sanction if the woman persisted. Tavernier, writing in the reign of Shah Jahan, observed that widows with children were not allowed in any circumstances to burn, and that in other cases governors did not readily give permission, but could be bribed to do so. Aurangzeb was most forthright in his efforts to stop sati. According to Manucci, on his return from Kashmir in December, 1663, he "issued an order that in all lands under Mughal control, never again should the officials allow a woman to be burnt." Manucci adds that "This order endures to this day." This order, though not mentioned in the formal histories, is recorded in the official guidebooks of the reign. Although the possibility of an evasion of government orders through payment of bribes existed, later European travellers record that sati was not much practiced by the end of Aurangzeb's reign. As Ovington says in his Voyage to Surat: "Since the Mahometans became Masters of the Indies, this execrable custom is much abated, and almost laid aside, by the orders which nabobs receive for suppressing and extinguishing it in all their provinces. And now it is very rare, except it be some Rajah's wives, that the Indian women burn at all."

FACTORS FOR URBAN EXPANSION

Five strength of the invader, of course, lay in combination and not in dispersal in an unfamiliar land and, thus, in initial stages, it was but natural for the members of the ruling class to prefer to stay at their iqta headquarters along with their cavalry. These iqta headquarters having the concentration of cavalry, its hangers-on and the retinue and household of the rnuqti thus emerged in the early phase as camp cities.

Most of the 13th century towns are infact defined as iqta headquarters in our sources; for example, Hansi, Kara, Anhilwara, etc. These towns were to be fed and provided for. In the beginning, the troops had to go for realising khar & j/mal by plundering the surrounding villages; but gradually by the 14th century, as pointed out by Moreland, cash nexus developed. The revenue was realised in cash from the peasants who were thus forced to sell their produce at the side of the field. The merchants catered to the needs of towns giving risk to what we will discuss below as-induced trade'.

The ruling class coming from a different cultural milieu had needs of leisure and comforts of a different type; they wanted songs in Persian and dances of a different style, books, silk to wear and arcuate light architecture (not !he stone edifices). Out of the resources that were indeed enormous by contemporary standards at its command, the new rulers naturally. Wanted to get luxuries and comforts of their taste which encouraged immigration from Islamic culture area. These immigrants were not only soldiers, but craftsman, artisans, singers, musicians, dancers, poets, physicians, astrologers and servicemen as described by Isami.

Urban Manufactures

It seems that the urban craft production received a twofold impetus with the establishment of the Delhi sultanate. First, the Sultanate ruling class remained town-centred and spent the enormous resources it appropriated in the form of land revenue mainly in towns, either on buying services or procuring manufacturers. Even the money spent on the service sector partly went to help the urban craft sector through multiplier effect. While the nobility created demand for high-priced skill-intensive luxury items, its hangers-on in all likelihood created a mass market for ordinary artisanal product.

The second factor that contributed to urban manufacturers was the introduction of a number of technological devices that reached India with the invaders. (You will learn, about them in detail in the next Unit). In the luxury sector, silk weaving expanded and carpet-weaving came from Persia. The other notable urban manufacture was paper making. Perhaps a major sector of urban employment was building industry. Barani says that Alauddin Khalji employed 7b,000 craftsmen for his buildings. One may well be justified in saying that there was considerably more masonary per acre of occupied space in the towns of 1400 than in those of 1200.

FOREIGN TRADE : SEABORNE AND OVERLAND

During the Sultanate period, overland and overseas trade were in a flourishing state.

Seaborne Trade

The Khalji annexation of Gujarat must have enlarged trade religions between the Delhi Sultanate and the Persian Gulf and the Red Sea Gujarat was connected with the Persian Gulf as well as the Red Sea.

Hormuz and Basra were the chief ports for the ships passing through the Persian Gulf, while the ports of Aden, Mocha and Jedda along the Red Sea were important for Gujarat. Through these ports, commodities moved on to Damascus and Aleppo, on the one hand, and Alexandria on the other. Aleppo and Alexandria opened upto the Mediterranean Sea with linkages to Europe. Merchandise of Gujarat were also carried towards the East-the port of Malacca situated at the Malacca straits and Bantam and Achin in the Indonesian archipelago.

A European traveller Tome Pires, who came to India in the first decade of the 16th century, comments on the trade of Cambay as follows : "Cambay chiefly stretches out two arms : with her right arm she reaches out towards Aden, with the other towards Malacca...." Pires further says :

"Malacca cannot live without Cambay, nor Cambay without Malacca, if they are to be very rich and very prosperous. If Cambay were cutoff from trading with Malacca, it could not live, for it would have no outlet for its merchandise." The main export from Gujarat to Malacca was the coloured cloths manufactured in Cambay and other Gujarat towns. These cloths were in demand in these places. In exchange, the Gujarati merchants came back with spices grown there. This pattern of "spices for coloured cloths" continued even after the Portuguese advent in the Asian waters.

Varthema, an Italian traveller, who came to India during the first decade of the 16th century says that about 300 ships (annually?) of different countries come and go from Cambay. He adds that about 400 "Turkish" merchants resided at Diu. The Khanid court historian Wassaf reports that 10,000 horses were annually exported to Cambay from Persia.

The Broach coin-hoards containing the coins of the Delhi Sultans along with the gold and silver coins of Egypt, Syria, Yeman, Persia, Genoa, Armenia and Venice further testifies to largerscale overseas trade.

THE MAJOR SEAPORTS

13th-15th Centuries, Imports and Exports

Ri of Urban Economy and Trade and Commerce

The two principal items of import were :

(a) horses-that were always in demand for cavalry since superior horses were not bredi? India and Indian climate was not wellsuited to Arabian and Central Asian horses. They were primarily imported from Zofar (Yemen), Kis, Hormuz, Aden and Persia;

(b) precious metals viz gold and silver, especially silver that was not at all mined in India but for which there was a high demand not only for metallic currency but also for fashioning luxury items.

Brocade and silk stuffs were imported from Alexandria, Iraq and China. Gujarat was the major centre from where the luxury articles from Europe used to enter. The Sultanate India mainly exported grain and textiles. Some of the Persian Gulf regions totally depended on India for their food supply. Besides, slaves were exported to Central Asia and indigo to Persia along with numerous other commodities. Precious stones like agates were exported from Cambay.

The Portuguese Advent

In spite of brisk trading activities, Indian merchants' share in the overseas trade was negligible. Only a small section of Gujarati Banias, Chettis of the South and domicile Indian Muslims used to take part in this large trading activity. Trade was mainly in the hands of the Arab Merchants. With the landing of the Portuguese at Calicut in A.D. 1498 after the rounding of the Cape of Good Hope, a new dimension was added to the Indian seaborne trade, that is, the 'element of force'. On account of better ships armed with cannons, the Portuguese soon imposed their commercial hegemony over the trading world of Asia, included the Indian seas, especially in Western part. This curtailed the Arabs' share of the Indian trade, though they survived in the Eastern part, especially at Malacca along with the Indian merchants. The Portuguese took Goa in 1510 which became their headquarters, Malacca fell in them hands in 1511. Hormuz in 1515; and Bassem and Diu In 1534 and 1537 respectively. Goa, under their patronage, soon developed as a major centre for import and export. The Portuguese well understood the strategic importance of Goa, which in their opinion, was essential to the maintenance of their position in India.. But the Portuguese possession of Goa was unfavourable to other Western Indian ports. Tome Presh ad rightly observed that the Muslim rulers of the Deccan and Gujarat had "a bad neighbour in Goa". Many ports on the west coast fell into decay during the hundred years of the Portuguese domination In the Indian waters.

Commercial Classes

Two types of merchants are mentioned in the sources of the Delhi Sultanate : the karwanis or nayaks and Multanis. The merchants specialising in carrying grains were designated by Barani as karwanis (a Persian word meaning those who moved together in large numbers). The contemporary mystic, Nasiruddin (Chiragh Delhi) calls them nayaks and describes them as those "who bring food grains from different parts to the city (Delhi)-some with ten thousand laden bullocks, some with twenty thousand" It can be said with a degree of certainty that these karwanis were the banjaras of succeeding centuries. As is clear from the Mughal sources, these were organised in groups and their headman called nayak.

The other important group of merchants mentioned in our sources was that of the Multanis. Barani says that the long distance trade was in the hands of these merchants. They were engorged in usury and commerce. It appears that the sahas and Multanis were rich enough to give loans even to nobles, who, according to Barani, were generally in need of cash. The sahas and Multanis were generally Hindu, but at least some Muslims also were among the Multani merchants: merchant). Besides these well defined merchant groups, others who had p chosen could take to trade : thus a Sufi (mystic) from Bihar became a slave-merchant trading between Delhi and Ghazni, and a number of pious men from Central Asia came to Delhi and became merchants.

Another important commercial class that emerged during the Sultanate period was that of the dallals ink between the buyer and the seller and took commission from both the parties. Barani says that they were the 'masters of market' (hakimnn bsenr) : they were instrumental in raising prices in the market. Alauddin Khalji used to conduct them about the cost of production of every article in the market in order to fix prices. But by Feroz Tughluq's reign, they seem to have regained their position.

Sads were yet another ambient group whose economic role was no less important than the brokers money changers, they were most sought after by the merchants, especially the foreign ones who came to India with their native coins. The sarapus tested the metallic party of the coins (indigenous and foreign) and established the exchange-ratio. They also issued bills of exchange or letters of credit, thereby acting as "bankers". The introduction of paper by the Turks into India accelerated the institution of bill of exchange. For all these troubles, the sarraf naturally charged his commission. Thus, both the brokers and the sarrafs occupied pivotal position in the commercial world of their period; they were the custodians of several basic economic institutions. Indeed, no merchant could have dispensed with their services.

Transport

It appears that the goods we transported both by pack animals and on bullock-carts. Perhaps the share of the pack animals was more than the latter. Ibn Battuta mentions 30,000 mans of grains being transported on the backs of 3,000 bullocks from Amroha to Delhi. Bullock-carts were also used, according to Afif, for carrying passengers on payment. The pack-oxen were of course a cheap mode of transport travelling slowly, grazing as they went and moving in large herds, thus reducing the cost of transport specially along the desert routes. Ibn Battuta describes that highways ran through the empire marked by minarets spaced at set distances. On the testimony of Shahabuddin a Umari, the author of the kasalik ul Abser, we may infer that efforts were made to create conditions conducive ko trade. Inns were built at each stage (mruudl). In Bengal, Iwaz Khalji built long embankments to safeguard from floods. Boats were employed for riverine routes to carry bulk goods, while large ships used for seabrone trade.

ORGANIZATION OF PRODUCTION

It is indeed important to know how production was organized. Whether the town artisans carried out production under the 'domestic system', that is, they owned their tools, raw material and the end product and also sold their product themselves; in other words, whether they were self employed or while tools were their own and they worked at their homes, raw material was provided to them by the merchants, that is whether they worked under the 'putting-out system'. The contemporary sources shed little light on these aspects. One can, however, legitimately assume that since the tools of production even after the introduction of new devices were still simple and mainly of wood and little of iron should have remained cheap. The artisan wish thus master of his own tools, though varied forms of labour organization seem to be prevalent. Certain artisans hawked or hired out their services such as cotton-card & who with a bow-string on his shoulder, went door to door selling his services as is evident from the account given in Khair-ul Majalis. Spinning was done usually by women staying at their homes.

The weavers too usually worked at their own looms at home weaving' cloth for sale, out of the yam bought or spun by the plosives. They also worked on wages to weave yarn supplied to them by customers. But if the raw material was expensive such as silk or gold of silver thread, etc. and the products were luxury items, the craftsmen were to work in karkhanas under supervision. We have definite information about the Sultans and high nobles maintaining these karkhanas where the production was to cater to their own needs and contrary to D.D.Kosambi's assumption was not for market. Shahabuddin al Umari records in his Masalik-ul Absar that in Mohammad Tughluq's karkhanas at Delhi, four thousand silk workers worked as embroiderers. According to Afif, Feroz Tughluq's karkhanas produced cloth and carpets in a big way. While there is no suggestion in our sources, we may only conjecture that perhaps merchants also maintained karkhanas where production was for sale.

Trade And Commerce

We have seen that there emerged some considerably big flourishing towns as well as numerous townships during the 13-14th centuries. These towns naturally needed to be fed and supplied raw material for craft production. At the same tinye, there was growing practice of lad revenue realization in cash. By the time of Alauddin Khalji, the cash-nexus came to be well developed and the-ruling class tended to claim almost the entire peasant suhlus by attempting to reduce the share of rural intermediaries, as we have seen in the previous Unit.

Both these factors were conducive to the development of inland trade. To pay the land revenue in cash, the peasantry was forced to sell its surplus produce while merchants had a market in newly emerged towns for agricultural products. This trade resulting from the compulsions of land revenue system is termed as 'induced trade'

Inland Trade

The inland trade developed at two levels : (a) the short distance village-town trade in commodities of bulk, and (b) long distance inter-town trade in high value goods. The village-town trade, as already explained, was a natural consequence of the emergence of towns of land revenue in cash. The urban centres were dependent for supply of food gardens and raw material for manufactures from the surrounding villages whereas the villages had to sell the agricultural products to receive cash for meeting the land revenue demand. The peculiar nature of this trade was the one-way flow of commodities. While the towns received grains and raw material from the villages in the vicinity they had no need to send their products in' exchange to the villages which were by and large self-sufficient. This one-way trade was owing to the land revenue demand imposed upon villages which naturally led to a continuous drain on rural sector and made the towns dependent on villages. The turnover of this trade was high in terms of volume but was low in terms of value. The commodities were food grains, that is wheat, rice gram, sugar cane, etc.

The inter-town trade was mainly in luxury articles and was thus high value trade. The manufactures of One town were taken to another : for example Barani reports that Delhi, the capita] itself, received distilled wines from Kol (Aligarh) and Meerut Muslin (fine cloth) from Devagiri and striped cloth from Lakhnauti (Bengal) while, according to Ibn Battota, ordinary cloth came from Awadh and betel-leaf from Malwa (twenty-four d!ays journey from Delhi). Candy sugar was supplied to Multan from Delhi and Laholie and ghi from Sirsa (in Haryana)., The long distance inter-town trade also carried goods coming from other countries exit-points.

INDUSTRY AND TRADE

Hindus occupied an important role in foreign, as in domestic, trade, although foreign Muslim merchants, known as khurasani, also had a large share of it. The rulers of the coastal kingdoms in the Deccan accorded to foreign merchants certain extra-territorial rights and special concessions, in consideration of the heavy taxes which they paid to the treasury. An organized class of brokers handled the business on the coast and inside the country. The imports consisted mainly of certain luxury items for the upper classes, and a general supply of all kinds of horses and mules, in which India was deficient. Hindus had never attached any importance to cavalry, but seeing the success of the Muslim horsemen, they started to substitute horses for elephants. The exports included large quantities of food-grains and cloth. Among the agricultural products were wheat, millet, rice, pulses, oilseeds, scents, medicinal herbs, and sugar. Some of the countries around the Persian Gulf depended on the subcontinent for their entire food supply. Cotton cloth and other textiles were especially important items of export, particularly to Southeast Asia and East Africa, although some reached Europe. They were carried by the Arabs to the Red Sea and from there found their way to Damascus and Alexandria, from where they were distributed to the Mediterranean countries and beyond.

Many industries of considerable size and importance developed during this period, the most important of which were textiles, various items of metal work, sugar, indigo, and in certain localities, paper. The Indian textile industry is very old, but the variety of cloth produced was originally limited. Taking advantage of the local talent, the Muslims introduced a number of fine varieties of textiles, most of which had Persian or Arabic origin. Bengal was the main centre of this industry, but Gujarat rivalled it as a supplier of the export trade during the sultanate period. Next in importance were a number of industries connected with metal work: the manufacture of swords, guns, and knives, as well as household needs such as trays and basins. Manufacture of sugar was also carried on a fairly large scale, and in Bengal enough was produced to leave a surplus for export after meeting the local demand. Paper-making was a minor industry, of which little is known except that Delhi was the centre of a considerable market.

These industries were mainly privately owned, but the government equipped and managed large-scale karkhanas, or factories, for supplying its requirements. The royal factories at Delhi sometimes employed as many as four thousand weavers for silk alone. The example of the sultan of Delhi was followed by the rulers of the regional kingdoms, and the contribution of the state to the development of the industry was not a minor one.

In certain aspects of social life, the Hindus had virtual autonomy during the sultanate. This was in accordance with the established axiom of Islamic law that while Muslims are governed by the Shariat, non-Muslim zimmis are subject to their own laws and social organization, but it was also a product of the Indian situation. The Muslim rulers from the days of the Arab occupation of Sind accepted the right of the village and caste panchayats to settle the affairs of their community. This meant that the Hindu villages remained small autonomous republics, as they had been since ancient times, and in commerce and industry the Hindu guilds were supreme. This position continued throughout the Muslim rule, but during the sultanate, when the provincial administration had not been properly organized, Hindu autonomy outside the principal towns was particularly effective.

It is often forgotten—and Muslim court chroniclers were not anxious to mention it—that a large number of independent or quasi-independent Hindu chiefs remained after the establishment of the sultanate. Some of them were rajas, or kings; others were only petty chieftains, controlling a few villages. Many of them belonged to old families, but new principalities grew up even after the establishment of Muslim power at Delhi. Rajputs often found new kingdoms for themselves in remote, easily defended areas in Rajputana and the Himalayas. From such movements during the sultanate come also some of the large landed estates still held by Rajputs in Oudh and in Bihar. In these predominantly Hindu areas the old religion was fostered, and its cultural expressions kept alive even in the periods of greatest Islamic power.

Learning, Literature, and the Arts

After the sack of Baghdad in 1258, Delhi was perhaps the most important cultural centre in the Muslim East. Heir to the traditions of Ghazni and Lahore, its importance increased when the Mongols destroyed the cultural centres of Central and Western Asia, and the poets, scholars and men of letters from these areas took refuge in Muslim India. Balban, who gave high offices of the state only to persons of good families, welcomed these distinguished refugees, and many illustrious families of Muslim India trace their origin to this period. This influx bore fruit in a large number of works, many of which are lost, but the contemporary historians attest to their worth. During the reign (1296–1316) of Alauddin Khalji the general prosperity engendered by his conquests enabled the nobles, and not just the sultan, to become literary patrons. This probably explains why Barani could devote fourteen pages to an account of the scholars, poets, preachers, philosophers, physicians, astronomers, and historians who thronged Delhi in the days of Alauddin Khalji. If the surviving poetry of Khusrau, the historical works of Barani, and the table talk of Hazrat Nizamuddin Auliya are any indication of the cultural vitality and richness of the age, one can well understand why Amir Khusrau and others felt that Delhi was the metropolis of the Muslim East.

Yet despite the cultural eminence of the capital, it cannot be claimed that the sultanate is a period marked by that solid scholarship and study of sciences which distinguished Baghdad and Cordova. The reason is obvious. Learned and gifted men had come to India, but without their libraries. Those who were escaping with their lives could not be expected to carry heavy loads of books over long distances. We get a glimpse of this in the case of Fakhr-i-Mudabbir, who fled from Ghazni without even his family papers, and had to wait for an opportunity to go back to reclaim them. The result was that only those cultural activities gained prominence which, like poetry, belles-lettres, local history, architecture, and music, were not dependent on accumulated stores of knowledge.

Probably for the same reason—the lack of libraries—great educational institutions of the kind found in Baghdad and Cairo did not develop in India. There were, however, schools and colleges in Delhi and all the important provincial capitals.

In Muslim society, teaching and the promotion of educational enterprises are regarded as necessary marks of religious vocation, and the Muslim state is expected to facilitate this by providing teachers with ample means of subsistence. This was the procedure generally adopted during Muslim rule in India, and the official in charge of religious endowments, the sadr-i-jahan, arranged for the grant of tax-free lands to Imams, Qazis, and other religious groups who provided education, particularly in Islamic subjects. This education was usually on the elementary level, but the system also provided for the maintenance of scholars who had specialized in different branches of learning. We find even nobles and distinguished men of affairs teaching subjects in which they had become proficient. Hazrat Nizamuddin Auliya, for example, studied under Shams-ul-Mulk, who became the wazir of Balban. The children of nobles were taught at their own residences by private tutors, whose guidance was often available for other students also.

For advanced students Madrasas, or colleges, were set up by pious and public-spirited rulers, and this activity received special attention during the early period. Two major Madrasas called Muizziya and Nasiriya were established during the beginning of Muslim rule at Delhi. Details about these Madrasas are lacking, but probably one of them was the college built by Iltutmish and repaired a century later by Firuz Tughluq. Similar steps to establish educational institutions were taken by Muslim rulers in the distant provinces, and we read of Mohammad Bakhtiyar Khalji setting up Madrasas at Devkot and other places in Bengal. Firuz Tughluq was unusual in that he looked after the institutions established by his predecessors; probably most of these establishments fell into decay when the original founders passed away, and the grants made for the Madrasas were diverted to other purposes.

Historians give little information about the staff or the curriculum of Madrasas, but some details are available for one founded by Firuz Tughluq near Hauz-i-Alai in Delhi. Barani has given a lengthy account of the beautiful building and gardens which provided a centre around which people built their houses. Both Barani and Mutahar, a well-known poet, praise the comprehensive knowledge of Maulana Jalauddin Rumi, the head of the institution. The main subjects taught seem to have been religious (interpretation of the Quran), hadith (tradition), and fish (jurisprudence). The intellectual activity of the schools owed much to the refugee scholars from Central Asia, Persia, and Iraq who came to Delhi in the thirteenth century.

After this influx had ceased and the Mongols had established their rule in the northwestern borderland, communication between Central Asia and northern India became difficult. It appears that in the Deccan, where contact was maintained with Iran by the sea route, intellectual activity during the later centuries encompassed a wider range than was the position in the north. In northern India, apart from religious subjects, literature, history, mysticism, and ethics were the principal subjects studied. In the Deccan, scientific subjects also received attention. The great Bahmani king, Firuz (1397–1422), for example, encouraged botany, geometry, and logic. He was interested also in astronomy, and in 1407 started work on an observatory near Daulatabad. The untimely death of Hakim Hashim Gilani, the astronomer who was to supervise the observatory, put an end to the project. When Sayyid Gisu Daraz, who has left a large number of books on mysticism and who was famous for his knowledge of religious subjects, reached the Deccan, Firuz went to meet him. The historian Firishta records that the sultan found the saint lacking in solid scholarship, and made no secret of his disappointment. The fact that Firuz was not alone in intellectual pursuits is evident from the account of a prince who used to teach students mathematics (including Euclid), theology, and rhetoric. Promotion of learning in the Deccan was largely the work of Persian statesmen and scholars whom the rulers had attracted from Iran, and an interesting monument to the age is the ruined college of the Bahmani minister, Mahmud Gawan, in Bidar. It was a magnificent building, as can be seen from its beautiful minarets and facade, but it was badly damaged during the wars of the Deccan kings with Aurangzeb.

The one scientific subject that received considerable attention in the schools was medicine. The earliest work on medicine, of which an imperfect manuscript copy has survived, was written about 1329 in the reign of Mohammad bin Tughluq. Its author, Zia Mohammad, went to the Deccan under the orders of the sultan. His book, Majmua-i-ziai, based on Arabic and Indian sources, gives local counterparts for Arabian medicines as well as the prescriptions of Hindu physicians. Following this work, other writers combined Greek and Indian works. The history of Indo-Islamic medicine has not yet been carefully studied, but it is reasonably certain that in the books written in India during the sultanate one sees the blending of the three streams of Greek, Arabic, and Hindu medical knowledge. The most famous of these works is the Tibb-i-Sikandari, written by the court physician Mian Bhuwa about 1512. It draws freely on the classical Sanskrit writers, and it long remained a standard textbook for followers of the indigenous medical systems.

Of the purely literary works of the early period, very few have survived. This is especially true of poetry, for barring the works of major poets like Amir Khusrau and Hasan, only those poems have been preserved which, because of their topical nature, were included in general histories. Examples are the poems of Sangreza on the arrival of Iltutmish's patent of sovereignty from the Abbasid caliphate and his verses on the accession of Iltutmish's son or Ruhani's poem on Iltutmish's conquest of Ranthambhor. While these poems have the usual limitations of occasional poetry, they indicate high poetic skill.

The early men of letters represented a trans-Indus tradition. Most of them had received their education beyond the border, and although they had settled down in Islamic India, an indigenous literary tradition was slow in developing. The two most important representatives of the early tradition were Mohammad Aufi and Mohammad bin Mansur Qureshi, generally known as Fakhr-i-Mudabbir. Aufi a native of Bukhara who lived in Lahore and Delhi, was the author of the earliest extant collection of biographies of Persian poets, Lubabul-Albab. He also completed the voluminous encyclopedia of anecdotes, Jawami-al-Hikayat, which, apart from its literary interest, is a mine of curious and interesting information relating to this and earlier periods. The major work of Fakhr-i-Mudabbir, who lived in Lahore at the beginning of the thirteenth century, was a study of statecraft; this has already been discussed in Chapter VII.

The first Persian poet of eminence who was born in India was Reza, or, as he was sometimes known, Sangreza. He was Iltutmish's secretary. The most distinguished writer of the early sultanate, however, was Amir Khusrau. His father, a junior Turkish officer under Iltutmish, had married a daughter of Rawat-i-Arz, Balban's famous minister. Khusrau showed literary promise at an early age, and, after spending some time at the provincial court of Oudh, became attached at first to Prince Bughra Khan, the governor of Samana and later of Bengal, and subsequently to Prince Mohammad, the heir-designate of Balban, who maintained a magnificent court at Multan. The prince lost his life in a skirmish with the Mongols in 1285, and the poet went to Delhi. Balban's successor, Kaiqubad, was Khusrau's first royal patron. In all, seven rulers were to be his patrons, but it is doubtful whether he was greatly concerned by the kaleidoscopic changes of royalty.

Apart from lyrics, Khusrau wrote poems relating to contemporary events. Qiran-us-Saadain, completed in 1289, gives an account of the historic meeting of Bughra Khan and Kaiqubad on the banks of the river Sarju, and contains an interesting description of the Delhi of those days. Miftah-ul-Futuh (1291) is a versified account of the exploits of Jalal-ud-din Firuz Khalji; in Ashiqa (1315) is an account of the romance of the Gujarati princess Deval Devi and Prince Khizr Khan, son of Alauddin Khalji.

The latter's conquests are the subject matter of Khazain-ul-Futuh (1311), an ornate prose work, while Nuh Sipihr, completed in 1318, celebrates the reign of Qutb-ud-din Mubarik Shah. In this book Amir Khusrau challenged the poets of Iran and sang of his native land, its hoary past, its love of learning, its flowers, and its fair, intelligent people. Tughlaq Nama describes the successful expedition of Ghiyasuddin Tughluq against the usurper Khusrau Khan. Khusrau was also among the earliest writers of Hindi poetry, and though the origins of the Hindi poems attributed to him are doubtful, he referred to his Hindi verses in the introduction to one of his Persian diwans. He also played a major role in the development of Indian music, as noted below.

The work of Hasan, a friend of Khusrau, was praised by Jami, the great

Persian poet, a rare distinction for an Indian writer. He wrote prose as well as verse, and his Fawaid-ul-Fuad, a record of the table-talk of his spiritual guide, Nizamuddin Auliya, is a literary classic. Equally interesting, though not so well known, was Ziya Nakhshabi, who was a master of simple and eloquent prose. His Tuti Nama (The Book of the Parrot) was based on a Sanskrit original. It has been translated into Turkish, German, English, and many Indian languages. His other translations include the Kok Shastra, a Sanskrit text on erotics.

While there were many distinguished names in poetry, perhaps the most important literary contribution during the sultanate was in the field of history. Since classical Hindu culture produced almost no historical literature, the Muslim works are of special significance for Indian historiography. Written by contemporaries who had taken part in the events they describe, these histories are of enormous value for an understanding of the period. They are marred, however, by certain defects which their very excellence tends to conceal. One is that many of the chronicles were written specifically for certain rulers and nobles whom the historians glorified at the expense of rivals; another is the tendency to picture the conquerors as actuated by unselfish and religious motives. These peculiarities of method can generally be discounted, however, and the historians do not seem to have falsified historical facts even when they were writing panegyrics.

The number of historical works of the sultanate period which have reached us is not large, but the works possess rich variety. The historians of the period, many of whom have already been mentioned, include Barani, Fakhr-i-Mudabbir, Hasan Nizami, Minhaj-us-Siraj, Aufi, Khusrau, Yahya, and Isami. Most of them occupied high official positions and wrote from personal knowledge. Barani is the most interesting, but he is not very particular about dates (normally the strong point of the Muslim historians), and this detracts from the value of his book, Tarikh-i-Firuz Shahi. But he wrote history as an artist, selecting and carefully arranging his material so that his book, instead of being a chronicle of events, emphasized the characteristics of various rulers and different reigns. He does not confine himself to the kings, but gives details about the political philosophies of different monarchs and leading men of the times, the literary and the religious history, the prices in the market, and other matters of concern to the ordinary people. Even more interesting is the gallery of portraits which he has brought to life by a skillful analysis of personalities and by providing those significant small details which most Indian historians omit.

As already noted, the rise of regional kingdoms in the fifteenth century played an extremely important role in the dissemination of Islamic culture. One significant feature of this disintegration of the central authority, with its dependence on Persian as the official language, was the rise of regional languages. Hindu kings had given their patronage to Sanskrit as the language of religion and the classics; Muslim rulers felt no such compulsion, and supported the common languages of the people. It was Muslim rulers, therefore, who were responsible for many of the first translations of the Sanskrit classics into the provincial languages. The Muslim rulers of Bengal engaged scholars to translate the Ramayana and the Mahabharata into Bengali. Maladhar Vasu translated the Bhagavata Purana into Bengali under the patronage of Sultan Husain Shah, and Chuti Khan, governor of Chittagong, employed Srikara Nadi to translate parts of the Asvamedha Parva of the Mahabharata into Bengali. In Kashmir, Hindu literature and philosophy were studied enthusiastically at the court of Zain-ul-Abidin (1420–1470). Rajatarangini, one of the few histories written in Sanskrit, was translated into Persian, with a supplement to bring the account up to date. Other works on music and mathematics were composed by Hindu scholars at the Kashmir court. In the south the Muslim rulers of Golkunda and Bijapur employed Hindus as ministers, and maintained the state records in the Marathi language. Cultural histories of the various provincial governments are yet to be written, but a similar process was at work at all places.

Among the nonliterary arts, music, rather than painting or sculpture, underwent important developments during the period of the sultanate. As already noted, Indian music had made an impact on the Arab systems as early as the conquest of Sind, and the interchange between the two forms was even more fruitful when the rich heritage of Persia and Central Asia was added. The result was the creation in North India of a new type of music, quite different from traditional Indian music which maintained its hold in South India.

Credit for this important work of synthesis is given to the poet Amir Khusrau, whose fame helped to give prestige to the new music, which had as its rival in the Delhi court the musical modes favoured by the Turkish rulers. The interest of the Chishti Sufis in "Hindustani" music and its practical cultivation by them further ensured its popularity. The next stage was reached during the establishment of the independent Muslim kingdom at Jaunpur, not far from Benares, and Kannauj, the old centres of Hindu arts. Here music received special attention, both at the royal court and in the Sufi monasteries. The two most important Indian Muslim musicians of the day were Sultan Husain Sharqi, the last king of Jaunpur, and the contemporary saint, Pir Bodhan of Barnawa. The saint's dwelling became a rendezvous for musicians from Delhi, the Deccan, and Jaunpur. The contribution of Sultan Husain to the development of Indian music was much more specific. He is regarded as the original founder of the khiyal (or romantic) school of music, which slowly matured and took its final shape in the days of the later Mughals, particularly under Mohammad Shah. Related to a Hindu devotional form that dealt with the love of Krishna for the milkmaids, the khiyal transformed the devotional theme to thinly veiled invocations of human love and romance.

Another regional kingdom where music was highly cultivated after the breakdown of the sultanate was Gwalior. Here the ruler, Raja Man Singh, was a Hindu, but the chief musician at his court, Nayak Mahmud, was a Muslim. Under his leadership a band of musicians systematized Indian music in the light of the changes it had undergone since the advent of the Muslims. This resulted in the compilation of Man Kautuhal, which contains almost all the airs introduced by the Muslim musicians.

Probably the greatest artistic achievement of the sultanate was neither literature nor music, but architecture. As with the musicians, the creativity of the Muslim architects was nourished by the mature styles of both the existing Islamic and Hindu traditions. The Muslims brought to India the experience gained in the great buildings of Cairo, Baghdad, Cordova, and Damascus, and they were able to draw upon the skill of Indian stonemasons. The result was a profusion of mosques, palaces, and tombs unmatched in any other Islamic country.

In the same year in which Delhi was occupied, the foundation of the mosque of Quwwat-ul-Islam was laid by Qutb-ud-din Aibak to commemorate the capture of Delhi and, as the name implies, to glorify the power of Islam. Aibak however spent most of his brief reign at Lahore, and adornment of the new Muslim capital was essentially the work of his successor, Iltutmish. He more than doubled the size of the Quwwat-ul-Islam mosque, built the Qutb Minar, one of the world's loveliest towers, erected the buildings for Nasiriya Madrasa, and, to meet the needs of the growing population of Delhi for water, excavated the great water reservoir, the Hauz-i-Shamsi. He also changed architectural methods. Previously material from Hindu buildings had been used for constructing mosques, but in 1230, when he extended the Quwwat-ul-Islam mosque, he used stone especially quarried for the purpose. This gave the addition a more Islamic appearance.

In architecture, as in other spheres of culture, the Indo-Islamic society was enriched by the dislocation in Central Asia and Persia caused by the Mongol invasion. Not only scholars but artisans as well came to Delhi as refugees, and they found a ready market for their skills in the expanding Muslim state. One important result was that the indigenous Indian artistic element ceased to be dominant in Delhi during this period. By the time of Alauddin Khalji, Muslim traditions had become firmly established on Indian soil, with the result that methods of construction were revolutionized and ornament became an integral part of the scheme, rather than a quasi-independent accessory, as was the case in the earlier buildings. The Jamaat

Khana mosque, constructed in the reign of Alauddin, is the earliest surviving example in India of a mosque built wholly in accordance with Muslim ideas.

In the provincial capitals, however, the influence of the refugee artisans was slight, and the indigenous styles remained important. In Bengal the Muslim rulers decorated their buildings with carving which is obviously the work of Hindu craftsmen, and in Gujarat they adapted the local style to Muslim needs to create some of India's most beautiful buildings. Yet even where most was owed to native Indian skills and tradition, the peculiar Muslim architectural characteristics of spaciousness and graceful forms are present.

Furthermore, the Muslims made full use of concrete and mortar, which were known but scarcely used before their arrival in India. "Thanks to the strength of their binding properties, it was possible for the Muslim rulers to span wide spaces with their arches, to roof immense areas with their domes, and in other ways to achieve effects of grandeur such as the Indians had never dreamt of."

The Tughluqs in the fourteenth century introduced a new and austere phase in architecture. Mohammad Tughluq, who shifted his capital from Delhi to Daulatabad, had no interest in the old city. The many buildings erected in Delhi during the reign of his successor Firuz show a severe simplicity, possibly due as much to the need for economy as Firuz's own strict orthodoxy. Hindu influences were reduced to the minimum, and Tughluq buildings are lacking in elegance and refinement. Under the Lodis there re-emerged a vigorous and catholic spirit of design, replete with creative energy and imagination. The explanation is probably that with the conversion of the Mongols to Islam and the reduction of chaos in Central Asia, inspiration from Persia was now available in architecture as in literature. The Lodis were soon replaced by the Mughals, under whom Persian influences became even more dominant.

TRADE BETWEEN WESTERN EUROPE AND THE MUGHAL EMPIRE IN THE 17TH CENTURY

Contact between Western Europe and the Mughal empire was put into practice in the very beginning of the 17th century. The Portuguese, English, and later on, the Dutch were the ones to communicate with the Mughal empire. As the first Islamic power on the Indian subcontinent, the Mughal empire was more interested in assimilating the land, studying the history, customs and religion of the people occupying this area, and communicating with the other two Islamic empires – the Saffavid and the Ottoman Empires.

The Mughal empire was blessed with very strong leaders, however, very different in approach and strategy. Akbar the Great was known for his tolerance towards unorthodox Muslims and Hindus. The Akbarnama, a book written by Abul Fazal on the life and rule of Akbar, gives a lot of evidence on how Hinduism was viewed and explained by the Muslims. Along with being tolerant towards his Hindu and Muslim subjects, Akbar welcomed Portuguese Jesuits, which allowed Portugal to enter the trade with Indian goods. At the very end of his rule, the British, Dutch, and Portuguese started trade with the Mughal empire as well. Even though the trade started during the reign of Akbar the Great, his son Jahangir was the one to strengthen this economic activity in the Indian subcontinent.

Premises of Western Europe for the trade

The English and Dutch were granted 21-year permission of monopoly in the "East Indies", which followed by the retorted answer from the Indian landlords – they encouraged the establishment of coastal posts for trade. Half a century afterwards, the competition for trade in the Indian Ocean was enhanced by the setting up of the French East India Company in 1664. It followed Jean-Baptiste Colbert's theory of Mercantilism that claimed to keep the national exports greater than the imports. In his Memorandum on English Alliances and Memorandum to the King on Finances written in 1669 and 1670 respectively, Jean-Baptiste Colbert defended his theory and tried to figure out a way of how to undercut the Dutch trade. This document gave evidence on the strength of the Netherlands' trade in the 17th century not only in India but also in the Caribbean. Moreover, it gave the precise numbers of the Dutch superiority over both the British and the French – 15,000 to 16,000 vessels per year versus 3,000 to 4,000 for the British and 500 to 600 for the French. The British managed to increase the trade with textile with 22.7 million square meters over a period of just twenty years. Ironically, they did that in the very same year that France intervened in the Indian trade..

The need for Alcohol Established the First Trading Contacts

One of the items traded was alcohol drinks. During Babur's and Jahangir's reign the trade was especially directed towards alcohol exchange. It probably was the same during the rest of the Great Mughals' reigns but the autobiographies and court chronicles had very little information about this issue. Moreover, these sources cannot be very reliable because the emperors reviewed them. However, there are records and journals written by individuals that were either travelling or were members of the Mughal court, which strongly suggest the overuse of alcohol and its social connection within the people and castes.

The Great Mughals were not only connoisseurs of alcohol, they were often overusing it, too. Jahangir died of alcohol abuse. Alcohol was also considered a gift of goodwill, especially between sailors and merchants. Evidence of that were the records and journals of the British East India company. Its employees often requested for wine supply for themselves and for gifts for the monarch. It was used not only for special occasions but also as a regular act of just revering the emperor. Jahangir was the emperor who was the most associated to alcohol but all the rest of the Great Mughals appreciated it too, with the exception of Jahangir's father Akbar. Wine and alcohol in general was as well used for negotiations and, was therefore a very important part of the trading process.

The Implementation of Trade

The trade in India was implemented mainly on the coast. During the 17th century there were two big Islamic empires between Western Europe and the Mughal empire – the Saffavid and the Ottoman Empires – their trade was implemented only by ships. Therefore, the main ports were on the coast of both the Arabian Sea and the Bay of Bengal with the small exception of Calcutta, located on the bank of river Hooghly, yet still accessible by water.

Bombay and Surat on the Arabian sea coast and Madras (today's Chennai) or - as the British named it - Fort St. George, were the four main locations of Indo-European trade during the 17th century. Trade as a tool for the Early World Globalization was very prosperous and profitable for both the European and the Indian merchants. Consequently, the local Indian landlords gained a lot of power and money.

Since the emperor's power was not as centralized and certainly was not recognized by all of the people of different origin living within the borders of the Mughal empire, the local potentates stood against the emperor and formed autonomous or semiautonomous states. This separation made it easy afterwards for the already penetrated British powers to put the end of the Mughal empire in the mid 19th century.

Trade on the Mughal Empire

Two and a half centuries of trade between India and Western Europe led to the downfall of an initially agriculturally-orientated empire with strong military forces and tolerance towards its subjects and their different religious beliefs (with the exception of Aurangzeb). All three Islamic empires found either their collapse or a significant weakening by the 19th century. European countries, however, were growing, expanding, developing, coming up with new movements, intentions, technology.

Even though they were essentially separated by the Ottoman and Safavid empire, the common interest, the trade, helped Europe to permanently settle into the Indian lands. The most comprehensive and clear sources about the Mughal empire were the factory records of the British East India company, which suggests that trade was the only way of communication between Western Europe and the Mughal empire. The trade was carried out by the same countries, only there were variations of the proportion of import for those countries, depending on what was going on at that time in Europe and on the alliances the countries tight themselves into.

The pattern of Globalization and World's entanglement was traced in 17th century through trade. This way the European countries found their place in the Mughal empire, gradually gaining more power over the trade and, consequently, over the empire until the British colonized the Indian subcontinent in the 19th century. The European language was primarily spread amongst coastal regions, in particular large trading centres and sometimes throughout big commercial towns which were based inland.

REFERENCES

Creswell, K. A. C.: *A Short Account of Early Muslim Architecture*, Aldershot, Adlohoc, 1989.

Heimann, Betty: *Facets of Indian Thought*, Geroge Allen & Unwin, London, 1964.

Ira Mervin Lapidus, *Muslim Cities in the Later Middle Ages,* Cambridge, Mass, 1967.

Hopkirk, Peter: *The Great Game: The Struggle for Empire in Central Asia*, Kodansha, 1992.

Chapter 7

Characteristics of Mughal Architecture

Mughal architecture, an amalgam of Islamic, Persian and Indian architecture, is the distinctive style developed by the Mughals in the 16th and 17th centuries in what is now India, Pakistan, and Bangladesh.

Some of the first and most characteristic examples that remain of early Mughal architecture were built in the short reign (1540–1545) of emperor Sher Shah Suri, who was not a Mughal; they include a mosque known as the Qila i Kuhna (1541) near Delhi, and the military architecture of the Old Fort in Delhi, Lal Bagh (Dhaka) in Bangladesh, and Rohtas Fort, near Jhelum in present-day Pakistan. His mausoleum, octagonal in plan and set upon a plinth in the middle of an artificial lake, is in Sasaram, and was completed by his son and successor Islam Shah Suri (1545AD-1553AD).

THE QUEST FOR A MUGHAL STYLE

Babur's memoirs indicate that the construction of permanent buildings assumed less importance for him than the construction of gardens. Just as he camped in gardens in Kabul when moving from site to site, so too in India the garden served as his camp. Moreover, his precarious financial situation - where the payment of troops had to be his first priority - left fewer resources for large stone monuments. Nevertheless, buildings were constructed, enough to employ almost 1,500 stone cutters at work on projects throughout his north Indian domain. Babur's view of indigenous Indian architecture is only partially reflected in his comment about a mosque within his Agra fort garden.

He considered the building unattractively constructed in the "Hindustani fashion." While his objections are vague, Zain Khan elaborates that the foundations as well as the walls of this Agra mosque were strong, constructed of brick and stone, but the "composition was not conformable,"16 that is, not harmonious, referring to the spatial organization, doubtless much less sophisticated than that of Timurid prototypes. But Babur did not dislike all Indian architecture, for he describes favorably at some length the palaces of the Gwalior fort, praising especially those of Man Singh Tomar discussed in the previous chapter. Its special appeal lay in the carved stone walls, tiled facades and exterior chattris. Just as Timur had admired Indian stone masons and some 225 years earlier had carried some back to work on his own buildings in Samarqand, so Babur - who had noted this in his memoirs - also favored the work of these artisans and employed them freely.

Still today the hand of Indian masons is evident on the tanks at the Dholpur Lotus garden. These masons had been rewarded with gifts by Babur, who admired their craft. He was astonished at the ability of Indian masons to inlay and bond pieces of colored stone without the use of mortar. In spite of his admiration for Indian craftsmen, Babur was concerned that the overall design of his structures in India should be modeled on Khurasani, that is, Timurid examples. Such models, for example, were probably followed in the design of one structure in the Agra Hasht Behisht garden. Although it is only known from textual description, it appears to have had a large pishtaq on each of four sides, connecting galleries and four small interior chambers. Possibly to insure fidelity to Timurid models, two artisans from Central Asia came to work for Babur in India. One was Mir Mirak Ghiyas, identified as a stone cutter in Babur's memoirs, possibly identical with Mirak Sayyid Ghiyas, the designer of Humayun's tomb, who came from Herat and owned much land in Khurasan.

A second stone cutter, Ustad Shah Muhammad, first had served Babur in Qandahar before his incursions into India and continued in his employ until at least 1529, the year before Babur's death. These men doubtless enjoyed a status far higher than that of ordinary craftsmen, for routine workers would not have been identified by name. Among the buildings of Babur's time that survive are one imperially patronized mosque and two others constructed by nobles on Babur's orders. These were all built in the final years of his reign. This is notable, for until Babur's conquest of India there is no evidence for his patronage of religious structures. The mosque that Babur himself provided is in Panipat, today in Karnal District of Haryana State (Plates 7-8).

Inscriptions indicate that the mosque was well under way, if not finished, by the end of 1527, and its gate, well and garden were finished by 1528. The mosque is not mentioned in literary sources; Babur's memoirs contain lacunae for this period, and Zain Khan's work ends abruptly with the events of early 1527. Nevertheless, we can certainly assume that the complex commemorates Babur's decisive victory over Sultan Ibrahim Lodi at Panipat and thus the Mughal conquest of Hindustan. Since the garden has disappeared, the mosque's location within it is not known. However, the building's large size suggests that it, rather than the garden, dominated the complex. The rectangular prayer chamber, measuring Plate 7.

Babur's mosque, today known as Kabuli Bagh mosque, Panipat 53. by 16. meters, is dominated by a large central domed bay flanked on either side by three-bayed triple-aisled side wings. Each bay of the side wings is entered by an arched opening supported on massive piers. Over the mosque's brick construction is a heavy stucco veneer, reminiscent of that covering much Sultanate architecture. The northwest and southwest corners of the mosque were marked by octagonal towers crowned by domed pavilions, although only one survives. Each of the mosque's bays is surmounted by a dome, those over the westernmost aisle being smaller than those on the east. The large central bay's qibla wall, the one oriented toward Mecca, is stonefaced, but elsewhere the veneer on the mosque's interior is stucco over a brick core.

This central bay is the mosque's focal point, visible even from the outside through the wide entrance. Attention is drawn to the mihrab by an epigraph - including the Throne Verse from the Quran, and an historical inscription dated 1527-28 - rendered dramatically in black stone against white marble. While the chamber itself is a simple domed structure, recalling the Lodi Bara Gumbad built in Delhi's Lodi Gardens in 1494, the appearance of net pendentives here used only decoratively, evokes a Timurid flavor. Each side wing is divided into two aisles by massive brick piers; the resulting bays are crowned by domes resting on brick pendentives that are covered by a thick stucco veneer modeled to resemble net squinches, introduced to north India by the Mughals. A stone gate stands in the courtyard's north wall. It is carved in the tradition of earlier Lodi gates, for example that at the Lodi-period tomb of Khwaja Khizr dated 1522-24 in nearby Sonepat. Most of the enclosure wall has disappeared, but remains suggest that the entire courtyard was walled and that each side had similar gates. The Panipat mosque's prayer chamber appears to have been loosely modeled on the type of congregational mosque used by the Timurids.

It also incorporates features of mosques built by the pre-Lodi sultans in this region. This mosque type, however, was favored by Babur not because of any earlier Indian associations, but for two rather different reasons. First, it is decidedly different from the single-aisled multi-bayed type used exclusively by Babur's immediate predecessors, the Afghan Lodis. Notably at Panipat, the site of this mosque, Babur had defeated the Lodis. Second, it is a type that, although somewhat transformed in the process of Indian translation, had been constructed by Timur, for example in his Bibi Khanum mosque in Samarqand. As the Mughal Babur was the only surviving Timurid ruler, it must have been especially important for him to preserve at least a vestige of Timurid architectural forms. A vestige it is, no more, surprising in light of Babur's admiration for the architecture of the great Central Asian Timurid cities Samarqand and Herat. Despite his regard for Timurid architecture, it could not be replicated on Indian soil. It appears that there were only a few artists trained in the Timurid homeland and probably no architect capable of introducing the complex Timurid engineering principles. Moreover, Babur lacked the wealth needed for such construction.

Instead, local architects and artisans relied closely on older but familiar Indian techniques. Two other mosques remain that were constructed by leading nobles following Babur's orders. Probably these orders were general ones, not commands to erect specific mosques. One of these mosques is at Sambhal (Plate 9), about 140 km east of Delhi. It was constructed in 15 26 by Mir Hindu Beg, an important noble in the court of both Babur and Humayun. Built a year before Babur's Kabuli Bagh mosque in Panipat, the Sambhal mosque is the first extant Mughal building in India. The complex is entered through a gate on the east that opens to a large walled courtyard. The prayer chamber, like the one of the Panipat mosque, is rectangular with a large square central bay. Its entrance is set into a high pishtaq, recalling those of Sharqi mosques at Jaunpur. The chamber is flanked on either side by three-bayed double-aisled side wings. A single dome surmounts the central bay, and a small flatish dome surmounts each bay of the side wings. The mosque's pishtaq and other features resembling fifteenthcentury Sharqi structures in nearby Jaunpur suggest a reliance on local artisans and designers. Even though the Sambhal mosque was renovated at least twice in the seventeenth century, enough of its original state remains to show that the plan and general appearance anticipate Babur's Panipat mosque commenced the following year. The size (40. by 12. meters), too, anticipates the scale of Babur's imperial mosque, thus making this mosque at Sambhal the largest one constructed in the Delhi region since Timur's sack of that city in 1398. This mosque is situated high on a hill and dominates the city for a considerable distance. According to Hindu lore that was known to the Mughals, the tenth and last incarnation of Vishnu will appear in Sambhal at the end of this era.

STARTING PERIOD OF MUGHAL ARCHITECTURE

By 1544, Humayun reached Iran and found refuge in the Safavid court of Shah Tahmasp. The relationship between the deposed Mughal and this Safavid ruler was not a comfortable one, since Shah Tahmasp insisted that Humayun embrace Shiism just as Babur had been forced to do some years earlier. Nevertheless, Shah Tahmasp's support eventually enabled Humayun to regain the Mughal throne in 1555. These years in Iran introduced Humayun not only to Safavid painters and painting but also to the architecture of Herat and Samarqand and to the Timurid-Safavid Iranian traditions that Babur had so admired. With the exception of a single inscribed mosque in Agra, no other surviving structure indisputably results from Humayun's patronage.

Some hold that the Delhi Purana Qalca, its mosque and octagonal pavilion (Plate n) also are his. Despite the dearth of remaining buildings from Humayun's time, contemporary sources refer to his architectural output. They describe, for example, his unique conceptions, although they are based on Timurid design concepts. One of them was a floating palace formed from four barges each bearing an inward facing arch and attached in such a manner that an octagonal pool formed the central portion. In addition, he designed three-storied collapsible palaces, gilded and domed. More traditional palaces were constructed at Gwalior, Agra and Delhi.

Neither the Gwalior palace, constructed of chiselled stones, nor the multistoried Agra palace, with its octagonal tank, connected via subterranean passages to other parts of the palaces, survives. Much controversy centers around Humayun's role in erecting the fortified enclosure today known as Delhi's Purana Qalca. Humayun commenced a walled city and imperial palace on this site in 1533. The city, named Din-Panah or Refuge of Religion, was auspiciously situated upon the age-old site known as Indraprastha, long associated with the traditional Hindu epic Mahabharata.

The city was also located in very close proximity to the shrine of Delhi's most revered saint, Nizam al-Din Auliya. The choice of the site must have been made with its history in mind, for Humayun, superstitious yet religious, sought advice from learned men as well as astrologers. Even after Humayun's victorious return to India in 1555, this site remained symbolic for the Mughals, for, as we shall see, Humayun's tomb was constructed in this same area. Khwand Amir, a noble in Humayun's court, reports that by 1534 the "walls, bastions, ramparts and gates" of Humayun's Din-Panah were nearly completed, adding that it was hoped that the "great and lofty buildings" of the city soon would be finished.

It is difficult to tell from Khwand Amir's bombastic prose exactly how much of the city in reality was ready by 1534; moreover, it is impossible to judge how much was completed before Sher Shah's accession to the Delhi throne in 1540, for Humayun was constantly engaged in defending the Mughal domain and struggling to maintain his crown. Sher Shah probably completed the fort and constructed its interior Qalca-i Kuhna mosque discussed in the previous chapter. Humayun almost certainly built the fort's small octagonal pavilion, known as the Sher Mandal (Plate 11) and traditionally associated with the library upon whose steps Humayun fatally fell in 1556, less than a year after his successful return to India. Abu al-Fazl, the official chronicler of Humayun's son and successor, Akbar, writes that the building in which Humayun had his fatal accident had only recently been completed,35 presumably by Humayun. The pavilion's design, close to Timurid garden pavilions and unlike Sultanate architectural types, suggests Mughal patronage. So does the appearance of the net pendentives in the structure's vaulting. The sole inscribed monument belonging to Humayun's patronage is a mosque in Agra known after the name of its locality, Kachpura (Plate 12). Two inscriptions indicate that the mosque was completed in 1530, the year of Humayun's accession to the throne. Its location, across the Jumna from the land on which the Taj Mahal was later built, may have been the site of the Hasht Behisht garden, or Garden of Eight Paradises, used for Babur's court.

This garden also most likely continued to serve as Humayun's court until he constructed his Delhi citadel. Like Babur's mosques, this one in Kachpura is mentioned in no text. It resembles Babur's Panipat mosque (Plates 7 and 8) in general plan and appearance, although the central pishtaq is much higher and the central vaulted chamber achieves a greater sense of open space than did the only slightly earlier Mughal mosques. The open character of the central bay with low flanking bays recalls earlier Timurid mosques, for example the Jamic mosque at Nishapur. As at Babur's Panipat mosque, stucco covers a brick core. On Humayun's mosque, eight-pointed stars and lozenge patterns are imprinted into the rectangular facade; possibly these were once painted to emphasize the design, evoking the brightly colored glazed tile ornamentation of Herat and Samarqand.

The mosque today is ruined, so it is unclear how many bays originally composed the double-aisled side wings. The interior central bay is surmounted by a dome supported on kite-shaped pedentives and net squinches. The smaller domes of the resulting side wings are similarly supported. While no traces of enclosure walls and entrance gates remain, they were almost certainly part of the original plan. The overall appearance and plan of this structure suggests that it, like Babur's Panipat mosque, was intended to emulate older Timurid types.

ARCHITECTURE IN DELHI

Delhi, the traditional capital of north Indian Islamic rulers, served as Akbar's capital until 1565, when he commenced his massive Agra fort. This was followed by the construction of other forts in strategically important locations signaling the diminishing importance of Delhi, until its revival in the midseventeenth century.

While ruling from Delhi, Akbar continued to reside in Humayun's citadel, Din-Panah. There is no example of Akbar's architecture from these early years, but leading members of his court built mosques and tombs close to the Din-Panah. For example, the Khair al-Manazil mosque and madrasa were constructed in 1561 by Maham Anga. She had been one of Akbar's wet-nurses and had considerable influence over the young king during this early period.

Erected under the supervision of Shihab al-Din Ahmad Khan, her son-in-law, the mosque closely follows the plan and elevation of the nearby Qalca-i Kuhna mosque probably built by Sher Shah. Her mosque is embellished with incised stucco and paint in lieu of inlaid stone. Its courtyard is enclosed with high cloistered walls used as a madrasa. The dominant feature of the mosque, however, is not the prayer chamber, but its monumental east gate (Plate 15).

It is faced with red and white stones like those on the entrance gates into the Din-Panah. This gate, which lay on a main thoroughfare linking the fort with the city walls, commanded a dominant position in the city. Nearby is the shrine (dargah) of Nizam al-Din Auliya. Restorations had been made there in Babur's and Humayun's reigns, and further renovations were made in Akbar's time.

In 1562 a noble of Akbar's court, Farid al-Khan, rebuilt Nizam al-Din's tomb. The walls of this square-plan tomb consist of marble screens (jalis) supported by intricately carved pillars; the carved geometric patterns are more finely rendered than those on the nearby tomb of Khusrau (Plate 13) carved in Humayun's reign. It is with this tomb that marble, probably in emulation of the tomb of Mucin al-Din in Ajmer, becomes an emblem of sanctity in Mughal architecture.

In the dargah of Nizam al-Din is the tomb of Ataga Khan (Plate 16), built in 1566-67 by his son Mirza Aziz Koka. Ataga Khan, Akbar's prime minister and the husband of one of his wet-nurses, was murdered in 1562 by the jealous son of Maham Anga. The square plan of this tomb follows the older Indian tombtypes, while its red sandstone exterior inlaid with multi-colored stones and white marble slabs carved with Quranic verses reflects the influence of the exquisite Qalca-i Kuhna mosque (Plate 5). This is the first Akbar-period monument for which we know the names of both the architect, Ustad Khuda Quli, and the calligrapher, Baqi Muhammad of Bukhara. The verses on the tomb were chosen carefully, referring specifically to the nature of Ataga Khan's demise, which Akbar's court chronicler Abu al-Fazl likens to martyrdom.

Ataga Khan's murderer, Adham Khan, was immediately punished by death. Adham Khan's large octagonal tomb (Plate 17), containing his grave and that of his mother, who died a few months later, was erected by imperial order 15 km south of Akbar's Delhi. By contrast to Ataga Khan's tomb, reflecting the apex of Mughal technology and taste, his murderer's tomb, stucco covered and octagonal in format, represents the end of this older type. Octagonal tombs once had been associated with royalty, for example by the Surs, considered traitors by the Mughals. Thus a tomb-type associated with traitors was particularly suitable for the once-leading, now disgraced, noble, Adham Khan. Timurid features are often evident in some of the most important Akbari buildings in Delhi, including his finest work there, his father's tomb. Many of these features are, however, largely dropped in Akbar's buildings constructed after moving the capital to Agra.

Among the works that recall architecture in the Mughal homeland is the Sabz Burj, located south of the citadel. The tomb is probably a product of Akbar's reign, although it may date as early as Humayun's reign. It is designed as a Baghdadi octagon (see glossary) with a high dome resting on an elongated neck; originally green tiles covered its surface. At least as clearly based on Timurid prototypes is the largest structure erected in Delhi during the early years of Akbar's reign, the tomb of the deceased emperor Humayun (Plates 18-19). Situated just south of the Din- Panah citadel and in close proximity to the esteemed dargah of Nizam al-Din, the mausoleum even today dominates its surroundings. A contemporary Mughal source indicates that the tomb was finished in 1571 after eight or nine years of work.

Tradition states that a devoted wife, Hajji Begum, was responsible for its construction; recently, however, Akbar has been proposed as the patron,5 even though the tomb resembles none of Akbar's other architectural enterprises. Its Timurid appearance must be credited to its Iranian architect, trained in the Timurid tradition and known from contemporary texts as both Mirak Sayyid Ghiyas and Mirak Mirza Ghiyas. His masterpiece came to be influential in the design of Mughal mausolea through the eighteenth century. Mirak Mirza Ghiyas, originally from Herat, may have been a stone cutter who had worked for Babur. He worked extensively in Bukhara, where he excelled at buildings and landscape architecture. Around 1562, he returned to India to design Humayun's tomb. Before its completion, however, he died. His son completed the great project in 1571.

Today the tomb complex is entered by a large gate on the west, although in Mughal times the southern gate was widely used. Upon entering any gate, the centrally situated tomb and its char bagh setting are visible. Each of the four garden plots is further sub-divided by narrower waterways. Based on the char bagh types established in Iran and more fully developed in Babur's own concept of the ideal garden, such formalized and geometrically planned garden settings became standard for all the imperial Mughal mausolea and for those of many nobles as well. Char bagh gardens long had been associated with paradisical imagery. But at Humayun's tomb, the association is all the more explicit, for the water channels appear to vanish beneath the actual mausoleum yet reappear in their same straight course on the opposite side. This evokes a Quranic verse which describes rivers flowing beneath gardens of paradise.

The mausoleum is square in plan, 45 meters on a side. Crowned with a white marble bulbous dome and flanking chattris, the tomb sits on a high elevated plinth 99 meters per side. Each facade, faced with red sandstone and trimmed with white marble, is nearly identical and meets at chamferred corners. The west, north and east facades are marked by a high central portal flanked on either side by lower wings with deeply recessed niches. The south entrance, probably the main one, consists of lower wings on either side of a high central pishtaq, underneath which is a deeply recessed niche.

The seeming simplicity of this tomb's exterior is belied by the interior. There, on the ground floor, the mausoleum has a central octagonal chamber containing a cenotaph. This chamber is surrounded by eight ancillary rooms, a radical departure from the single chamber of earlier Indian tombs. Passages connect these smaller chambers with the main one and with the outside. The second story of the tomb is similar. Such a spatial arrangement is based on geometric principles first applied in Timurid architecture and seen in structures such as the cIshrat Khana built about 1464 and used as a dynastic mausoleum for women.

These eight ancillary chambers are intended to evoke the paradises of Islamic cosmology. The passages connecting them are probably intended to facilitate circumambulation of the cenotaph in the central chamber. This ritual, drawn from sufic rites, was a common practice at Mughal imperial tombs. The tomb's adherence to geometric principle and the complexity of its internal organization bear a clear imprint of Timurid tradition. This is not surprising since the architect himself had worked extensively in Bukhara, the last bastion of Timurid artistic traditions. Coupled with the fact that Humayun and his wife had long been exiled in Iran and developed a taste for an Iranian aesthetic, this easily explains the tomb's appearance.

Moreover, the Mughals were extremely proud of their Timurid ancestry, and it is not without significance that this Timurid-inspired tomb and setting continued for the most part to serve as an important model for imperial tombs. Some believe that Humayun's tomb was conceived as a Mughal dynastic mausoleum in the tradition of the great Timurid dynastic mausolea, for example, the Gur-i Amir in Samarqand. It was, however, not used as the tomb for subsequent rulers, although some members of the royal house were buried there. In 1565, only three years after its commencement, Akbar began construction on his massive Agra fort and moved his administration there.

Moving the imperial headquarters from Delhi did not signal its abandonment by either the emperor or highly influential court members. For example, Akbar in 1571 visited his father's tomb upon its completion and in 1572-73 gave orders for the restoration of the Jamacat Khana mosque at the Nizam al-Din dargah. In 1575-76, Akbar's chief theologian (sadr), Shaikh Abd al-Nabi Khan, who wielded tremendous power until his fall from favor about 1580, constructed a mosque not in Agra or Fatehpur Sikri, then imperial residences, but in Delhi, suggesting that the city still was envisioned as a major urban center. This mosque, situated north of the Mughal Din-Panah, closely resembled Maham Anga's madrasa, although today few of its original features remain. The structure's epigraph, composed by Akbar's poet laureate, Faizi, the brother of Abu al-Fazl, does not specifically identify the structure's function, but its close adherence to the earlier madrasa suggests that it was intended as a theological school, indicating Delhi's continuing role as an intellectual center.

HUMAYUN'S TOMB

Humayun's tomb is a complex of buildings built as the Mughal Emperor Humayun's tomb, commissioned by Humayun's wife Hamida Banu Begum in 1562 CE, and designed by Mirak Mirza Ghiyath, a Persian architect. It was the first garden-tomb on the Indian subcontinent, and is located in Nizamuddin East, Delhi, India, close to the *Dina-panah* nothing also known as *Purana Qila*, that Humayun founded in 1533. It was also the first structure to use red sandstone at such a scale The complex was declared a UNESCO World Heritage Site in 1993, and since then has undergone extensive restoration work, which is still undergoing.

The complex encompasses the main tomb of the Emperor Humayun, which houses the graves of his wife, Hamida Begum, and also Dara Shikoh, son of the later Emperor Shah Jahan, as well as numerous other subsequent Mughals, including Emperor Jahandar Shah, Farrukhsiyar, Rafi Ul-Darjat, Rafi Ud-Daulat and Alamgir II. It represented a leap in Mughal architecture, and together with its accomplished Charbagh garden, typical of Persian gardens, but never seen before in India, it set a precedent for subsequent Mughal architecture. It is seen as a clear departure from the fairly modest mausoleum of his father, the first Mughal Emperor, Babur, called *Bagh-e Babur* (Gardens of Babur) in Kabul (Afghanistan). Though the latter was the first Emperor to start the tradition of being buried in a paradise garden. Modelled on *Gur-e Amir*, the tomb of his ancestor and Asia's conqueror Timur in Samarkand, it created a precedent for future Mughal architecture of royal mausolea, which reached its zenith with the Taj Mahal, at Agra. The site was chosen on the banks of Yamuna river, due to its proximity to Nizamuddin Dargah, the mausoleum of the celebrated Sufi saint of Delhi, Nizamuddin Auliya, who was much revered by the rulers of Delhi, and whose residence, *Chilla Nizamuddin Auliya* lies just north-east of the tomb. In later Mughal history, the last Mughal Emperor, Bahadur Shah Zafar took refuge here, during the Indian Rebellion of 1857, along with three princes, and was captured by Captain Hodson before being exiled to Rangoon. At the time of the Slave Dynasty this land was under the 'KiloKheri Fort' which was capital of Sultan Kequbad, son of Nasiruddin (1268-1287).

Gardens and Hunting Pavilions

In 1619 Jahangir returned to Agra after a five-year absence. There he once again found greatest delight in the mansions and gardens of his highest-ranking nobles and those of his wife, Nur Jahan. Jahangir was highly pleased with his Gul Afshan garden, probably the same garden later owned by Nur Jahan and renamed the Nur Afshan Bagh. But at this time Jahangir clearly regarded it his own project, for he personally rewarded the architect, Khwaja Jahan, by increasing his rank. This is yet another indication of the emperor's regard for architects and garden settings. The Nur Manazil garden, also in Agra, was well under way about the time of the emperor's return to the city and appears to be another of Khwaja Jahan's designs. Delighted with its appearance, Jahangir describes a large walled garden with richly embellished dwellings, water basins, canals and planted plots. The emperor mentions that a large sum had already been expended on the project and more was to be spent. Clearly this was done, for later he mentions this garden as an entertainment site.

In Kashmir's capital city, Srinagar, Akbar had constructed a massive fort on a high hill known as the Koh-i Maran or Hari Parbat overlooking Dal lake. There Jahangir ordered the completion of the unfinished portion of the fortifications and the restoration of the palace buildings in it, especially a garden and Public Audience Hall. Muctamad Khan was charged with this work. He created a three-tiered garden. There he had its pavilion embellished with the work of master painters, as was done at Jahangir's palaces in Ajmer, Agra and Lahore. Again, in keeping with many of his earlier works, Jahangir renamed this garden Nur Afza, Light Increasing, after himself, continuing his long-standing fascination with light imagery. The banks of Srinagar's Dal lake are famed for their magnificent Mughal gardens. Although Jahangir visited Kashmir more times than any other Mughal ruler, his role in the construction of the gardens around Dal lake is less clear. However, in 1620 Jahangir ordered his son, the prince Shah Jahan, to block up the stream in an area known as Shalimar, near the banks of Dal lake. While the choice of the setting was Jahangir's, the garden is Shahjahan's (Plate 129).

Jahangir gave special attention to gardens in the valley south of Srinagar. He loved the natural streams and springs, and so added to them canals, fountains and buildings to create terraced gardens. At Loka Bhavan, some 40 km south of Srinagar, Jahangir ordered the restoration of the reservoir in front of the springs, indicating that he was not the spring's first patron, and constructed a new building there. In fact, few of these gardens are the result of a single patron. In close proximity to Loka Bhavan are the springs of Macchi Bhavan and Inch. Here the patronage is not imperial but that of high-ranking Hindu nobles; Jahangir descri Ram Das Kachhwaha's Macchi Bhavan garden and spring with crys clear waters, large fish and splendid trees beautiful beyond words. It see likely that imperial example stimulated the construction of the numerous rdens through this valley.

About 8 km north of Loka Bhavan are the natural spring and terfall of Achibal (Plate 66). Jahangir describes its water, magnificent t s and enchanting pavilions. He notes a garden with beautiful flow s, not necessarily one he constructed. Although the garden later was as ciated with Jahan Ara, Shah Jahan's favorite daughter, its appearance was bably established by Jahangir's time. At the summit of the terraced g den is the natural spring which still today is gathered in a large poo hat is dammed so that water pressure produces a powerfully impressive terfall gushing into lower terraced canals. The water chutes, carved to emble rushing water, are of Mughal origin as are the pavilion bases; wever, the pavilions' superstructures, as in most Mughal gardens, are more cently constructed. Achibal, more than any other Mughal garden, preserves the natural beauty of the falls and dense foliage, set against the towering hills.

The site in Kashmir most often mentioned by Jahangir is the spring at Vernag (Plate 67), about 10 km north of Achibal. When still a prince Jahangir visited Vernag twice. Then the crystal clear waters of the spring, the source of the powerful Jhelum river, were contained within an octagonal reservoir with cells nearby for recluses. In 1606 Jahangir ordered that the sides of the spring be faced with stone and that a garden, canal and splendid edifices be constructed. However, both epigraphical and literary sources indicate that they were not completed until his fifteenth regnal year, 1619-20. Even then, the canal and its watercourses were not fully finished, for a second inscription, dated 1626-27, describes the construction of a water course and cascade by the architect Haider. While much of the garden and surrounding pavilions have disappeared, the tank, with low walls containing arched apertures and blind arched niches, still exists as do descendants of the large fish that swim in the lucid waters, creating a spectacle of royal splendor.

Jahangir twice mentions a tower, tank and pavilion used as a hunting palace about 29 km from Lahore. Today the site is known as Sheikhupura, but Jahangir in 1606 refers to it as Jahangirpura and then in 1620 calls it Jahangirabad, both meaning City of Jahangir, the latter a more Persianate form. Here the emperor's favorite tame antelope died before 1606; it was buried in a grave above which a sculpted antelope and eulogy written by Mulla Muhammad Husain of Kashmir were placed. Adjacent to this gravestone, a tower was constructed around 1606 (Plate 68) under the supervision of Sikandar Mucin Khan, the landholder of the area. On Jahangir's orders, Sikandar Mucin Khan also built a tank and royal residence. Despite Mucin's death while the work was in progress, the complex was handsomely completed by 1620, the later stages of construction having been supervised by Iradat Khan. The expenses incurred were sufficiently awesome that the emperor recorded the amount in his memoirs. Jahangir considered the site a "kingly hunting place,"25 although his successor found the place inadequate and in 1634 spent another sizable sum rebuilding the pavilion.

The tank, tower and pavilion are well preserved. Situated to the west of the tank, the tower resembles closely the plan and elevation the so-called Hiran Minar at Fatehpur Sikri and the Nim Serai Minar at Malda, both datable to Akbar's reign (Plates 27 and 53). Built about 1606, the Sheikhupura tower belongs to the very early part of Jahangir's reign; hence, the close resemblance to Akbari prototypes is not surprising. Missing are the tusk-like projections around the sides, but holes that would have accommodated them remain. The tower's brick fabric was originally covered with a thick stucco veneer which retained traces of red, yellow and green polychrome until recently, when it was plastered anew. The tower sits on an octagonal base and was possibly used as an observation post for hunting. Aligned with the tower is a three-storied octagonal pavilion situated in the center of a large square tank. The tank was constructed in Jahangir's reign, but the three-storied octagonal pavilion in its current state is a product of Shah Jahan's patronage (Plate 128).

GARDENS OF SHAH JAHAN

Shah Jahan had a life-long interest in the construction of superbly well-ordered gardens. Many of these served as the setting for major structural works, for example the tomb of Mumtaz Mahal, better known today as the Taj Mahal, or Jahangir's tomb in Lahore. Palaces also incorporated gardens into their layout. Other gardens, however, were developed independently of tombs and palaces. Structures enhanced these gardens, but they were not the reason for the gardens' existence. Most of the gardens Shah Jahan built or renovated were situated between Agra and Kabul. They thus could double as camps or as an imperial serai along the road to Kashmir and further to Kabul. In 1634 when Shah Jahan was en route from Agra to Kashmir via Lahore, he stopped at a number of gardens, including one in Ambala. Shah Jahan had constructed a garden there when he was still a prince. Upon his accession he gave the garden to Jahan Ara, his eldest and favorite daughter, and ordered that suitable buildings be erected there for the women serving as imperial wetnurses. Continuing his travels to Kashmir in 1634, Shah Jahan proceeded from Ambala to Sirhind and there pitched camp in the Bagh-i Hafiz Rakhna. It had been initially constructed by Akbar and later renewed under Jahangir. During this visit Shah Jahan ordered

Diyanat Khan, the faujdar (law and order official) of Sirhind, to add several structures including private quarters, an audience hall, a viewing balcony and terraced platforms on the banks of the garden's tank.

These buildings, completed in 1635, were visited by Shah Jahan at that time. The garden, today known as the Amm Khass Bagh, was divided into four sections, one for fruit trees, another for flowers, the third for vegetables and the fourth for the royal palace. Several structures there retain the imprint of Shah Jahan's patronage. The most notable of these is a two-storied building with a curved bangala roof, a type associated with imperial structures. The climate and natural beauty of Kashmir made it the Mughal seat of rest and leisure. Shah Jahan enjoyed the many Mughal gardens there - some imperially sponsored, others built by princes and high-ranking officials. Among those he praised were the one at Avantipur constructed by Dara Shukoh, Asaf Khan's Nishat Bagh, and Nur Jahan's Bagh-i Nur Afza, all located within the Srinagar Valley. But the most impressive of all are Shah Jahan's own gardens in Kashmir, especially the world famous Shalimar garden.

Shalimar garden, situated on the edge of Dal lake in Srinagar and set against the Pir Panjal mountain range, was termed by the Frenchman Bernier the most beautiful of all the gardens. While this site long had served as a garden, its conversion into a terraced Mughal-type garden commenced in 1620, when Jahangir ordered the prince Shah Jahan to dam the stream near Shalimar. In 1634 Shah Jahan further enlarged the garden. It was extended to reach the foot of the mountains, and additional pavilions were then built. Although the older name Shalimar was never abandoned, the Mughals called their new garden the Bagh-i Faiz Bakhsh and Farah Bakhsh, reflecting its division into two parts. The lower terraces, used for imperial audiences, formed the Farah Bakhsh garden (Garden of the Bestower of Pleasure). The higher terraces nearer the mountains, intended for private use, were known as the Faiz Bakhsh (Bestower of Plenty). The garden was approached from Dal lake. According to Bernier, a tree-lined canal led to a small fore-garden that originally fronted Shalimar proper.

The entire garden is divided laterally by a wide stream that commences from the mountains behind and runs the entire length of the garden through the terraced levels. Carved water chutes enhance the effect of rapidly running water. Recessed niches for lamps were carved into the terraced walls over which cascading water fell, illuminating the water at night, for the gardens were used as much then as during the day. Pools with spouting fountains further embellish the garden. In the center of each part of the garden is a black stone pavilion (Plate 129) covered with a tiered roof. Serving as imperial seats, these pavilions stretch across the canal overlooking cascading waterfalls. In the lower garden a centrally placed black platform, serving as the imperial throne, is situated across the water between bracketed pillars. Shah Jahan's Shalimar garden epitomizes the long-standing Mughal love of architectural setting within ordered nature.

Although the most famous Shalimar garden is the one in Kashmir, another Shalimar, also known in contemporary times as the Bagh-i Faiz Bakhsh and Farah Bakhsh, was constructed by Shah Jahan in Lahore. In Mughal times, it was on the city's outskirts, though now it is well within modern Lahore. Modeled generally on Shah Jahan's Kashmir Shalimar, it is a large terraced garden, though not situated on a river bank; instead, its water supply derived from a great canal that originated considerably north of Lahore and brought water to this Mughal city. In 1641, Khalil Allah Khan was ordered to commence the garden. A year and a half later it was completed at considerable time.

This garden consists of three terraces divided laterally by a wide canal. The lowest terrace is essentially a square four-part garden of the standard Mughal type. Marble imperial residences and audience halls are located on the second terrace on the edges of the large central tank filled with spouting fountains (Plate 130). One marble platform is even located in the center of the tank and linked to each of the banks by narrow red stone bridges supported on cusped arches. Included in the garden were seats for public audiences, baths inlaid with stones, and residences for the emperor and his daughter. During Shah Jahan's time there were so many buildings that according to contemporary historians tents were not pitched when the imperial camp was in residence. When Shah Jahan visited Lahore, he often stayed here rather than at the imperial residence in the fort.

TAJ MAHAL : MUGHAL MONUMENTS

Of all Mughal monuments, the renowned Taj Mahal (Plate 131) best represents the continuing imperial fascination with paradisical imagery. It was built as the tomb of Shah Jahan's favorite wife, Mumtaz Mahal; after his d h Shah Jahan was interred there as well, as probably he had long inter d. While it is often said that Shah Jahan planned to construct for him a structure similar to the Taj Mahal in black stone across the river, ther no evidence to support this. The Taj Mahal has become one of the worl best known monuments. This domed white marble structure is situ l on a high plinth at the northern end of a four-quartered garden, evok the gardens of paradise, enclosed within walls measuring 305 by 549 ters. Outside the walls, in an area known as Mumtazabad, were livin uarters for attendants, markets, serais and other structures built by l merchants and nobles.

tomb complex and the other imperial structures of Mumtazabad wer intained by the income of thirty villages given specifically for the tomb's support. The name Taj Mahal is unknown in Mughal chronicles, but it is used by contemporary Europeans in India, suggesting that this was the tomb's popular name. In contemporary texts, it is generally called simply the Illumined Tomb (Rauza-i Munawara). Mumtaz Mahal died shortly after delivering her fourteenth child in 1631. The Mughal court was then residing in Burhanpur. Her remains were temporarily buried by the grief-stricken emperor in a spacious garden known as Zainabad on the bank of the river Tapti. Six months later her body was transported to Agra, where it was interred in land chosen for the mausoleum. This land, situated south of the Mughal city on the bank of the Jumna, had belonged to the Kachhwaha rajas since the time of Raja Man Singh and was purchased from the then current raja, Jai Singh. Although contemporary chronicles indicate Jai Singh's willing cooperation in this exchange, extant farmans (imperial commands) indicate that the final price was not settled until almost two years after the mausoleum's commencement. Jai Singh's further cooperation was insured by imperial orders issued between 1632 and 1637 demanding that he provide stone masons and carts to transport marble from the mines at Makranaj within his ancestral domain, to Agra where both the Taj Mahal and Shah Jahan's additions to the Agra fort were constructed concurrently.

Work on the mausoleum was commenced early in 1632. Inscriptional evidence indicates much of the tomb was completed by 1636. By 1643, when Shah Jahan most lavishly celebrated the cUrs ceremony for Mumtaz Mahal, the entire complex was virtually complete. Some of the numerous artists who worked on the Taj Mahal are known from contemporary sources. Makramat Khan, later associated with the supervision of Shahjahanabad, and Abd al-Karim, a master architect in Jahangir's reign and subsequently responsible for the Shah Burj in the Lahore fort completed in 1631-32, supervised the project. Amanat Khan was the chief calligrapher. No architect's name is recorded in the contemporary chronicles; however, a work by the poet Lutf Allah identifies the poet's father, Ustad Ahmad, later Shahjahanabad's architect, as the designer of Mumtaz Mahal's tomb. Shah Jahan himself doubtless played a major role in the design and execution of this tomb, as he did in his other architectural enterprises. Possibly the emperor's active role in design explains why Ustad Ahmad's name is omitted in the official chronicle written by Lahauri. The entire complex was proportionally designed according to a series of geometrically related grids, hence explaining not only the tomb's perfect balance but also that of the entire complex. The initial part of the complex is a red sandstone forecourt (chowk-i jilo khana) south of the walled garden. This area, like its counterpart at Jahangir's tomb, was intended for the imperial retinue. A magnificent red sandstone gateway, about 30 meters high and leading into the walled garden, also serves as the northern wall of the forecourt. The entrance is within a deeply recessed central arch that is surmounted by small domed chattris recalling Akbar's ceremonial entrance, the Buland Darwaza, to his Jamic mosque at Fatehpur Sikri (Plate 23). The entire central pishtaq is framed by a rectangular panel composed of black Arabic lettering inlaid into a white marble ground and dated 1647. Four chapters from the Quran comprise this text, including the final verses from a chapter entitled Daybreak that invites the faithful to enter paradise (89: 28-30). This message is similar to that given not in Quranic verse but in a Persian poem on the gateway to Akbar's tomb in nearby Sikandra (Plate j8). This parallel is not fortuitous, for the calligrapher responsible for both these gates was Abd al-Haqq Shirazi, who had been awarded the title Amanat Khan early in Shah Jahan's reign. Although Amanat Khan died about two years before the calligraphy on the gate was completed, the close stylistic similarities and the programmatic unity of all the verses on the complex suggest that his design continued to be followed.

Beyond the forecourt is a four-part garden divided into quadrants by wide waterways that resemble the streams of paradise mentioned in the Quran more than the much narrower courses at earlier Mughal tombs. They meet at a large tank in the garden's center. The garden is clearly modeled on a wellestablished concept, the garden of paradise. At the garden's northern end, not in its center, is the splendid tomb. It is flanked on the west by a red sandstone mosque surmounted by white marble domes and on the east by a nearly identical structure called in contemporary texts a guest house or mehman khana. The mosque's facade is delicately inlaid with white marble and in its spandrels are colored stones, while the interior is richly polychromed.

Mumtaz Mahal's superbly proportioned mausoleum is seated on the center of a high square marble plinth that elevates the tomb above the garden. The plinth is at the river's edge, and to compensate for the effects of flooding it rests on deeply sunk wells. At each corner of the plinth is a four-storied marble minaret recalling those used in earlier Timurid funereal architecture, for example the Gur-i Amir at Samarqand, as well as at Jahangir's tomb (Plate 103) whose construction was commenced by Shah Jahan only a few years before the Taj Mahal. Surmounted by a bulbous white dome, the tomb is essentially square in plan with corners chamfered to form a Baghdadi octagon. Each of the tomb's four faces is marked by a high central pishtaq flanked by deeply recessed arched apertures. The design is controlled and balanced, creating a unique architectural achievement that many consider one of the wonders of the world.

The Taj Mahal has often been likened to Humayun's tomb (Plates 18 and 19), a building essentially Timurid in character and designed by an architect trained in the Timurid homeland. This form, quite different from more nearly contemporary multi-tiered Mughal tombs, was probably adopted because Shah Jahan was immensely proud of his Timurid ancestry (upon his accession, remember, he adopted the very titles used by Timur). The exterior of the mausoleum is primarily white marble. Inlaid colored stones are more sparsely used here than on his palace architecture constructed at the same time. As on the gate facade, rectangular panels with black calligraphy rendering verses from the Quran are inlaid into the tomb's white surface. The play of light, reflected and absorbed by the marble surface, is a dominant decorative device. Light continues to have a metaphoric role, associated with God's presence, as it did in Jahangir's monuments. While Islam teaches that God is everywhere, nowhere would God's presence be more appropriate than in the gardens of paradise, that is, the ultimate abode of the true believer. A series of panels carved with sprays of floral motifs form dadoes along the tomb's base. Although the matching of flowers with the leaves on a single spray defies botanical identification, the flowers depicted - roses, narcissus and tulips among others - came in Persianate culture to be associated with the flowers of paradise; moreover, they are the flowers used to describe the features of the beloved in Persian mystic poetry. The beloved on the most profound level is a metaphor for God and also might refer to the beloved of the emperor, his deceased wife here entombed.

The layout of the tomb's ground floor is similar to that at Humayun's tomb, although here the surrounding chambers are linked in a more fluid fashion. As at Humayun's tomb, they are intended to represent the eight levels of paradise in Islamic cosmology. The central chamber is octagonal. In its center is a magnificent inlaid marble cenotaph marking the placement of Mumtaz Mahal's interred body in the crypt below. Shah Jahan's cenotaph, similarly embellished, is to the west of the deceased queen's. The off-center position of Shah Jahan's cenotaph in no way indicates that it was added as an afterthought. In the tomb of Ictimad al-Daula, built in 1626, his wife's cenotaph, not his, occupies the more prominent central position. Surrounding the cenotaphs of Shah Jahan and Mumtaz Mahal is a carved latticed marble screen that Shah Jahan ordered to replace the gold one designed by Bebadal Khan, his master goldsmith. Shah Jahan became worried that the gold one would be looted.

The interior, like the exterior, bears rectangular bands of Quranic verses, more than on any earlier Mughal building. Quranic passages, many of them entire chapters, are inscribed on the tomb complex. All those chosen for inclusion here have a common theme, the reward promised to believers and the fate of eternal doom that awaits non-believers on the Day of Judgment. This theme is appropriate for funereal architecture. The number of Quranic verses and their emphasis on the Day of Judgment is reinforced by the location of the mausoleum, not only at the end of the paradisical gardens but also on the platform above them.

That position matches the very location of God's throne, which, according to Islamic tradition, will be above the gardens of paradise. This is illustrated in a diagrammatic drawing that Shah Jahan owned depicting the assembled on the Day of Judgment. This drawing possibly served as a model for the design of the Taj Mahal, intended not only as a tomb for his beloved wife and himself, but also as a visual replica of the throne of God on that momentous day. Although such an interpretation may seem radical, in fact, evoking God's throne was not an innovation here.

Earlier it was a common poetic conceit and continued in contemporary writing to be used as an image for tombs, gardens, palaces and mosques. All the designers of this unique tomb were highly educated not only in mathematics, engineering and astrology, but also in literature and, of course, theology. They were thus well prepared to formulate the tomb's symbolic program as the ultimate vision of paradise on earth. That such a program would appeal to Shah Jahan is not difficult to accept, for paradisical imagery is found in nearly every work he commissioned.

PATRONAGE OF AURANGZEBN

Attitude toward Hindu construction Condemned by some as a religious zealot and praised by others as an upholder of Islam, Aurangzeb and his religious policies are among the most misunderstood of all Mughal history. There is no doubt that Aurangzeb was a devout Sunni Muslim. Highly educated, he spent his leisure reading the Quran and in prayer. Aurangzeb's court also assumed an increasingly orthodox atmosphere. For example, the practice of jharoka, the daily presentation of the emperor to his subjects, was abandoned since it was derived from the Hindu notion of darshan. Court dancing girls and musicians were released, but only ostensibly for religious reasons.

Aurangzeb did not have the resources to maintain them. More controversial than the increasing austerity of the court and its ritual is Aurangzeb's attitude toward Hindu construction, especially temples. Common belief holds that he destroyed massive numbers of Hindu temples and banned the construction of new ones. True, he did not encourage the construction of new temples, continuing a policy already in practice under his father, Shah Jahan. But when Aurangzeb did destroy temples, he did so not out of bigotry but as a political response when his authority was challenged. For example, the Keshava Deva temple in Mathura, built by the Mughal amir Raja Bir Singh and supported by imperial grants, was destroyed to retaliate for seriously disruptive Jat uprisings in the Mathura area in 1669-70.' Mughal losses were heavy. Abd al-Nabi Khan, the commandant of Mathura (faujdar) and the patron of that city's Jamic mosque (Plate 177), was among the Mughals killed. Temples in Cooch Behar were destroyed in 1661 after the local rajas there had defied Mughal authority. Those Hindus who remained loyal were rewarded, indicating that temple destruction in Cooch Behar was politically motivated, not simply an aggressive act against Hindus. The demolition of temples as Udaipur, Jodhpur and other places in Rajasthan in 1679 and 1680, too, was a response to long-term recalcitrance on the part of the ranas there. Similarly the destruction of Raja Man Singh's famous Vishvanath temple in Benares was largely to punish Hindus, especially those related to the temple's patron, who were suspected of supporting the Maratha Shivaji. Many of these temples desecrated by Aurangzeb, including the largest and most notable among them, had been built by Mughal amirs. In each case, Aurangzeb reacted to the violation of a long-established allegiance system binding emperor and nobility by destroying property maintained previously with Mughal support. Thus in a sense Aurangzeb destroyed state-endowed property, not private works.

Some of Aurangzeb's alleged destruction is more legendary than real. He is commonly accused of destroying the caves at Ellora and other sites in modern Maharashtra, but these assertions are made in considerably later sources. They are not mentioned in any contemporary Persian chronicle, where such destruction is generally reported in terms of glorious holy war (jihad). Rather, Aurangzeb's own writings praise the beauty of Ellora. Aurangzeb himself says the caves must be the work of Almighty God,7 indicating that he had an aesthetic sensitivity that many assume he lacked, in fact, a sensitivity not limited to Islamic patronized structures. Moreover, decrees (farman) testify that imperial support was provided for temples throughout Aurangzeb's reign. These orders were issued either to protect the rights of Hindu subjects or to reward service rendered by Hindus. Imperial mosques

Contemporary histories relate that Aurangzeb repaired numerous older mosques. The frequent mention of his repair and construction of mosques suggests that this was the architectural enterprise he most highly valued. He reputedly repaired more mosques than any of his predecessors, not just Mughal mosques but also those built under the Tughluq, Lodi and Deccani sultans as well. In other cases Aurangzeb was attentive to the maintenance of mosques. Once he ordered a lamp for a mosque in an old outpost, and on another occasion he wrote to his prime minister (wazir) to express dismay that the carpets and other furnishings of the palace were in better condition than those of the palace's mosque. After capturing Maratha forts, Aurangzeb often ordered the construction of a mosque. In part they were erected from religious fervor and in part they served as a symbol of Mughal conquest. These mosques were probably constructed quickly of locally available materials. Other mosques he built filled a genuine need. For example, in Bijapur city he built an cIdgah since there was no suitable one there. In the Bijapur palace he added a mosque for his personal use. To gain special merit, the emperor even laid some of the stones himself. Concerned that all remaining materials should not be used for impious purposes, Aurangzeb ordered them buried.

Shortly after his accession, Aurangzeb ordered a small marble chapel, known today as the Moti or Pearl mosque, to be constructed inside the Shahjahanabad fort (Plate 160). Shah Jahan had built no mosque inside this fort, using instead the large Jamic mosque for congregational prayers. Aurangzeb, however, wanted a mosque close to his private quarters. Five years under construction, his exquisite mosque was completed in 1662-63 a t considerable personal expense. It is enclosed by red sandstone walls that vary in thickness to compensate for the mosque's angle, necessary to orient the building toward Mecca, and at the same time to align it with the other palace buildings. Entered on the east, the compound consists of a courtyard with a recessed pool and the mosque building.

Although the mosque and its courtyard are small, about 9 by 15 meters internally, the high walls, over which nothing can be seen, emphasize the sense of compact verticality creating a sense of spatial tension, a characteristic of Aurangzeb's architecture. This is further underscored by the three bulbous domes on constricted necks, the central one rising above the others. These domes were originally gilt-covered copper that resembled gold, drawing attention to the height. They later were replaced with white marble domes, still in place. Closely modeled on the Nagina mosque (Plate 114), the prayer chamber, entered through three cusped arches, is divided into two aisles of three bays each with an ancillary corridor on the north for use by the court ladies. The marble surfaces here and on the courtyard walls (Plate 161) are more ornately rendered than those on Shah Jahan's mosques (Plates 105, 114, 115 and 124). Here arabesque foliate forms - unique during this period to imperial palace mosques - cusped arches, and even architectural members are elegantly carved. They serve as a contrast to the much more sedate ornamentation of Shah Jahan's religious edifices. The immediate source of this ornate decor is surely Plate 161. Courtyard walls, Moti mosque, Shahjahanabad, Delhi the organic carving on Shah Jahan's later palace architecture, for example, the nearby throne of Shah Jahan's Public Audience Hall (Plate 119). Aurangzeb's Badshahi mosque (Plate 162) also reveals an ornateness and emphasis on spatial tension seen in the Moti mosque, but on a much larger scale. Adjoining the Lahore fort, the Badshahi mosque remains the largest mosque in the subcontinent. An inscription over the east entrance gate indicates that it was built in 1673-74 by Aurangzeb under the supervision of Fidai Khan Koka, the emperor's foster brother. Prior to this time Lahore had no monumental mosque capable of serving the population. Aurangzeb's construction of this mosque follows Shah Jahan's provision of large mosques close to the Agra and Delhi forts.

Situated on a raised platform, the mosque is approached by high steps. The east entrance is a large vaulted gatehouse made of red Sikri sandstone. It opens to an enormous courtyard. Built to hold 60,000 persons, the mosque served an unusual dual function of cIdgah and Jamic mosque. The prayer chamber adheres generally to the plan of Shah Jahan's Delhi mosque (Plate 124) constructed about two decades earlier, although it is considerably larger. While closely modeled on Shah Jahan-period congregational mosques, the Badshahi mosque reveals a greater sense of spatial tension in keeping with the new aesthetic established early in Aurangzeb's reign. This is achieved, in part, by the sheer scale of the complex and by the facade's arched openings that are small in comparison to the building's overall massive size. Further underscoring this spatial tension are the bulbous domes and the minarets at the compound corners that emphasize the sense of verticality.

The ornamentation, like that on Aurangzeb's Moti mosque, is less chaste than on Shah Jahan's religious buildings. Here floral designs, cusped arches and cartouche motifs are outlined with white marble inlaid into the red surface. In lieu of the smooth flowing lines that characterized ornament on Shah Jahan's mosques, a series of short curved lines form the designs, thus creating a sense of ornateness that becomes characteristic of later Mughal design.

The mosque's stucco interior relief, including baluster columns (Plate 163), is polychromed to achieve the effect of inlaid stone seen earlier in Shah Jahan's architecture. Aurangzeb's mosques built in close association with palaces - primarily those dating to the time of his father, Shah Jahan - are considerably more ornate than the mosques of Shah Jahan's reign. Their decor, however, is inspired by Shah Jahan's palace architecture. Ornateness formerly reserved for palaces is now found in mosques which to Aurangzeb were the most significant architectural type. As palaces were less important to him, he curtailed some of the earlier court ritual; for example, in his eleventh regnal year he abolished the practice oijharoka. Significantly after this time, his most elaborate mosque, the Badshahi mosque, was built.

For Aurangzeb, personal devotion and the ritual of prayer were more meaningful than courtly ritual such as the viewing of the emperor at the jharoka that had developed to bolster the semi-divine character of earlier Mughal rulers. Thus, by extension, features formerly associated with royalty were now associated with piety and Islam. Most telling is the use of the baluster column and fulsome floral forms found earlier on the marble throne in the Shahjahanabad palace's Public Audience Hall, but now found in what Aurangzeb must have considered a strictly religious realm.

By contrast to the ornateness of Aurangzeb's palace mosques is the impressive red sandstone cIdgah at Mathura (Plate 164), also certainly sponsored by Aurangzeb. This cIdgah, a mosque for the annual cId celebration, replaced the temple of Keshava Deva, destroyed in 1669-70 by Aurangzeb's command to avenge on-going insubordination by Jats. One chronicler notes that after the temple's destruction a large sum was spent on the construction of a mosque. The patron's name is not mentioned by the Mughal chronicler, but a European visiting Mathura within the decade states that it was built by Aurangzeb himself. The structure's size, 52 by 20 meters, as well as its appearance suggest imperial patronage. Situated high on a hill, the cIdgah is built on the foundations of the destroyed temple. The facade is similar to that of the contemporary Badshahi mosque. For example, all the entrances are cusped, but they have no inlaid marble work. The mosque's double-aisled multi-bayed interior also bears little ornamentation; a large recessed tri-partite central mihrab is its most striking feature.

This mosque bears considerably less ornamentation than do the other two built by Aurangzeb, but they were associated with imperial palaces. The Mathura cIdgah, however, was situated nowhere near a palace. Rather, it was built at Mathura, a city then of secondary importance, on top of a demolished temple, to remind rebel forces that non-Muslims would be tolerated only so long as Mughal authority was obeyed. Tombs Like his predecessors, Aurangzeb visited the dargahs of esteemed saints and contributed sizable sums for their maintenance, especially those of Gesu Daraz in Gulbarga, Mucin al-Din in Ajmer and Khwaja Qutb Sahib Bakhtiyar Kaki in Delhi. But unlike the earlier Mughal rulers, his attitude toward building at these shrines is ambiguous. At one point he comments that the erection of mausolea over graves is not in accordance with orthodox Islamic practice. In fact, he provided no buildings at the Ajmer or Gulbarga shrines. Yet he did order renovation of Bakhtiyar Kaki's tomb in Delhi and had a drawing made of the shrine's layout. Although the dargah dates to the thirteenth century, active Mughal patronage of it commenced under Aurangzeb, when several princes were buried there. The colored tiles with floral sprays inlaid into the west wall of the saint's tomb are probably Aurangzeb's contribution. Toward the end of his life, Aurangzeb noted that visiting graves was not acceptable in orthodox Islam. Nevertheless, the location of his own tomb indicates that he personally never lost esteem for saints. For just before he died, Aurangzeb ordered the construction of his tomb at the dargah of Shaikh Burhan al-Din in Khuldabad, meaning the Abode of Eternity, not far from Aurangabad and the Ellora caves. This area long had been the burial site of esteemed saints as well as some Deccani and Mughal princes. The emperor's open-air grave, in accordance with his final wishes, was marked by a simple stone cenotaph, although in the early twentieth century it was faced with white marble. The top was filled with earth so plants might grow. Its original simplicity followed a form used earlier at Jahan Ara's tomb (Plate 167), one that in the eighteenth century became common.

Throughout his life Aurangzeb was concerned about the maintenance of royal tombs, foreshadowing the interest in his own. He protested bitterly when land containing the grave of one of his deceased daughters was purchased. When a prince, Aurangzeb had written Shah Jahan regarding repairs that he felt were mandatory for the preservation of his mother's tomb, the Taj Mahal (Plate 131). After Shah Jahan's death, Aurangzeb ordered the governor of every province to send 2,000 rupees for the maintenance of this tomb.

Fortification, Palace and Garden Architecture

Despite his primary concern with religious building, Aurangzeb maintained a lifelong interest in secular structures. For example, he built and repaired serais, wells and bridges - structures all necessary for the welfare of the state. In addition, the construction of fortifications was well in keeping with this emperor's interests in territorial expansion. During the first few years of his reign, Aurangzeb constructed outer defensive gates before Shah Jahan's Lahore and Delhi gates of the Shahjahanabad palace. Reputedly the imprisoned Shah Jahan, upon hearing of this, wrote, "You have made the fort a bride and set a veil before her face."19 These monumental gates, composed of red sandstone, obscured Shah Jahan's ceremonial entrances into the fort and their original direct alignment with the city's main bazaar, its canal and Jahan Ara's gardens. They did, however, lend military strength to the fort. Aurangzeb also ordered an outer defensive wall (sher hajji) erected around the Agra fort. It was built in three years under the supervision of Ictibar Khan. Later in his reign, Aurangzeb ordered forts constructed during the campaign against the Afghans, and in 1705 another was built in conjunction with the campaign against the Marathas. In various Deccani cities additional fortification was provided. In 1683 Ihtamam Khan was charged with building walls around the city of Aurangabad. These masonry walls today have virtually disappeared, but several of the original thirteen gates still exist. The Delhi gate (Plate 165), marked by a wide entrance arch and engaged polygonal turrets surmounted by a domed chattri on each side, follows an older regional form, not one characteristic of contemporary Mughal structures elsewhere in India.

Aurangzeb's concerns extended beyond the military security of a locale. In Delhi he banned any construction that did not have his prior approval and went so far as to dismantle a structure erected by a lady of the court without his permission. Even after his permanent departure from Shahjahanabad, Aurangzeb ordered Aqil Khan, governor (subadar) of Delhi, to maintain its gardens, palaces and serais. The emperor ordered reports on their condition and had drawings of them prepared. The rooms of the palace were cleaned, locked and the carpets stored to prevent damage.

Once Aurangzeb had moved permanently to the Deccan he did not reside in older palaces of the Deccani sultans. He had new ones built, including the palace at Aurangabad. In addition, Aurangzeb repaired the residences of others. For example, in 1685 he ordered renovations to an earlier palace near Ahmadnagar. Aurangzeb, like his predecessors, clearly felt that palatial residences were a necessity for a king. He objected, however, to the misuse of palatial settings, stating that dissipated rulers spent inordinate time in the pleasures of a palace. Like his predecessors, Aurangzeb loved garden settings and rewarded gardeners for good work. He built only a few, mostly when still a prince, including a garden and tank in the vicinity of Bijapur as well as one in Ujjain. Aurangzeb, again like his predecessors, was taken by the beauty of Kashmir and its gardens, although he decreed in the sixth year of his reign that no king should visit there unless on military or administrative business; the pursuit of pleasure, he believed, was inadequate reason for going to Kashmir.

During Aurangzeb's reign, most members of the imperial family were more devoted to the patronage of literature and religion than to the construction of grand edifices and gardens. However, several notable tombs and mosques were constructed by the royal family, including the Bibi-ka Maqbara, or Tomb of the Queen, built in Aurangabad (Plate 166). This monumental white tomb, completed in 1660-61, was built for Rabica Daurani, Aurangzeb's wife, also known as Dilrus Banu, who died in 1657. At Aurangzeb's command, their eldest son, Prince Aczam Shah, built this tomb closely modeled on the Taj Mahal (Plate 131).

Persian inscriptions on the tomb's south entrance gate give the names of the architect, Ata Allah, the supervisor, Aqa Abu al-Qasim Beg, and the engineer, Haspat Rai. Other contemporary documents indicate that the supervisor and others in responsible positions were at the site continuously during this time, Plate 166. Tomb of Rabica Daurani, also known as the Bibi-ka Maqbara, Aurangabad thus resulting in the tomb's completion within four years of the queen's death. The architect, Ata Allah, was the son of Ustad Ahmad, architect of the Taj Mahal and Shahjahanabad fort. This does much to explain the tomb's close resemblance to the Taj. Rabica Daurani's tomb is situated in the middle of a char bagb, typical of most imperial Mughal tombs (Plate 19). Approximately half the size of the Taj Mahal, this tomb is different in notable ways. At Rabica Daurani's tomb there is an emphasis on the building's verticality, not the harmonious balance of proportions as at the Taj. This rapid shift in spatial arrangement occurring shortly after Aurangzeb's accession triggers innovative directions for eighteenth- and nineteenth-century architecture.

While marble is the predominant building material for the Taj, burnished stucco covers the Bibi-ka Maqbara and its adjacent mosques. Only on the tomb's interior is marble used. Unlike the Taj, Rabica Daurani's tomb has no inlaid work. Instead, the tomb's ornate surfaces are carved with panels of intricate floral sprays. Although the mausoleum itself is not painted, rich polychrome decorates the elaborate net vaulting of the entrance gates. The carving, polychrome and the emphasis on the tomb's verticality are characteristic of late seventeenth- and eighteenth-century tombs and elaborate dwellings. By contrast the two mosques inside the tomb's compound bear little elaborate ornament, recalling more the private mosques of Shah Jahan (Plates 105, 106, 114 and 115) than Aurangzeb's contemporary Moti mosque in the Shahjahanabad fort (Plates 160 and 161). Rabica Daurani's tomb is the last imperial Mughal tomb built in the tradition of monumental covered mausolea set in a char bagh. Raushan Ara's structural tomb had been built in Shah Jahan's time with an opening in the roof exposing the cenotaph to the elements. The taste for simple graves uncovered by any superstructure, hence in accordance with orthodox practice, increases throughout the late seventeenth and eighteenth centuries. Aurangzeb's own grave was of this type. So was the one built by Shah Jahan's devoted daughter, Jahan Ara, for many years the most powerful woman in the empire. She is buried in Delhi at Nizam al-Din's dargab, not far from the tomb of the esteemed saint. Enclosed by beautifully carved marble screens, her white marble cenotaph serves as a planter (Plate 167). It is marked by a marble slab carved with a verse demonstrating her humble piety and devotion to the Chishti saints. Forgiven by Aurangzeb after Shah Jahan's death, Jahan Ara regained her position as a significant cultural force. She lived the rest of her life in Delhi writing a biography of Mucin al-Din Chishti and died in 1681.

Simple graves and cenotaphs now mark the burial sites of imperial princesses. Among them was Zeb al-Nisa, who died in 1702, the oldest of Aurangzeb's children and a beneficent patron of poetry and literature, and Zinat al-Nisa, Aurangzeb's second daughter, who was noted for her piety and charity. Each was buried in separate grave sites near or in Shahjahanabad. Their tombs, each destroyed, had simple graves marked by a cenotaph and headstone carved with Quranic verses similar to those at Jahan Ara's grave. In conjunction with her simple tomb, dated 1711-12, Zinat al-Nisa constructed a large mosque in Shahjahanabad (Plate 168). Located due south of the palace and overlooking the Jumna river, it was built on a high plinth. The location and size of this mosque, along with those constructed by earlier ladies of the court (cf. Plate 116), underscore the status of the patron. The mosque's red and white striped domes and high centralpishtaq, among other features, are modeled closely on Shah Jahan's Jamic mosque (Plate 124). Typical of Aurangzeb's architecture, however, are the tightly constricted necks of the domes and cusped entrance arches supported on slender piers, emphasizing the structure's height.

SAFDARJUNG'S TOMB

Safdarjung's Tomb is a garden tomb in a marble mausoleum in Delhi, India. It was built in 1754 in the style of late Mughal architecture. The top story of the edifice houses the Archaeological Survey of India. The garden, in the style evolved by the Mughal Empire that is now known as the Mughal gardens style known as a *charbagh*, is entered through an ornate gate. Its facade is decorated with elaborate plaster carvings.

Description

The tomb was built for Safdarjung, the powerful prime minister of Muhammad Shah who was the weak Mughal emperor from 1719 to 1748. The central tomb has a huge dome. There are four water canals leading to four buildings. One has an ornately decorated gateway while the other three are pavilions, with living quarters built into the walls. Octagonal towers are in the corners. The canals are four oblong tanks, one on each side of the tomb

SHALIMAR BAGH (SRINAGAR)

Shalimar Bagh, is a Mughal garden linked through a channel to the northeast of Dal Lake. Its other names are Shalamar Garden, Shalamar Bagh, Farah Baksh and Faiz Baksh, and the other famous shore line garden in the vicinity is the Nishat Bagh. The Bagh was built by Mughal Emperor Jahangir for his wife Nur Jahan, in 1619. The Bagh is considered the high point of Mughal horticulture. It is now public park.

History

While the recent history and development of the Mughal types of gardens is credited to Emperor Jahangir of the Mughal Dynasty, the ancient history of the garden that existed here is traced to the 2nd century when it was built during the reign of Pravarsena II. Praversena II founded the city of Srinagar and ruled in Kashmir from 79 AD to 139 AD. He had built a cottage for his stay at the northeastern corner of the Dal Lake and had named it as Shalimar ('Shalimar' in Sanskrit means "Abode or Hall of Love").

The King, on his visits to a local saint by the name Sukarma Swami at Harwan, used to halt at this cottage. Over the years, the cottage fell into ruins and later could not be located also. However, the village name remained as 'Shalimar'. It is at this location that Emperor Jahangir built his celebrated Shalimar Bagh, his dream project to please his queen. He enlarged the ancient garden in 1619 into a royal garden and called it as

'Farah Baksh' (meaning: 'the delightful'). He built this for his wife Nur Jahan (meaning: 'light of the world'). In 1630, under Emperor Shah Jahan's orders, Zafar Khan the Governor of Kashmir got it extended He named it 'Faiz Baksh' ('the bountiful'). It then became a pleasure place for the Pathan and Sikh governors who followed Zafar Khan. During the rule of Maharaja Ranjit Singh the marble pavilion was the guest house for the European visitors. Electrification of the premises was done during Maharaja Hari Singh's rule. Thus, over the years, the garden was extended and improved by many rulers and called by different names, but the most popular name 'Shalimar Bagh' continues to this day.

During the Mughal period in particular, Emperor Jahangir and his wife Nur Jahan were so enamoured of Kashmir that during summer they moved to Srinagar with their full court entourage from Delhi, at least 13 times. Shalimar Bagh was their imperial summer residence, and also the Royal Court. They used to cross the arduous snowy passes of the Pir Panjal mountain range on elephants to reach Srinagar.

Layout

The layout of the garden is an adaptation of another Islamic garden layout known as the Chahar Bagh in Persia. This garden built on a flat land on a square plan with four radiating arms from a central location as the water source, could not be exactly replicated to the hilly conditions in the Kashmir valley. It needed to be modified to suit the hilly terrain and availability of a source of water, which could be diverted from a higher elevation by gravity to the planned gardens. Thus, modifications to suit the location were designed, which involved the main channel running through the garden axially from top to the lowest point. This central channel, known as the Shah Nahar, is the main axis of the garden. It runs through three terraces. This layout saved on radial arms and the shape became rectangular, instead of a square plan of the Chahar Bagh.

The garden, as finally laid, extends to an area of 12.4 hectares (31 acres) built with a size of 587 metres (1,930 ft) length on the main axis channel and with a total width of 251 metres (820 ft). The garden has three terraces fitted with fountains and with chinar (sycamore) tree-lined vistas. The Shahnahar is the main feeder channel to all the terraces. Each one of the three terraces has a specific role.

The garden was linked to the open Dal Lake water through a canal of about 1 mile (1.6 km) length and 12 yards (11 m) in width that ran through swampy quagmire. Willow groves and rice terraces fringed the lake edge. Broad green paths bordered the lake with rows of chinar trees. The garden was laid in trellised walkways lined by avenues of aspen trees planted at 2 feet (0.61 m) interval.

Architecture

The architectural details of the three terraces of the garden are elaborated.

The first terrace is a public garden or the outer garden ending in the Diwan-e-Aam (public audience hall). In this hall, a small black marble throne was installed over the waterfall. The second terrace garden along the axial canal, slightly broader, has two shallow terraces. The Diwan-i-Khas (the Hall of Private Audience), which was accessible only to the noblemen or guests of the court, now derelict, is in its centre. However, the carved stone bases and a fine platform surrounded by fountains are still seen. The royal bathrooms are located on the north-west boundary of this enclosure. The fountain pools of the Diwan-i Khas, the Diwan-i-Amm, and in turn, the Zenana terrace are supplied in succession.

In the third terrace, the axial water channel flows through the Zenana garden, which is flanked by the Diwan-i-Khas and chinar trees. At the entrance to this terrace, there are two small pavilions or guard rooms (built in Kashmir style on stone plinth) that is the restricted and controlled entry zone of the royal harem. Shahajahan built a baradari of black marble, called the Black Pavilion in the zenana garden. It is encircled by a fountain pool that receives its supply from a higher terrace.

A double cascade falls against a low wall carved with small niches (chini khanas), behind the pavilion. Two smaller, secondary water canals lead from the Black Pavilion to a small baradari. Above the third level, two octagonal pavilions define the end wall of the garden. The baradari has a lovely backdrop of the snow mountains, which is considered a befitting setting for the Bagh. The Shalimar Bagh is well known for *chini khanas*, or arched niches, behind garden waterfalls. They are a unique feature in the Bagh. These niches were lighted at night with oil lamps, which gave a fairy tale appearance to the water falls. However, now the niches hold pots of flower pots that reflect their colours behind the cascading water.

Another unusual architectural feature mentioned is about the doors of the Baradari. In the garden complex, the Baradari had four exquisite doors made of stones supported by pillars. It is conjectured that these stone doors were ruins from old temples that were demolished by Shahajahan. The garden also provided large water troughs where a variety of fountains were fixed.

It has been aptly described by a chronicler glowingly:

A subtle air of leisure and repose, a romantic indefinable spell, pervades the royal Shalimar: this leafy garden of dim vistas, shallow terraces, smooth sheets of falling water, and wide canals, with calm reflections broken only by the stepping stones across the streams.

Even in later years, during Maharaja's rule, the gardens were well maintained and continue to be so even now as it is one of the prominent visitor attractions around the Dal Lake. The garden is considered to be very beautiful during the autumn and spring seasons due to the colour change in leaves of the famed Chinar trees.

The gardens were the inspiration for other gardens of the same name, notably the Shalimar Bagh, Delhi in Delhi (built in 1653, which now also has an upscale colony) and Shalimar Gardens in Lahore, Pakistan built by Emperor Shah Jahan in 1641.

RED FORT

The Red Fort is a 17th century fort complex constructed by the Mughal emperor Shahjahan in the walled city of Old Delhi (in present day Delhi, India). It served as the capital of the Mughals until 1857, when Mughal emperor Bahadur Shah Zafar was exiled by the British Indian government. The British used it as a military camp until India was made independent in 1947. It is now a popular tourist site, as well as a powerful symbol of India's sovereignty: the Prime Minister of India raises the flag of India on the rampants of the Lahori Gate of the fort complex every year on Independence Day. It was designated a UNESCO World Heritage Site in 2007.

History

Mughal Emperor Shahjahan started construction of the massive fort in 1638 and work was completed in 1648. The Red Fort was originally referred to as "Qila-i-Mubarak" (the blessed fort), because it was the residence of the royal family. The layout of the Red Fort was organised to retain and integrate this site with the Salimgarh Fort. The fortress palace is an important focal point of the medieval city of Shahjahanabad. The planning and aesthetics of the Red Fort represent the zenith of Mughal creativity which prevailed during the reign of Emperor Shah Jahan.

This Fort has had many developments added on after its construction by Emperor Shahjahan. The significant phases of development were under Aurangzeb and later Mughal rulers. Important physical changes were carried out in the overall settings of the site after the First War of Independence during British Rule in 1857. After Independence, the site experienced a few changes in terms of addition/alteration to the structures. During the British period the Fort was mainly used as a cantonment and even after Independence, a significant part of the Fort remained under the control of the Indian Army until the year 2003.

The Red Fort was the palace for Mughal Emperor Shah Jahan's new capital, Shahjahanabad, the seventh greatcity in the Delhi site. He moved his capital from Agra in a move designed to bring prestige to his reign, and to provide ample opportunity to apply his ambitious building schemes and interests.

The fort lies along the Yamuna River, which fed the moats that surround most of the wall. The wall at its north-eastern corner is adjacent to an older fort, the Salimgarh Fort, a defense built by Islam Shah Suri in 1546.The construction of the Red Fort began in 1638 and was completed by 1648.

On 11 March 1783, Sikhs briefly entered Red Fort in Delhi and occupied the Diwan-i-Am. The city was essentially surrendered by the Mughal wazir in cahoots with his Sikh Allies. This task was carried out under the command of the Sardar Baghel Singh Dhaliwal of the Karor Singhia misl.

The last Mughal emperor to occupy the fort was Bahadur Shah II "Zafar". Despite being the seat of Mughal power and its defensive capabilities, the Red Fort was not defended during the 1857 uprising against the British. After the failure of the 1857 rebellion, Zafar left the fort on 17 September. He returned to Red Fort as a prisoner of the British. Zafar was tried on in a trial starting on 27 January 1858, and was exiled on 7 October.

On 15 August 1947, India became an independent nation. This was marked by Jawahar Lal Nehru, the Prime Minister of India, unveiling the flag of independent India on 15 August 1947. This practice of unfurling the national flag with a speech by the Prime Minister on Independence Day continues to this day. Just after World War II, the Red Fort had been the scene of the famous trial of the Indian National Army.

Architectural Design

Red Fort showcases the very high level of art form and ornamental work. The art work in the Fort is a synthesis of Persian, European and Indian art which resulted in the development of unique Shahjahani style which is very rich in form, expression and colour. Red Fort, Delhi is one of the important building complexes of India which encapsulates a long period of Indian history and its arts. Its significance has transcended time and space. It is relevant as a symbol of architectural brilliance and power. Even before its notification as a monument of national importance in the year 1913, efforts were made to preserve and conserve the Red Fort, for posterity. The walls of the fort are smoothly dressed, articulated by heavy string-courses along the upper section. They open at two major gates, the Delhi and the Lahore gates. The Lahore Gate is the main entrance; it leads to a long covered bazaar street, the Chatta Chowk, whose walls are lined with stalls for shops. The Chatta Chowk leads to a large open space where it crosses the large north-south street that was originally the division between the fort's military functions, to its west, and the palaces, to its east. The southern end of this street is the Delhi Gate.

IMPORTANT BUILDINGS INSIDE FORT

Diwan-i-Aam

Beyond this gate is another, larger open space, which originally served as the courtyard of the Diwan-i-Aam, the large pavilion for public imperial audiences with an ornate throne-balcony (*jharokha*) for the emperor. The columns were painted in gold and there was a gold and silver railing separating the throne from the public.

Diwan-i-Khas

The Diwan-i-Khas is a pavilion clad completely in marble, the pillars decorated with floral carvings and inlay work with semi-precious stones.

Nahr-i-Behisht

The imperial private apartments lie behind the throne. The apartments consist of a row of pavilions that sits on a raised platform along the eastern edge of the fort, looking out onto the river Yamuna.

The pavilions are connected by a continuous water channel, known as the Nahr-i-Behisht, or the "Stream of Paradise", that runs through the centre of each pavilion. The water is drawn from the river Yamuna, from a tower, the *Shah Burj*, at the north-eastern corner of the fort. The palace is designed as an imitation of paradise as it is described in the Koran; a couplet repeatedly inscribed in the palace reads, "If there be a paradise on earth, it is here, it is here". The planning of the palace is based on Islamic prototypes, but each pavilion reveals in its architectural elements the Hindu influences typical of Mughal building. The palace complex of the Red Fort is counted among the best examples of the Mughal style.

Zenana

The two southernmost pavilions of the palace are *zenana*s, or women's quarters: the Mumtaz Mahal (now a museum), and the larger, lavish Rang Mahal, which has been famous for its gilded, decorated ceiling and marble pool, fed by the *Nahr-i-Behisht*.

Moti Masjid

To the west of the hammam is the Moti Masjid, the Pearl Mosque. This was a later addition, built in 1659 as a private mosque for Aurangzeb, Shah Jahan's successor. It is a small, three-domed mosque in carved white marble, with a three-arched screen which steps down to the courtyard.

Hayat Bakhsh Bagh

To its north lies a large formal garden, the Hayat Bakhsh Bagh, or "Life-Bestowing Garden", which is cut through by two bisecting channels of water. A pavilion stands at either end of the north-south channel, and a third, built in 1842 by the last emperor, Bahadur Shah Zafar, stands at the centre of the pool where the two channels meet.

The Fort Today

The Red Fort is one of the most popular tourist destinations in Old Delhi, attracting thousands of visitors every year. The fort is also the site from which the Prime Minister of India addresses the nation on 15 August, the day India achieved independence from the British.

It also happens to be the largest monument in Old Delhi. At one point in time, more than 3,000 people lived within the premises of the Delhi Fort complex. But after the Sepoy Mutiny of 1857, the fort was captured by Britain and the residential palaces destroyed. It was made the headquarters of the British Indian Army. Immediately after the mutiny, Bahadur Shah Zafar was tried at the Red Fort.

JAMA MASJID, DELHI

The Masjid-i Jahan-Numa commonly known as the Jama Masjid of Delhi, is the principal mosque of Old Delhi in India. Commissioned by the Mughal Emperor Shah Jahan, builder of the Taj Mahal, and completed in the year 1656 AD, it is the largest and best-known mosque in India. The name Jahan-Numa comes from Persian meaning "World-reflecting". It lies at the origin of a very busy central street of Old Delhi, Chandni Chowk.

The later name, Jami Masjid, is a reference to the weekly Friday noon congregation prayers of Muslims, Jummah, which are usually done at a mosque, the "congregational mosque" or "jami' masjid". The courtyard of the mosque can hold up to twenty-five thousand worshippers. The mosque also houses several relics in a closet in the north gate, including an antique copy of the Qur'an written on deer skin.

Construction

The foundation of the historic Jama Masjid (Friday Mosque) was laid on a hillock in Shahjahanabad by fifth Mughal Emperor of India, Shahjahan, on Friday the October 6, 1650 AD, (10th Shawwal 1060 AH). The mosque was the result of the efforts of over 5,000 workers, over a period of six years.. The cost incurred on the construction in those times was 10 lakh (1 million) Rupees, and it was same Emperor who also built the Taj Mahal, at Agra and the Red Fort, which stands across the Jama Masjid, which was finally ready in 1656 AD (1066 AH), complete with three great gates, four towers and two 40 m-high minarets constructed of strips of red sandstone and white marble.

Shah Jahan built several important mosques in Delhi, Agra, Ajmer and Lahore. The Jama Masjid's floorplan is very similar to the Jama Masjid, Fatehpur Sikri near Agra, but the Jamia Masjid is the bigger and more imposing of the two. Its majesty is further enhanced because of the high ground that he selected for building this mosque. The architecture and design of the slightly larger Badshahi Mosque of Lahore built by Shah Jahan's son Aurangzeb in 1673 is closely related to the Jamia Masjid in Delhi.

Architecture

The courtyard of the mosque can be reached from the east, north and south by three flights of steps, all built of red sandstone. The northern gate of the mosque has 39 steps. The southern side of the mosque has 33 steps. The eastern gate of the mosque was the royal entrance and it has 35 steps. These steps used to house food stalls, shops and street entertainers. In the evening, the eastern side of the mosque used to be converted into a bazaar for poultry and birds in general. Prior to the 1857 War of Indian Independence, there was a madrassah near the southern side of the mosque, which was pulled down after the mutiny.

The mosque faces west. Its three sides are covered with open arched colonnades, each having a lofty tower-like gateway in the centre. The mosque is about 261 feet (80 m) long and 90 feet (27 m) wide, and its roof is covered with three domes with alternate stripes of black and white marble, with its topmost parts covered with gold. Two lofty minarets, 130 feet (41 m) high, and containing 130 steps, longitudinally striped with white marble and red sandstone, flank the domes on either side. The minarets are divided by three projecting galleries and are surmounted by open twelve-sided domed pavilions. On the back of the mosque, there are four small minarets crowned like those in the front.

Under the domes of the mosque, is a hall with seven arched entrances facing the west and the walls of the mosque, up to the height of the waist, are covered with marble. Beyond this is a prayer hall, which is about 61 meters X 27.5 meters, with eleven arched entrances, of which the centre arch is wide and lofty, and in the form of a massive gateway, with slim minarets in each corner, with the usual octagonal pavilion surmounting it. Over these arched entrances there are tablets of white marble, four feet (1.2 m) long and 2.5 feet (760 mm) wide, inlaid with inscriptions in black marble. These inscriptions give the history of the building of the mosque, and glorify the reign and virtues of Shah Jahan. The slab over the centre arch contains simply the words "The Guide!"

The mosque stands on a platform of about five feet (1.5 m) from the pavement of the terrace, and three flight of steps lead to the interior of the mosque from the east, north, and the south. The floor of the mosque is covered with white and black marble ornamented to imitate the Muslim prayer mat; a thin black marble border is marked for the worshippers, which is three feet long and 1 ½ feet wide. In total there are 899 such spaces marked in the floor of the mosque. The back of the mosque is cased over to the height of the rock on which the mosque stands with large hewn stones.

Aurangzeb and Later Mughal Architecture

In Aurangzeb's reign (1658–1707) squared stone and marble gave way to brick or rubble with stucco ornament. Srirangapatna and Lucknow have examples of later Indo-Muslim architecture. He also added his mark to the Lahore Fort. He also built one of the thirteen gates, and it was later named after him, Alamgir. The most impressive building of Aurangzeb's reign, is the Badshahi Mosque which was constructed in 1674 under the supervision of Fida'i Koka. This mosque is adjacent to the Lahore Fort.

Badshahi Mosque is the last in the series of great congregational mosques in red sandstone and is closely modeled on the one Shah Jahan built at Shahjahanabad. The red sandstone of the walls contrasts with the white marble of the domes and the subtle intarsia decoration. The materials depart from the local tradition of tile revetment that is seen in the Wazir Khan Mosque. According to Blair and Bloom, the cusped arches and arabesque floral patterns inlaid in white marble give the building, despite its vast proportions, a lighter appearance than its prototype.

Additional monuments from this period are associated with women from Aurangzeb's imperial family. The construction of the elegant Zinat al-Masjid in Daryaganij was overseen by Aurangzeb's second daughter Zinat al-Nisa. The delicate brick and plaster mausoleum in the Roshan-Ara-Bagh in Sabzimandi was for Aurangzeb's sister Roshan-Ara who died in 1671. Unfortunately, the tomb of Roshanara Begum and the beautiful garden surrounding it were neglected for a long time and are now in an advanced state of decay. Bibi Ka Maqbara a mausoleum was built by Prince Azam Shah, son of Emperor Aurangzeb, in the late 17th century as a loving tribute to his mother, Dilras Bano Begam in Aurangabad, Maharashtra. The Alamgiri Gate, built in 1673 A.D., is the main entrance to the Lahore Fort in present day Lahore, Pakistan. It was constructed to face west towards the Badshahi Mosque in the days of the Mughal Emperor Aurangzeb. The monumental gateway is an imposing vestibule flanked by two semi-circular bastions that have boldly fluted shafts and lotus petalled bases and are crowned with domed pavilions.

MUSIC IN MUGHAL INDIA

Tansen the famous singer at Akbar's court is credited with having enriched the Hindustani school by composing many new melodies or ragas. One of the most popular of these was the raga Darbari. Jahangir and ShahJahan continued patronizing music in the royal court. New styles of singing such as the khayal and thumri became popular. However music in all forms continued to be patronized by Aurangzeb's queens and by the nobles. That is the reason for largest number of books on classical Indian music in Persian were written during Aurangzeb's reign. But some of the most important developments in the field of music took place only in the 18th century during the reign of Muhammad Shah.

Considered as the greatest musician in India, Tansen (1506-1589) is instrumental in the creation of the classical music that dominates the north of India. He was considered as one of the Navaratnas (Nine Gems) in the court of Emperor Akbar. Tansen was born in a Hindu family in a place called Gwalior located in Madhya Pradesh. His father was a famous poet by the name of Mukund Mishra. Tansen was named Tannu Mishra when he was born. To know more about the fascinating life history of this great musician, go through this biography of Mian Tansen.

He received the prefix "Mian" from Emperor Akbar. As a young boy, Tansen learnt music from his Guru, Shri Haridas Swamy. He was considered to be a legendary teacher of that time. It is said that Tansen has no equal apart from his teacher. Such was his passion for music that he is said to have performed astonishing miracles merely by singing. He could bring rain by singing in a particular Raag known as Megh Malhar. Similarly he could start a fire by singing in Raag Deepak. He has also composed several Ragas that have been the foundation of classical music like Bhairav, Darbari Todi, Darbari Kanada, Malhar, Sarang and Rageshwari. There is no particular evidence of the origin of each and every school of music. Since he is the greatest musician, every school of music tries to trace its origin from him. The Dhrupad style of music is likely to have been started by him and his Guru. Some of his important works on music are the Rajmala and Sangeet Sara. Such was the power of his music that when he used to sing in the court of Akbar, candles used to light up automatically. Even today, Tansen is considered to be the greatest of all and there is no comparison when it comes to his style of singing. His contribution to the world of music is priceless and is still worshipped by leading singers and composers of the world.

Persian Influence on Mughal Music

The advent of Islamic rule under the Delhi Sultanate and later the Mughal Empire over northern India caused considerable cultural interchange. Increasingly, musicians received patronage in the courts of the new rulers, who in their turn, started taking increasing interest in local music forms. While the initial generations may have been rooted in cultural traditions outside India, they gradually adopted many aspects from their kingdoms which retained the traditional Hindu culture. This helped spur the fusion of Hindu and Muslim ideas to bring forth new forms of musical synthesis like qawwali and khayal.

The most influential musician from the Delhi Sultanate period was Amir Khusrau (1253-1325), sometimes called the father of modern Hindustani classical music. A prolific composer in Persian, Turkish, Arabic, as well as Braj Bhasha, he is credited with systematizing many aspects of Hindustani music, and also introducing several ragas such as Yaman Kalyan, Zeelaf and Sarpada. He created the qawwali genre, which fuses Persian melody and beat on a dhrupad like structure. A number of instruments (such as the sitar and tabla) were also introduced in his time.

Amir Khusrau is sometimes credited with the origins of the khayal form, but the record of his compositions do not appear to support this. The compositions by the court musician Niyamat Khan (*Sadarang*) in the court of Muhammad Shah 'Rangiley' bear a closer affinity to the modern khyal, and suggests that while khyal already existed in some form, 'Sadarang' may have been the father of modern day khyal. Much of the musical forms innovated by these pioneers merged with the Hindu tradition, composed in the popular language of the people (as opposed to Sanskrit) in the work of composers like Kabir or Nanak. This can be seen as part of a larger Bhakti tradition, (strongly related to the Vaishnavite movement) which remained influential across several centuries; notable figures include Jayadeva (11th century), Vidyapati (1375 AD), Chandidas (14th-15th century), and Meerabai (1555-1603 AD).

As the Mughal Empire came into closer contact with Hindus, especially under Jalal ud-Din Akbar, music and dance also flourished. Particularly, the legendary musician Tansen is recognized as having introduced a number of innovations, ragas as well as particular compositions. Legend has it that upon his rendition of a night-time raga in the morning, the entire city fell under a hush and clouds gathered in the sky, or that he could light fires by singing raga Deepak, which is supposed to be composed of notes in high octaves. At the royal house of Gwalior, Raja Mansingh Tomar (1486-1516 AD) also participated in the shift from Sanskrit to the local idiom (Hindi) as the language for classical songs. He himself penned several volumes of compositions on religious and secular themes, and was also responsible for the major compilation, the *Mankutuhal* (book of curiosity), which outlined the major forms of music prevalent at the time. In particular, the musical form known as dhrupad saw considerable development in his court and remained a strong point of the Gwalior gharana for many centuries.

MUGHAL PAINTING

Mughal painting is a particular style of South Asian painting, generally confined to miniatures either as book illustrations or as single works to be kept in albums, which emerged from Persian miniature painting, with Indian Hindu, Jain, and Buddhist influences, and developed during the period of the Mughal Empire (16th-19th centuries).

Genesis

When the second Mughal emperor, Humayun (reigned 1530–1540 and 1555-1556) was in Tabriz in the Safavid court of Shah Tahmasp I, he was exposed to Persian miniature painting. When Humayun returned to India, he brought with him two accomplished Persian artists, *Sayyid Ali* and *Abdus Samad*. Their works, and the assimilation of local styles during succeeding decades, gave shape to a distinct style, which became known as Mughal painting. The *Tutinama* (literal meaning "Tales of a Parrot"), now in the Cleveland Museum of Art, is among the earliest examples of Mughal painting. The manuscript was made in the reign of Humayun's son, Akbar (r. 1556-1605). Another manuscript the Hamzanama, also made early in Akbar's reign, is said to have contained about 1400 large paintings on cotton (only a fraction have survived) and took about 15 years to complete.

Themes

Mughal painting was rich in variety and included portraits, events and scenes from court life, wild life and hunting scenes, and illustrations of battles.

Development

Mughal painting developed and flourished during the reigns of Akbar, Jahangir and Shah Jahan. During the reign of Akbar (1556-1605), the imperial court, apart from being the centre of administrative authority to manage and rule the vast Mughal empire, also emerged as a centre of cultural excellence. Mughal painting thrived and hundreds of painters created innumerable paintings depicting scenes from various Hindu epics including the Ramayana and the Mahabharata; themes with animal fables; individual portraits; and paintings on scores of different themes. Mughal style during this period continued to refine itself with elements of realism and naturalism coming to the fore. Jahangir (1605-27) had an artistic inclination and during his reign Mughal painting developed further. Brushwork became finer and the colors lighter. Jahangir was also deeply influenced by European painting. During his reign he came into direct contact with the English Crown and was sent gifts of oil paintings, which included portraits of the King and Queen. He encouraged his royal atelier to take up the single point perspective favoured by European artists, unlike the flattened multi-layered style used in traditional miniatures. He particularly encouraged paintings depicting events of his own life, individual portraits, and studies of birds, flowers and animals. The Jahangirnama, written during his lifetime, which is a biographical account of Jahangir, has several paintings, including some unusual subjects such as the sexual union of a saint with a tigress, and fights between spiders. During the reign of Shah Jahan (1628-58), Mughal paintings continued to develop, but they gradually became cold and rigid. Themes including musical parties; lovers, sometimes in intimate positions, on terraces and gardens; and ascetics gathered around a fire, abound in the Mughal paintings of this period. Govardhan was a noted painter during the reigns of Akbar, Jahangir and Shah Jahan.

Decline

Aurangzeb (1658-1707) did not actively encourage Mughal paintings, but as this art form had gathered momentum and had a number of patrons, Mughal paintings continued to survive, but the decline had set in. Some sources however note that a few of the best Mughal paintings were made for Aurangzeb, speculating that the painters may have realized that he was about to close the workshops and thus exceeded themselves in his behalf. A brief revival was noticed during the reign of Muhammad Shah 'Rangeela' (1719-48), but by the time of Shah Alam II (1759-1806), the art of Mughal painting had lost its glory. By that time, other schools of Indian painting had developed, including, in the royal courts of the Rajput kingdoms of Rajputana, Rajput painting and in the cities ruled by the British East India Company, the Company style under Western influence.

REFERENCES

Asher, Catherine: *Architecture of Mughal India*, Cambridge, New York, 1992.

Bednorz, A. : *Moorish Architecture in Andalusia*, Cologne, London, 1992.

Jonathan Bloom: *The Art and Architecture of Islam, 1250-1800,* Pelican History of Art. New Haven, 1994.

Koch, Ebba: *Mughal Architecture: An Outline of Its History and Development (1526-1858),* Munich, London, 1991.

Bibliography

Asher, Catherine: *Architecture of Mughal India*, Cambridge, New York, 1992.

Bednorz, A. : *Moorish Architecture in Andalusia*, Cologne, London, 1992.

Borchert, Bruno: *Mysticism: Its History and Challenge,* Samuel Wiser, York Beach, 1994.

Bosworth, C.E., *The Ghaznavids*, Edinburgh University Press, Edinburgh, 1963.

Creswell, K. A. C.: *A Short Account of Early Muslim Architecture*, Aldershot, Adlohoc, 1989.

Crowe, S.: "*The Gardens of Mughal India*", Oxford, London, 1972.

Currie, P.M. *The Shrine and Cult of Muin-ul-din Chishti of Ajmer*, Oxford, Delhi, 1989.

Duboi, Abbe: *Hindu Manners, Customs and Ceremonies*, Fifth Indian Impression, CUP, 1985.

Edwin, M.: *Social Pathology A Systematic Approach to the Theory of Sociopathic Behaviour,* New York: McGraw-Hill, 1951.

Elizabeth B.: *Paradise as a Garden In Persia and Mughal India*. New York, George Braziller, 1979.

Evans, T.F. : *On Three Copper Cakes found at Bryndu*, Oxford, Anglesey, 1873.

Goodwin, Godfrey: *A History of Ottoman Architecture,* Oxford, New York, 1992.

Hambly, G.: "*Cities of Mughal India*", New York: G. P. Putnam's Sons, 1968.

Heimann, Betty: *Facets of Indian Thought*, Geroge Allen & Unwin, London, 1964.

Hopkirk, Peter: *The Great Game: The Struggle for Empire in Central Asia*, Kodansha, 1992.

Ira Mervin Lapidus, *Muslim Cities in the Later Middle Ages,* Cambridge, Mass, 1967.

Jonathan Bloom: *The Art and Architecture of Islam, 1250-1800,* Pelican History of Art. New Haven, 1994.

Koch, Ebba: *Mughal Architecture: An Outline of Its History and Development (1526-1858),* Munich, London, 1991.

Lai, K.S., *History of the Khaljis*, Asia Publishing House, Bombay, 1967.

MacIver R.M. : *Society, An Introductory Analysis*, Rinehart and Company, New York 1949.

Michell, George, and Mark Zebrowski: *Architecture and Art of the Deccan Sultanates,* Cambridge, London, 1999.

Okada, Amina: *Indian Miniatures of the Mughal Court*, New York, Harry N. Abrahms, Inc. Publishers, 1992.

Peter S.: *The Early Islamic Architecture of the East African Coast*, British Institute of History and Archaeology in East Africa, Nairobi, 1966.

Sharma, K. L.: *Caste, Class and Social Movements*, Rawat Publications, Jaipur, 1986.

Sharma, Sri Ram, *The Religious Policy of the Mughal Emperors*, Asia Publishing House, Bombay, 1962.

Stein, Burton : *Peasant State and Society in Medieval South India*, Oxford University Press, Delhi, 1980.

Sunder, Prem : *Caste Class and Society : Then and Now*, Educational Pub, Delhi, 2010.

Tillotson, G. H. R.: *Mughal India*, New York, Penguin Books, 1990

Vivian, W. : *Mine Managers Reports 1855-57*, Unpublished UCNW Archives, Bangor, 1856.

Yadav, Kripal Chandra : *India's Unequal Citizens : A Study of Other Backward Classes,* Manohar, New Delhi, 1994.

Zaidi, A. Moin: *Evolution of Muslim Political Thought in India,* New Delhi: S. Chand, 1975.

Index